Poor Richard's Women

Poor Richard's Women

Deborah Read Franklin and the Other Women behind the Founding Father

NANCY RUBIN STUART

BEACON PRESS, BOSTON

Beacon Press
Boston, Massachusetts
www.beacon.org

Beacon Press books
are published under the auspices of
the Unitarian Universalist Association of Congregations.

25 24 23 22   8 7 6 5 4 3 2 1

This book is printed on acid-free paper that meets the uncoated paper
ANSI/NISO specifications for permanence as revised in 1992.

Text design by Kim Arney
Composition by Wilsted & Taylor Publishing Services

Author's Note: Spelling and punctuation have been modernized
in many quotations to enhance readability.

Library of Congress Cataloging-in-Publication Data

Names: Stuart, Nancy Rubin, 1944– author.
Title: Poor Richard's women : Deborah Read Franklin and the other women
  behind the Founding Father / Nancy Rubin Stuart.
Other titles: Deborah Read Franklin and the other women behind the Founding Father
Description: Boston : Beacon Press, [2022] | Includes bibliographical
  references and index | Summary: "Poor Richard's women describes
  Deborah's common-law marriage to Ben Franklin and his romances with
  other women"—Provided by publisher.
Identifiers: LCCN 2021039138 | ISBN 9780807011300 (hardcover) |
  ISBN 9780807011409 (ebook)
Subjects: LCSH: Franklin, Benjamin, 1706–1790—Relations with women. |
  Franklin, Deborah Read Rogers, 1708–1774. | Franklin, Benjamin,
  1706–1790—Friends and associates. | Franklin, Benjamin,
  1706–1790—Family. | Man-woman relationship—United
  States—History—18th century. | Mistresses—Europe—History—18th
  century. | Statesmen—United States—Biography. | Philadelphia
  (Pa.)—Biography.
Classification: LCC E302.6.F8 S93 2022 | DDC 973.3092
  [B]—dc23/eng/20211013
LC record available at https://lccn.loc.gov/2021039138

To Wendy

CONTENTS

Poor Richard's Women

Introduction

BENJAMIN FRANKLIN LIKED WOMEN. Occasionally, he even loved them. Throughout his life Ben was fascinated by the fair sex but considered the currents between them as dangerous as electricity. Still he pursued women as boldly and persistently as he conducted scientific experiments. There was one difference. Experiments required close attention, but Ben kept his sweethearts "at a distance of ten leagues."[1] To the distinguished scientist-statesman, their appeal was so strong it threatened his composure. As he warned readers of *Poor Richard's Almanack*, "If passion drives you, let reason hold the reins."[2]

While Ben's iconic image remains that of a man who embraced reason over emotion, a second, more erotic image persists: as a womanizer who fathered at least a dozen children and left a string of broken hearts in his wake. Neither of these images is realistic; Ben's life was neither wholly pragmatic nor preoccupied with prurient intrigues.

For generations his flirtations with women have been exploited in popular culture, diminishing his achievements and the complexity of his personal attachments. By examining Ben's correspondence with his wife, Deborah; his writings on sexuality; and his relationships with his sweethearts Catharine Ray, Madame Brillon, and Madame Helvétius, this book attempts to portray a man who privately struggled with prudence and passion. It also depicts his dependence upon the women who served as nurturers, caretakers, companions, financial assistants, and sexual objects. By doing so, these pages reveal the importance of Ben's women to his happiness and well-being, deepening our understanding of him beyond traditional analyses of his commercial, scientific, and political achievements.

One event that earlier historians acknowledged was the birth of Ben's son William, who was born out of wedlock. Despite the public taunts over William's birth directed at Ben by his political enemies, he never apologized for his sexual behavior. Even when newly married to Deborah, Ben's "Rules and Maxims for Promoting Marital Happiness" in the *Pennsylvania Gazette* warned wives that their spouses had flaws, for "her husband is a man, not an angel."[3]

Thousands of books have been written about Benjamin Franklin, most by male historians: scholars and biographers who focused upon his scientific, diplomatic, and political achievements. Many of those biographies portrayed his wife, Deborah, as a dull, even stupid woman. Several factors contributed to that image. Ben's *Autobiography* mentions her only briefly and with little emotion. Exacerbating Deborah's shadowy image is an absence of historical information about her youth and the early years of her marriage to Ben. Unfortunately, even the letters she wrote from 1757 to 1762, during Ben's first assignment as a colonial agent to England, are lost. It was only from his second London trip, 1764 to 1775, that Deborah's letters were preserved. Finally we hear her voice, although only in the last decade of her life.

Replete with spelling and grammatical errors, her letters were often cited by historians as proof that Deborah was an ignorant, provincial woman, hardly a suitable mate for the future founding father. Only recently, thanks to scholarship on women's history, has it been established that Deborah, like most colonial women, was never taught the rudiments of syntax or spelling, since that skill was considered unnecessary for future wives and mothers. "Now I am to returne your thankes for the Pictuer for the Hankeshcer I gave Salley al of them thay is verey hansum . . ." is just one example of Deborah's writing.[4] Since her letters can be difficult to decipher, I have modernized spelling and syntax in these pages.

Nevertheless, Deborah's correspondence reveals a woman far more capable than earlier historians originally assumed. While not intellectually brilliant like Ben, Deborah was an astute businesswoman and devoted helpmate who not only contributed to his early success but also attended to his complex business affairs during his years overseas. In Ben's absence she shouldered many duties men traditionally performed. Ben trusted her competence so thoroughly that he awarded her power of attorney two times before embarking on trips. During his long absences overseas, Deborah also fulfilled other obligations men usually assumed. These included supervision of construction for the half-built Franklin house, defense of that house at gunpoint during a Stamp Act riot, purchase of a costly property that enlarged Franklin Court, and management of the colonial postmastership while Ben's substitute was being trained.

On a personal level, Deborah was equally remarkable. While raising Ben's son, William, and her own daughter, Sally, Deborah managed a successful store, hosted and entertained visitors who admired Ben's work, nursed sick friends and relatives, managed Ben's financial affairs when he traveled, and won the friendship of Philadelphia's leading citizens. A devoted wife, she nursed Ben when he was ill, sent him home-cooked foods on the Pennsylvania frontier, wrote regularly to him in London (despite his infrequent responses), and diplomatically exchanged gifts with his English female companion. Even during Deborah's last illness, she relayed colonial news and shipped gifts and food to Ben in London.

These pages depict other women important to Ben's life. Among them was twenty-three-year-old Catharine Ray, with whom the middle-aged Ben had a fleetingly passionate relationship. Even later, when Catharine was married and the mother of six children, she maintained a warm friendship with the scientist-statesman.

Historians have also dismissed Ben's beloved companion, the widowed Margaret Stevenson, the landlady he lived with during his two assignments in England, from 1757 to 1762 and from 1764 to 1775. During their fifteen years together, she served as a kind of "second wife" who nursed Ben when he was ill; provided meals; outfitted him in stylish English clothes; attended plays, concerts, and dinners with him; and hosted their friends in her Craven Street townhouse. For all Margaret's urban sophistication, she had many qualities similar to Deborah's. A warm and devoted companion with a spirited temperament, she, too, wrote and spelled poorly. Like Deborah, Margaret had only one child, a daughter, Polly, upon whom she doted. During Ben's years in London he became so attached to the mother and daughter that he considered them his "English family." Ben's deep affection for Margaret has led historians to suspect they became lovers. One of his letters even admitted that he considered his years with Margaret "some of the happiest years of my life."[5]

Historians have also glossed over Ben's love affairs with two other women during his diplomatic assignment in France from 1776 to 1785. His first sweetheart was the gifted and beautiful musician Anne-Louise Boyvin d'Hardancourt Brillon de Jouy, known as Madame Brillon. Then in his early seventies, Ben played chess, attended dinners, and devoted his Wednesdays and Saturdays to the musician during the late 1770s. For decades scholars have downplayed his well-documented pleas for intimacy as nothing more than a parlor game, witty flirtations meant to charm a younger woman with few expectations of sexual rewards. But the dozens of letters that passed between Ben and Madame Brillon, some cited in these pages, suggest his pleas were sincere and revealed a lonely man longing for love.

No less poignant was Ben's subsequent pursuit of Anne-Catherine de Ligniville d'Autricourt, or Madame Helvétius, the unconventional widow of the philosopher Claude-Adrien Helvétius. Intrigued by her wit, gaiety, and friendships with the *philosophes* of pre-revolutionary France, Ben pursued her relentlessly in hopes of a marriage. Stunned by his proposal and finally alarmed by his passionate persistence, the usually poised Madame Helvétius fled to the countryside.

These pages consequently illustrate that Ben's romances with his French sweethearts were far from trivial and revealed his sincere longing for love. His letters brim with an intensity that reveals a previously ignored dimension of Ben's private life.

I am not the first author to examine the founding father's romantic attachments. In 1966 Yale University Press published *Mon Cher Papa: Franklin and the Ladies of Paris*, by Claude-Anne Lopez. Nine years later W. W. Norton published *The Private Franklin: The Man and His Family*, by Claude-Anne Lopez and Eugenia W. Herbert. In 2000 Yale University Press published Lopez's *My Life with Benjamin Franklin*. Lopez's familiarity with his letters was encyclopedic, a result of her work as editor in chief of *The Papers of Benjamin Franklin* project at Yale University.

The idea for this book grew out of my long interest in women's lives. Today, as during previous waves of feminism, it is again acknowledged that women are the forgotten sex and that many of their deeds and influence have been dismissed or at best reduced to historical footnotes. Unfortunately, this loss of information has left a frustrating gap in our understanding about the lives of men as well. That became painfully obvious in the early 1990s as I first read traditional accounts of Ben's life. The questions abounded. Why didn't Deborah accompany him to England? What led her to remain in Philadelphia, far from the man she adored? Was that her decision, or Ben's? Was their marriage filled with dissension? Was their separation an eighteenth-century version of divorce?

Perplexed, I began searching through Yale University's bound volumes of the Franklin papers at the New York Public Library. That led to more questions. Why were Deborah's letters between 1757 and 1762, during Ben's first trip to England, missing? And why, if the Franklins were estranged, were the letters they exchanged between 1764 and 1774 so affectionate?

Finally, in late 1996 I met with Dr. Larry E. Tise, then executive director of the Benjamin Franklin National Memorial at the Franklin Institute, who answered some of my questions and recommended several books by Claude-Anne Lopez. Dr. Tise also suggested the work of other scholars whose essays later appeared in his 2002 collection, *Benjamin Franklin and Women*.

My initial proposal on Deborah Franklin elicited lukewarm enthusiasm from commercial publishers, who still considered her a marginal figure in Ben's life. Discouraged, I relegated the idea to a back file drawer. Fast-forward fifteen years. With renewed interest in women's rights and history, I revisited that proposal. By then the time seemed right to correct historical misconceptions about Deborah Franklin.

"Lost time is never regained," Ben once observed in *Poor Richard's Almanack*.[6] Two hundred and forty years ago he could not have imagined the advent of the electronic age, although that surely would have pleased "the Father of Electricity." In 2006, thanks to technology, *The Papers of Benjamin Franklin* were digitized through a joint effort of the American

Philosophical Society and Yale University, then posted on the websites of the Library of Congress and the National Archives. Obtaining access to those documents greatly enhanced my research on Franklin's women.

Here then is a contemporary interpretation of Ben's passions—his wife and sweethearts—through a postfeminist lens.

1

"A Most Awkward Ridiculous Appearance"

ON SUNDAY MORNING, OCTOBER 6, 1723, fifteen-year-old Deborah Read stood outside the door of her home on Philadelphia's Market Street between Third and Fourth. People in their Sunday best strolled past, their pace slowed by clouds of dust from horse-drawn carriages bumping along the wide roads. As the air cleared, the weathervane on the cupola of the brick courthouse gleamed in the late-morning sun. The new stone jail and workhouse stood at the southwest corner of Third and Market and near the small brick Anglican Christ Church where Deborah's family prayed.

A young man walked along Market Street toward the Read home. As he drew closer, Deborah noticed the stranger's clothes were disheveled and his pockets bulging. Added to his unkempt appearance was the ravenous way he was eating a roll. Two others were tucked beneath his arm.

Years later Ben Franklin admitted he had arrived in Philadelphia in less than respectable circumstances as a fugitive apprentice from Boston: "I was dirty from my journey, my pockets were stuffed with shirts and stockings . . . I was fatigued with traveling . . . and very hungry." To appease his stomach, Ben had purchased "three great puffy rolls" from a baker. As he strolled past Deborah, she giggled. It was understandable, Ben reflected forty years later in his *Autobiography*, for "I made a most awkward ridiculous appearance."[1, 2]

Laughter was Deborah's first reaction to the man who would become America's most inventive founding father and the love of her life. Had someone predicted Ben's future, she would have not only giggled but laughed out loud. After all, Deborah was the dutiful daughter of carpenter John Read and his wife, Sarah White, from Birmingham, England, who sailed with her to Philadelphia in 1711 on a difficult transatlantic journey. The idea of marrying a vagabond was as outrageous as the thought of crossing the Atlantic again.

Months later a handsome, brown-haired, and blue-eyed teenager appeared at the Read home and asked to speak to Deborah's father. The young man looked vaguely familiar, but Deborah could not place him. Then something reminded her of the fugitive who had walked by the Read home in October eating a roll. Could he be that same person? It seemed impossible, for this young man was well dressed and well spoken. But he was that same person, as Ben triumphantly noted in his *Autobiography* forty-eight years later. By the time he appeared before Deborah's father, John, Ben's trunk and clothes had long since arrived. "I made rather a more respectable appearance in the eyes of Miss Read, than . . . when she first happened to see me eating my roll in the streets."[3]

At that time Ben was working for the eccentric, long-bearded Samuel Keimer, owner of a nearby print shop. The employer was fuming because Ben was living in the home of his rival, the printer Andrew Bradford. Keimer rented a house from Deborah's father and suggested Ben board with the Reads. Once comfortably settled, Ben probably told the Reads a little about his past. Born January 6, 1706, in Boston, he was the youngest son in a brood of seventeen siblings. Ben's pious father, Josiah, was a soap and tallow candlemaker and former cloth dyer from Ecton, Lancashire, in the Midlands of England. His mother, Josiah's second wife, was the sturdy Abiah Folder of Nantucket. By the time Ben was twelve, Josiah had apprenticed him to his older brother James, master printer and owner of the controversial *New England Courant*. After months of dissension with James and intrigues over leadership of the newspaper, Ben broke his apprenticeship contract and fled from Boston on September 23, 1723.

Nearly two weeks later he arrived in Philadelphia and looked for work. The city was located on a wide plain near the confluence of the Schuylkill and Delaware Rivers and surrounded by fertile farmlands. In 1681

Charles II had granted Quaker William Penn the province of Pennsylvania in repayment for a debt. Founded by Penn as a place for religious tolerance, Pennsylvania attracted thousands of English, Lutheran Germans, Quakers, Moravians, Scots-Irish Presbyterians, Irish Catholics, and enslaved Africans. By the time Ben arrived, the City of Brotherly Love had six thousand residents and would soon become the fastest-growing commercial center in North America. While a recent recession in Britain left abandoned houses and empty lots in Philadelphia's broad streets, the community was still lined with shops, taverns, and brick-front homes. Moreover, the port on the Delaware bustled with stores of wheat, flour, biscuit, barrels of beef and port, butter, cheese, cider, and apples for trade with England and the West Indies. Despite Philadelphia's busy port and expanding size, the city had just two printers.

The first was the crotchety Samuel Keimer; the second Andrew Bradford, publisher of the *American Mercury* newspaper. Only Keimer had an opening. In desperation Ben had accepted the job but immediately had misgivings about his employer, whom he later described as an "odd fish, ignorant, rude . . . and a little knavish." Disheartening, too, was Keimer's shop, equipped only with an "old shattered press and one small worn-out fount of English." The shop was greatly inferior to his brother James's printing house in Boston, but at least it provided paying work.[4]

Chances are Ben did not describe to the Reads the intrigues at the *Courant* that prompted his flight from Boston. By the usual terms of colonial apprentice contracts Ben, then only seventeen, still owed years of service until his twenty-first birthday. Deborah may have wondered about that, but it was not her place to ask. Such questions were left to her father, John. If questioned, Ben would have mentioned that his brother James whipped him when he made a mistake and how deeply he resented it. Nearly five decades later, Ben's *Autobiography* reflected his youthful anger. For James, "though a brother . . . considered himself my master."[5]

As a boarder at the Reads', Ben was polite, well-behaved, and friendly. His weekdays were spent working at Keimer's and his nights reading books by candlelight in his room. Gradually, as he became more acquainted with Deborah, he found her not only attractive but endowed with a convivial, cheerful personality. Only one portrait of Deborah exists. Commissioned by Ben and painted by an unknown American artist, when his wife was in her early fifties, the painting was later copied in oil by Benjamin Wilson in England. In the portrait Deborah was depicted as a plump, chestnut-haired brunette with blue eyes, slightly coarse features, and a firm expression—an attractive, or "handsome" woman, in the terms of her era, but probably not beautiful. Nevertheless, as one of the daughters of a moderately prosperous carpenter, Deborah had a dowry, an advantage the pragmatic Ben must have known about.

Occasionally Ben must have entertained Deborah with stories. One of his favorites was his description of himself as a foolish child who finally saved enough money to buy a longed-for whistle, only to be teased by his older siblings for paying too much. In another Ben told how he rescued a drunken passenger who fell off a boat. Once again aboard, the gasping man asked Ben to dry out his book. Coincidentally it turned out to be one of his favorites, John Bunyan's moralistic *Pilgrim's Progress*.

Ben never seemed to run out of stories about his youthful ventures. His most brazen involved letters he wrote in a woman's voice, which appeared in his brother James's *New England Courant*. Known as Silence Dogood, Ben's fictitious character was a widow devoted to exposing the intolerance of dour clergymen like Cotton Mather and the hypocrisies of prim Bostonians. Nothing corrupt, unfair, or vain escaped the widow's sharp eye, among them alcoholism, women's lack of education, and the folly of fashionable hoop skirts. James, who assumed the letters were penned by a distinguished citizen, had published them to an enthusiastic readership.

One of Silence's most titillating letters defended prostitutes. "Nightwalkers are a set of people who contribute very much to the health and satisfaction of those who have been fatigued with business or study," Ben had declared in Silence's voice. The "widow" even insisted that prostitutes were an economic asset to the community. "Men of business, the shoemakers and other dealers in leather are doubly obliged to them . . . as they exceedingly promote the consumption of their wares." When a shoemaker was asked how long a nightwalker's shoes might last, he replied that "he knew how many days she might wear them but not how many nights," for that depended upon "how many hours she spent on the streets."[6]

When James eventually discovered that his brother had authored Silence's letters, he exploded and accused Ben of becoming conceited from the praise they received.

Given the racy subject of the widow's "nightwalker" letter, Ben may not have shared it with Deborah. Not that it mattered, for the young woman was already fascinated by his wit, worldliness, and liberal ideas. None of the young men she knew were like Ben. Rarely did they travel to other colonies, their days spent learning a trade, shopkeeping, or working at the port on the Delaware. Deborah's life was equally provincial, limited to domestic chores, church meetings, and friends. The Reads, like other Pennsylvanians, owned a household slave, but Deborah's mother, Sarah, taught her to cook, clean, weave, and sew clothes. Like other daughters of tradesmen, she had also learned to read and write but not spell, since that was considered unnecessary for women. Deborah, however, became adept at bookkeeping, a skill Sarah probably taught her to keep the ledgers for her homemade ointment and salve business.

In contrast, Ben, who had been trained as a printer, was fascinated with books and considered them so important that he had his collection shipped from Boston to Philadelphia. Already well read by the time he arrived there, his literary tastes ranged from Homer, Plutarch, Shakespeare, Bunyan, and Hobbes to contemporary English writers Jonathan Swift, William Congreve, and Alexander Pope. As a child Ben had been so drawn to books that his father, Josiah, intending him for the ministry, sent him to the Boston Latin School.

Ben excelled there, but after Josiah discovered that Ben disliked formal religion and avoided attending church, he removed his son from school and insisted he learn a trade. To the youth, books were a lifeline to a world outside the narrow constraints of puritanical Boston, a means of stimulating his imagination and widening his ambitions. While apprenticing to James, Ben read through his library, then persuaded other Boston apprentices to "borrow" books from the libraries of their masters.

Ben's literary bent soon enabled him to befriend other young Philadelphians who were "lovers of reading."[7] Often they met after work in taverns to discuss books. On Sundays they strolled the grassy banks of the Schuylkill to compare the ideas promoted in those volumes. To today's reader, the education gap between Ben and Deborah may suggest incompatibility, but not in colonial America. A woman's place was in the home.

Deborah was not the only one who admired Ben. Soon after moving to the Reads' home, Ben's brother-in-law, the sea captain Robert Holmes, shared Ben's letter praising Philadelphia to Pennsylvania's Lieutenant Governor William Keith. The official was so impressed with Ben's writing he declared him "a young man of promising parts, who should be encouraged."[8] Soon afterward, the elegantly dressed and bewigged lieutenant governor and his aide, Colonel John French, a former Speaker of the Delaware Assembly, arrived at Keimer's shop one day. To the printer's astonishment, the two officials brushed past him and asked for Ben.

"I was not a little surprised and Keimer stared like a pig poisoned," Ben gleefully recalled.[9] After whisking the young man off to a tavern for a glass of Madeira, the officials insisted they intended to support Ben's establishment of his own print shop. To ensure its success, they promised to use their "interest and influence in procuring the public [government] business."[10] There was only one caveat: Ben must ask his father to fund his shop. The youth was thrilled.

In late April 1725 Ben sailed to Boston with Sir Keith's flattering proposal in hand, worried that Josiah would think the venture impractical. He also wondered how his parent would receive him, for when Ben bolted from Boston, he had upset the extended Franklin clan. Deborah had her own worries, because by then she was attracted to Ben, if not already in love with him. As he recalled in his *Autobiography*, "I had made some courtship to Miss Read. I had a great respect and affection for her, and had some reason to believe she had the same for me."[11]

Ben's journey to Boston was ultimately disappointing. His parents and other relatives had warmly welcomed him, but again he offended James. Determined to avenge himself, Ben had arrived at the *Courant* puffed up with self-importance. Mocking himself years later in his *Autobiography,*

Ben admitted he was "dressed better than ever while in his service, having a genteel new suit . . . a watch and my pockets lined with near five pounds sterling in silver." However, James was unimpressed and received Ben "not very frankly, looked me over and turned to his work again."[12] Despite the snub, the *Courant*'s journeymen crowded around Ben and asked him about Philadelphia. Gloating, Ben praised the town, displayed his watch, and presented the workers with silver coins for drinks.

Ben's visit to the Franklins' three-story clapboard home on the corner of Union and Hanover Streets was equally unsettling. At first Josiah seemed surprised by Sir Keith's proposal and praised Ben for "advancing in so short a time," but privately he questioned the sincerity of the proposal.[13] Ben returned to Philadelphia empty-handed. Josiah had agreed to help establish his printing shop, but only after his son turned twenty-one.

Sir Keith, who often invited Ben for dinners and for whom "setting me up was always mentioned as a fixed thing," then proposed a new idea.[14] "Since he [Josiah] will not set you up, says he, I will do it myself."[15] Initially, the lieutenant governor offered to buy printing equipment for Ben in London but then changed his mind. Instead he promised to fund Ben's trip to England so that he could select the equipment himself. Ben was thrilled, because to learn the latest advances in London would make him one of the most expert printers in North America. Sir Keith ordered him to sail on the London Hope on November 5. There was only one obstacle, for Ben planned to marry Deborah.

Whatever turmoil that stirred in the couple was promptly put aside when on September 2 Deborah's forty-seven-year-old father died. His death must have stunned Sarah, for soon afterward she insisted to her daughter and Ben that she felt it "most prudent" to postpone the wedding. The young lovers were still very young. Besides, Ben was "barely eighteen" and "about to take a long voyage." The marriage "if it was to take place would be more convenient" after his return.[16]

The reader can only imagine Deborah's despair. In a matter of days, one of the two important men in her life had died and the second was about to leave. Added to that was the Reads' sudden loss of income. Although John was considered "a man of some substance, owning two adjacent lots and two houses on High [Market] Street," and his estate was valued at a moderate eighty-eight pounds, British law allowed a widow only a third of her husband's property.[17] Moreover, because John had left debts, Sarah began hawking her ointments and salves more aggressively and probably relied on Deborah for assistance.

Meanwhile Ben, ecstatic with the idea of sailing to England, fancied he was destined to become a great success. Years later his *Poor Richard's Almanack* warned readers about the dangers of high hopes. "Blessed be he who expects nothing, for he will never be disappointed." Then in a more folksy version, "Cut the wings of your hopes and your hens, let they lead you to weary dance after them."[18]

On November 5, after "interchanging some promises with Miss Read," Ben agreed to write frequently from London. Deborah had no reason to doubt him. Before departing, he repeated his intention to marry her "when I should be, as I expected, set up in my business."[19]

Among Sir Keith's promises were letters of credit that would fund the journey and still others that recommended Ben to his English friends. But as soon as Ben boarded the ironically named *London Hope*, he realized the letters were missing. Initially he assumed it was an oversight. Surely Sir Keith would send them when the ship stopped in New Castle, Delaware, before heading into the Atlantic.

Hours before the ship was to sail from Delaware, an aide to the lieutenant governor came aboard and promised delivery of the letters. Still Ben did not see them, and once the *London Hope* was at sea, he asked Captain Annis for them. Important documents, the captain replied, were stored in a mail pouch for safekeeping but would be retrieved just before they landed. When the ship finally approached England, Ben obtained the pouch and rifled through it. Nothing was there from Sir Keith.

In a panic, Ben expressed his rage and predicament to fellow passenger Thomas Denham, a Quaker merchant from Philadelphia. With a wry smile, the older man "let me into Keith's character, told me there was not the least probability that he had written any letters for me, that no one who knew him had the smallest dependence on him . . . laughed at the notion of the governor giving me a letter of credit, having no credit to give."[20]

Immediately, the merchant suggested Ben find work at one of London's printing houses.

A half-century later Ben described Sir Keith as a well-meaning man and attributed his betrayal to a character flaw. The official was a people pleaser, who "having little to give . . . he gave expectations."[21] To Ben it was a stern lesson in self-sufficiency. "In things of moment, on thy self depend / Nor trust too far thy servant or thy friend," Ben later wrote in the *Almanack*.[22]

Soon he found a job at the Samuel Palmers publishing house. His friend, the poetic James Ralph who had accompanied him to London, had failed to find work as an actor and writer, so Ben paid the rent for their shared rooms. James, meanwhile, dazzled by London's wide offering of plays and other entertainments, gadded about town and enticed Ben to join him— until Ben realized the costs.

James's giddiness also extended to his personal relations. Having deliberately abandoned his wife and child in Philadelphia, he persuaded Ben to forget his commitment to Deborah. "I never wrote but one letter and that was to let her know I was not likely soon to return," Ben admitted. The letter, he added, "was another of the great errata [a printer's term for error] of my life which I should wish to correct if I were to live it over again."[23]

By late spring 1725 Deborah had received the letter. She was heartbroken. How could he forget her? Part of her wanted to wait for Ben, but for how long? Her mother, other relatives, and friends pointed out he might never return. Moreover, since Deborah was of marriageable age, they reminded her she had no time to waste. After weeks of tears and regrets her "friends [mother, relatives, and confidants], despairing with reason of my [Ben's] return," finally persuaded Deborah to accept other suitors. Among them was a sweet-talking English potter named John Rogers, whom her family and friends "persuaded her to marry."[24] On August 5, 1725, Deborah wed Rogers at Philadelphia's Anglican Christ Church.

Ben, meanwhile, pursued other women in London. One of his favorites was a Mrs. T, who boarded with her child in the same house where he and James lived. A "genteelly bred" milliner who kept a shop in fashionable Chelsea, Ben thought her "sensible . . . lively and of most pleasing conversation."[25] Mrs. T, however, favored James, and after they became lovers, they moved to different quarters. Unable to find work in London, James found a teaching job sixty miles from the city.

In his absence, Mrs. T appealed to Ben for money to help with her struggling finances. "I grew fond of her company and being at this time under no religious restraints and presuming on my importance to her, I attempted familiarities (another Erratum)," he recalled. The woman was appalled and after showing a "proper resentment," wrote James about Ben's behavior.[26] Storming back to London, James confronted his friend and claimed Ben's dishonesty so enraged him that he refused to pay his debts. For Ben it was another lesson on the importance of financial independence. "If you'd know the value of money, go and borrow some" he later warned readers of *Poor Richard's Almanack*.[27]

Ben soon found a better job at the publishing company of John Watts in Lincoln's Inn Fields. London was then in the midst of a golden literary age. Publishers churned out pamphlets and essays in the style of Steele and Addison's *Tatler,* satirists like Alexander Pope and Jonathan Swift debunked social customs, and editorial cartoonists like Hogarth illustrated the follies of society. Fascinated, Ben frequented London's coffeehouses and taverns where distinguished writers, editors, and thinkers met to debate current events. By late 1726, despite his acquaintance with men like writer-philosopher Bernard Mandeville, botanist and secretary of the Royal Society Sir Hans Sloane, and future publisher of the *London Magazine* Charles Ackers, he claimed that he had "tired of London, remembered with pleasure the happy months . . . spent in Pennsylvania and wished again to see it."[28]

Deborah must have been part of those memories, although Ben's *Autobiography* never explained what he meant by those "happy months." During his trip to London he remained friendly with Thomas Denham, whom he had met on his voyage. The merchant persuaded Ben to give up printing with the promise of joining his importing business back in Philadelphia. So kind and fatherly was Denham, even loaning Ben money for the passage home, that the young printer agreed. On October 11, 1726, after nearly three months at sea, their ship finally arrived in Philadelphia.

During Ben's eighteen months abroad, circumstances for some of his friends and acquaintances had changed. Surprisingly, his old boss Keimer "now had a better house, a shop well supplied . . . plenty of new type . . . and seemed to have a great deal of business." In contrast Sir Keith was no longer the deputy governor. Once Ben saw him walking by as an ordinary citizen and almost stopped to greet him. The former official saw him too but "seemed a little ashamed to see me but passed without saying anything."[29]

Even more painful was seeing Deborah again. Soon after her marriage to Rogers she learned he had a wife and child in England, and she angrily declared she would no longer live with him or bear his name. After that Rogers disappeared.

Knowing that must have made Ben's first trip to the Reads awkward. Even so, he later claimed in his *Autobiography* that "a friendly correspondence as neighbors and old acquaintances had continued between me and Mrs. Read's family, who all had a regard for me from the time of my first lodging in their home." They were remarkably forgiving toward the man who had jilted Deborah, but Ben claimed he was "often invited there and consulted in their affairs, wherein I sometimes was of service."[30] More than likely he offered Mrs. Read financial advice, for by 1728 Ben and a partner had established a successful printing business.

Even so, Deborah remained in the background. No longer was she the high-spirited, sociable, and trusting young woman Ben had left behind but was "generally dejected, seldom cheerful and avoided company."[31] It was understandable, for Rogers had not only squandered her dowry but was also rumored to be in heavy debt. Legally Deborah was still his wife, but without proof of Rogers's earlier marriage, she could not obtain an annulment. Nor did the Colony of Pennsylvania provide recourse for a divorce. Despite her predicament, she still loved Ben even though a marriage to him now seemed impossible.

2

"A Man and Not an Angel"

ONE SUMMER DAY IN 1730, as Ben visited with the Reads, he told Sarah that he blamed himself for Deborah's plight. Guiltily, he confessed that "his giddiness and inconstancy when in London [was] in a great degree the cause of her unhappiness."[1] Privately, Deborah must have agreed.

To Ben's surprise, Deborah's mother "was good enough to think the fault more her own than mine." It was she, after all, who "had prevented our marrying before I went thither" and in Ben's absence, "persuaded the other match."[2] Sarah's words spread over Ben like one of her medicinal ointments, soothing the guilt he felt about Deborah since returning from London.

"Soon afterwards our affection was revived," Ben recalled. Like other key emotional moments in his writings, Ben omitted the details of his reconciliation with Deborah. What motivated him? Was he still attracted to his former sweetheart, perhaps even passionately so? Or was there a practical reason for his renewed interest in Deborah? Historians have never been able to settle upon an answer. The only comment Ben wrote in his *Autobiography* reads, "I took her to wife September 1, 1730."[3]

There was no church wedding. Deborah simply moved into Ben's rented house on the north side of Market Street at Second in a "common law" marriage. Informal unions like that were not unusual, even in Quaker-dominated Philadelphia. Pragmatically, Deborah had no other option. She was still Rogers's wife, so a legal marriage was out of the question. Still, as Ben recalled in his *Autobiography*, there were "great objections to our union."[4] Among the reasons were rumors that Rogers, who fled to the West Indies, had died in a barroom brawl. If that could be proven and Ben married Deborah, he could be liable for Rogers's debts. Had she and Ben formally wed and Rogers then reappeared, the couple would have been convicted of bigamy, subjected to thirty-nine lashes on their bare backs and imprisoned with hard labor for life.

"We ventured however, over all these difficulties . . . [and] none of the inconveniences happened." Deborah "proved a good and faithful helpmate . . . we throve together and have ever mutually endeavored to make each other happy," Ben wrote decades later. "Thus I corrected that great erratum as well as I could."[5]

In comparison to Deborah's disastrous first marriage, her second one seemed promising. As a bride she lived with Ben in his rented house just down the street from her widowed mother and siblings. From the first days of their union, Deborah exuded pride in her husband. No longer was Ben the unsettled young man who once boarded at her parents' home. By the time he married, he had become a respected businessman, owner of the *Pennsylvania Gazette*, a print shop, and a stationery store that he ran from his home.

As he had matured Ben learned that being "industrious and frugal" was not enough. It was also important to appear that way. "I dressed plainly; I was seen at no places of idle diversion; I never went out a-fishing or shooting; a book, indeed, sometimes debauched [distracted] me from my work: but that was seldom . . . [I] gave no scandal . . . thus being esteemed an industrious, thriving young man."[6]

The path to Ben's success had been rocky. After returning to Philadelphia in October 1726, he became Thomas Denham's junior partner in an importing shop near the Delaware wharves, but that winter they both became ill. "My distemper was a pleurisy which nearly carried me off. I suffered a good deal, gave up . . . and was rather disappointed when I found myself recovering," Ben recalled in his *Autobiography*. Denham, however, continued to suffer for over a year and passed away in July 1728. In his will, his employer forgave Ben the money borrowed for the return passage to

Philadelphia, but either Denham's failing health or creditor possession of his business left Ben "once more to the wide world."[7]

Today medical experts consider pleurisy secondary to a viral infection. A major symptom is chest pain, especially while taking a deep breath, a result of inflamed pleura, the membrane lining the inner chest cavity and lung. Possibly Ben and Denham had contracted pneumonia or even influenza, then beginning to spread from Europe to America. Ben, a strong swimmer and wrestler in his youth, never forgot the horror of that illness and subsequently became an advocate for fresh air. Even on the coldest winter days the future founding father opened his windows and sat by them, often in the nude. In summer, Ben took long walks. He exercised vigorously, lifted weights, and engaged in what today is called "aerobics."

Denham's failing health meant Ben had to find a new job. Reluctantly he returned to work as a printer for Samuel Keimer, who lured him back with promises of higher wages and a promotion. First, though, Ben was obliged to mix inks, prepare engravings, manage the warehouse, and teach Keimer's workers new printing skills. Gradually the printer's warmth cooled, and he began criticizing Ben's work. "The wolf sheds his coat once a year, his disposition never," as Ben later wrote in *Poor Richard's Almanack*.[8] Six months into the job, Keimer began grumbling that Ben's wages were too high and complained about his work. One afternoon when Keimer bellowed at him in public, Ben quit.

That same night, his fellow worker, Hugh Meredith, proposed they partner in a print shop funded by his father, Simon. Ben brightened at the thought. Only later did he realize Meredith's father had an ulterior motive, secretly hoping Ben's temperance would cure Hugh of his "wretched habit of dram drinking."[9] Suspecting nothing, Ben embraced the idea of a partnership. During the months before the printing equipment arrived, he reluctantly returned to work with Keimer. By then the printer had a contract with the Colony of New Jersey to print paper money, but the task exceeded his skills. To save his employer's reputation, Ben fashioned "a copper plate, the first that had been seen in the country," and then "successfully completed the job."[10]

In the gossipy, tight-knit neighborhood around Market Street, the newly single Deborah must have known about Ben's sporadic employment with Keimer, but not about his personal life. During the years before he married her, Ben pursued other women. By June 1728, after he and Hugh rented a three-story brick house on Second Street near Market to house their printing press (now 139 Market Street), they rented out part of it to the glazier and mathematician Thomas Godfrey and his wife and two daughters. At the suggestion of Godfrey's wife, Ben found one of her daughters "very deserving" and courted her.[11]

At first all went well. The Godfreys often invited Ben to dinner, then discreetly left him and their daughter alone. Before long Ben proposed and the girl accepted. Then he demanded her parents pay off his business debts. Outraged, the Godfreys shut their daughter in her room, canceled the match, and moved out of the house.

Ben remained determined to find a wife. Bachelors were looked upon with suspicion as potential troublemakers, and thus almost everyone in colonial America married. In confirmation of that view, Ben later wrote, "Marriage is the natural state of man. A bachelor is not a complete human being. He is like the odd half of a pair of scissors . . . therefore is not even half so useful as they [he and a woman] might be together."[12] To find that "other half," Ben consequently "looked round me and made overtures in other places."[13]

Yet none of the fathers whose daughters Ben favored welcomed his courtship, reasoning that printers were poor providers. If Ben wanted to marry he was told "not to expect money with a wife unless with such a one, as I should not otherwise think agreeable."[14] Simultaneously, Ben was privately struggling with what he termed that "hard-to-be-governed passion of youth." In a passage remarkably candid for an eighteenth-century memoir, Ben admitted in his *Autobiography* that his urges "hurried me frequently into low intrigues with low women . . . attended with some expense and great inconvenience, besides a continual risk to my health by a distemper . . . though by great good luck I escaped."[15] Marriage was the obvious—and practical—remedy.

After Ben and Hugh set up their shop, they dumped Keimer. As Ben gleefully reported in his *Autobiography,* he and Hugh "left him . . . before he heard of it."[16] Their revolt shocked others, who predicted the upstart company would fail. To that Ben scoffed. "Croakers there are in every country, always boding ruin."[17] Despite the doubters, the new publishing house thrived. The highlight was Ben and Hugh's October 3, 1729, purchase of Keimer's dull newspaper, the *Universal Instructor in all Arts and Sciences; and Pennsylvania Gazette,* whose title they shortened to the *Pennsylvania Gazette.*

Despite that triumph, the young printing house had debts. In addition, since Hugh was "a poor pressman and seldom sober," Ben assumed most of the work.[18] In desperation he appealed to friends, who agreed to lend him money on one condition: Ben must dismiss Hugh, who was "often seen drunk in the streets and playing at low games in alehouses."[19] Out of loyalty to his partner, Ben hesitated.

The timing could not have been worse, for by then the shop's solidity was further threatened by a colony-wide scarcity of hard currency. Without coinage, bills and debts remained unpaid, creating a panic among the merchants of Pennsylvania. "There was a cry among the people for more paper money. Only £15000 being extant in the Province and that soon to be sunk," as Ben recalled.[20] Something had to be done, and soon. On October 3, Ben consequently wrote and circulated "The Need and Necessity of a Paper Currency," which explained how "the want of money . . . reduces trade and discourages production."[21] After reading the article, the Pennsylvania Assembly voted his suggestion into law and designated Ben and Hugh their official printers.

Still Hugh's drinking increased, and at last he agreed to end the partnership in the summer of 1730. In return, Ben repaid his father's loans and provided Hugh with "thirty pounds and a new saddle" to begin a new life in the Carolinas.[22] On July 14 the partnership formally ended. Ben thus became the sole owner of the *Gazette* and print shop, which he called simply B. Franklin, Printer.

To boost profits, Ben opened a stationery store in his home. By autumn 1730 his bride Deborah—or Debby or Debbie, as Ben fondly called her—took over the store, kept the books for his printing business, and attended to related tasks. Decades later Ben attributed much of his financial success to her. "It was lucky for me that I had one [a wife] as disposed to industry and frugality as myself. She assisted me cheerfully in my business, folding and stitching pamphlets, tending shop, purchasing old linen rags for the paper-makers, etc. etc."[23]

To a natural saleswoman like Deborah, the goods in Ben's stationery store—quills, sealing wax, inkhorns, and books—seemed unlikely to produce a big profit. More items with a broader appeal were needed. Deborah consequently stocked dozens of other items, many brought by wagon from nearby farmlands and the Delaware wharves, shipped from distant colonies and England. Among the goods were coffee, tea, chocolate, palm oil, saffron, linseed, Rhode Island cheese, codfish, mackerel, and mustard powder. Included too was the Franklins' "crown soap," made by Ben's Boston relatives. Ben also promoted Widow Read's ointments in the *Gazette* as "sufficient to remove the most inveterate itch."[24] Occasionally Deborah sold other items, such as scales, lampblack, goose feathers, and white stockings, effectively transforming Ben's stationery shop into what later became known as a general store.

Despite Ben's subsequent praise for Deborah, some of his writings suggest their adjustment to marriage was challenging. Six weeks after their union, Ben's October 6 *Pennsylvania Gazette* published his "Rules and Maxims for Promoting Matrimonial Happiness." He urged women especially to read it, explaining "all females that would be married, or already [are] ... not that I suppose their sex more faulty than the other, and most to want advice, for I assure them, upon my honor, I believe the quite contrary, but I esteem them better disposed to receive and practice" his advice.[25]

First, a wife must give up "all thoughts of managing your husband. Never ... deceive or impose on his understanding ... not try his temper but treat him always ... with sincerity ... and afterwards with affection and respect." Moreover, she should neither be "overly sanguine before marriage" nor expect perfection afterward, for her husband was "a man and not an angel." If she found "anything in his humor or behavior that is not altogether so agreeable as ... expected, pass it over as a human frailty, smooth your brow; compose your temper; and try to amend it by cheerfulness and good nature."[26]

Ben listed still other rules. Among them was the importance of wives to be cheerful, to faithfully wear her wedding ring, and to remember that her

power and happiness had "no other foundation but her husband's esteem
and love." Above all Ben urged her to read the matrimonial service frequently and "take care . . . not to overlook the word *obey*."[27]

The reader may wonder what prompted Ben's article. If asked, he probably would have replied that he was merely providing a public service for
Gazette readers. The timing so soon after his marriage, however, suggests
Ben's expectations as a husband. Moreover, the rules later served as his defense against a situation he did not yet dare broach with Deborah.

One day in March 1731, Ben arrived home with a squirming bundle.
Within it was his infant son, William, the probable result of his earlier association with one of the "low women" he later mentioned in his *Autobiography*. Deborah was shocked—and hurt. Already she had been betrayed
by her first husband. Now the second one had dealt her a humiliating blow.

Ben's presentation of his infant contradicted everything she knew about
him. Piety had been drummed into him as a child. Ben's father, Josiah, had
served as constable, or chief of moral marshals, at Boston's South Church.
He and his wife, Abiah, had a library of theological books and often opened
their house for prayer meetings. While Deborah knew Ben disliked attending religious services, he was a moral, civic-minded man. Few could dis-
pute that. Philadelphians considered him an upstanding businessman; to his
fellow tradesmen Ben was a leader; to Deborah's family, a wise and courte-
ous adviser. Yet despite her husband's gentlemanly demeanor, the baby was
proof that he had dallied with another woman—and rather recently at that.

By bringing the baby home, Ben implicitly expected Deborah to raise
him. She was stunned and at first she balked. Beyond that, little is known
about her reaction. Yet like anyone confronted with a similar situation,
Deborah must have asked about the child's mother. Who was she? How did
Ben know her? Why couldn't she raise the baby herself? Then or perhaps
later, Deborah may even have asked the most painful question of all: Had
Ben married her in September because he expected the birth of the child
and needed a responsible caretaker? Had he wed Deborah as a practical
solution rather than out of love?

Given the subsequent forty-three years of their affectionate marriage, Ben
surely reassured Deborah of the latter. Possibly, too, he pleaded tolerance

because of his years as a bachelor. Nor could Deborah argue against his "Rules and Maxims for Promoting Matrimonial Happiness," especially the warning that a husband was "a man and not an angel" and thus might occasionally stray. Even so, a wife was obliged to remember she held a unique position in her husband's heart. As a result, she must conduct herself with dignity and "let the tenderness of conjugal love be expressed with decency, delicacy and prudence [as] distinct from the designing fondness of a harlot."[28]

Deborah ultimately complied. According to her great-granddaughter's memoir, she agreed because Ben's "tenderness towards herself at last overcame her objections."[29] Ben had rescued her from a poor and lonely future. She owed him for that. While she accepted the baby because of her love for Ben, she never loved or accepted the child as her own. Years later when "Billy" (as his family called him) was in his early twenties, a visitor noted that Deborah regarded him "coldly, even with open hostility."[30]

Scholars and historians have long debated the timing and circumstances of his birth. Pulitzer Prize–winning biographer Carl Van Doren believed Deborah was Billy's real mother. He believed the claim of illegitimacy was a lie, that more than likely it was a way to hide Ben and Deborah's premarital intimacy and preserve her honor.

Several factors argue against that. Deborah never acknowledged Billy as her son. Nor did she ever deny that he was Ben's child. As Ben became politically prominent, his enemies spread rumors through the colonies and England about Billy's origins as Franklin's "bastard." Some of them even accused the founding father of treating Billy's mother cruelly.

In 1763, after years of those rumors, George Roberts, the son of Ben's close friend Hugh Roberts, attempted to end them. "It is generally known here that his [William's] birth is illegitimate and that his mother is not in good circumstances," but any report of her "begging bread in the streets . . . is without the least foundation of truth . . . some small provision is made by him [Ben]." Since, however, she was "none of the most agreeable women . . . the father and son [were not] acknowledging any connection with her," Roberts wrote to an influential English friend.[31]

Other biographers, among them the distinguished scholar J. A. Leo Lemay, argued that Billy was born several years before Ben wed. As proof he cited the dates of the youth's service in the army, then insisted the claim of promotion for the sixteen- or seventeen-year-old Billy from ensign to captain in 1747 was unlikely. Lemay consequently concluded Ben's son must have been born in 1728 or 1729. He also disputed the idea that the boy's mother was a prostitute, theorizing that she was a woman of higher rank, since Ben claimed that William was his son. Quite likely, Lemay reasoned, she may have been the wife of one of his friends or acquaintances who was away for many months. Other historians believe William was born after 1729. Sheila Skemp believed that William was born in 1730 or 1731, joined the army at sixteen, and was prematurely promoted a year later.

Equally tantalizing was Ben's April 12, 1750, boast to his mother, Abiah, that Billy was "now 19 years of age, a tall, proper youth and much of a beau."[32] By writing, Ben may have attempted to hide the real age of his son from his pious and elderly mother. But that might have been true, for even late in life Billy maintained that was his age.

Other historians maintain that Billy's imminent birth prompted Ben to marry Deborah. For proof they cite his June 1730 letter to his older sister, Sarah Franklin Davenport. In it, Ben insisted, "I am not to be married, as you have heard."[33] If so, he must have written it just a few days or weeks before his mistress announced her pregnancy. According to that theory, Ben was so alarmed at the prospect of having no one to care for the newborn that he suddenly proposed to Deborah.

That too seems possible, for Ben was a practical man. Yet beneath his famous image as a calm, highly reasoned person, he privately wavered between passion and prudence throughout his life.

During the first months of Ben's marriage to Deborah, he must have worried about the baby's welfare. What woman would be willing to raise his bastard? It would have to be someone in an unusual situation; someone young, longing for a husband; someone who loved him enough to forgive him. The answer was obvious: Miss Read.

Only decades later would Deborah come to terms with the unspoken contract she had accepted as Ben's wife.

3

"Like a Faithful Pair of Doves"

CRADLES MUST BE ROCKED, a baby's hunger relieved with breast milk, diapers washed in boiling water, and herbs ground with mortar and pestle to make medicines. If a colonial era infant survived to become a toddler, he or she was tethered by leather straps to furniture to prevent exploration of dangerous open-hearth fireplaces, iron grates, and teapots on stands. These were among the tasks Deborah reluctantly performed during the first years of Billy's life. Simultaneously, she hoped for a child of her own.

Nearly another year would pass before Ben's wife discovered she was pregnant, then she waited another seven or eight months before giving birth. Nearly two years: a long time for the twenty-four-year-old Deborah to care for another woman's child.

On October 20, 1732, she delivered Francis Folger Franklin. "Franky," his parents called him. From the start, the infant was vibrant and curious, a son whom Ben believed was destined for greatness. To the enthralled father, interrupted sleep, crying spells, coughs, and fevers seemed a small sacrifice to pay. Babies were one of "the most delightful cares in the world," he wrote a father who had recently lost an infant.[1] Those "cares" were almost certainly Deborah's responsibility. By the time Franky was two, Ben was so proud that he had the child's portrait painted. Convinced the boy was highly intelligent, he even hired a tutor for the toddler. He also arranged for a tutor for four-year-old Billy.

Later, when his older son became a teenager, Ben doted upon Billy too. Still, as historian Sheila Skemp noted, Ben probably spent little time with the child in his early years because of long hours as a printer, publisher, and civic innovator. That in turn left Deborah as the boy's consistent, if less than open-hearted, caregiver. Maybe that was to be expected, for in the early eighteenth century discipline, rather than tender expressions of love, was considered the measure of good parenting. "Let thy child's first lesson be obedience / and the second will be what thou wilt," as Ben later advised readers of the *Almanack*.[2]

Deborah's life as a young mother has not been recorded, but her duties in the home and the shop suggest that she, too, had little extra time. Four months after Ben brought Billy home, Deborah's mother, Sarah, moved into the Franklins' small home. That made their quarters more crowded, but the matron undoubtedly helped with the housekeeping duties and care for the two Franklin boys. Deborah was then free to stand at the counter of her store and to respond to a knock on the door or the clang of a bell announcing the arrival of customers. In between those visits, she took stock of her goods and arranged delivery of new ones from nearby farms and the Delaware wharves. The combination of shopkeeping, marriage, and motherhood was not unique to Deborah. By then a small but growing group of other enterprising women juggled those duties around Market Street, Philadelphia's commercial center. Running a store not only introduced Deborah to a wide range of people but also refined her bookkeeping skills to the point that Ben considered her an important factor in his financial success.

As her shop and Ben's print business thrived, Deborah became increasingly proud of her husband. Ben, who rarely wrote about his wife's emotions, recorded one instance of her admiration in his *Autobiography*. One morning when he appeared at the table for breakfast, he found a china bowl and silver spoon set for his porridge in place of his usual two-penny earthen bowl and pewter spoon. "They had been bought for me without my knowledge by my wife, and cost her the enormous sum of three and twenty shillings, for which she had no other excuse or apology . . . but that she thought her husband deserved a silver spoon and china bowl as well as any of his neighbors," Ben explained.[3]

Deborah's pride was justified. Back in 1727 Ben had organized a dozen tradesmen and artisans into a club to discuss moral and "natural philosophy"; the group was dedicated to self-improvement and community welfare. Known as the Leather Apron Club from its origin among tradesmen, the twelve original members soon changed its name to the Junto. A year after his marriage, Ben urged members of the Junto to establish the Library Company so that Philadelphians could borrow books. In 1736 the Pennsylvania legislature, or Assembly, appointed Ben their clerk as well and their official printer. One wonders how Ben managed all those duties along with his newspaper, print shop, and role as a young parent. While he later hired a foreman, it was Deborah who assisted him when urgent obligations—Assembly meetings, legislative papers and bills, and newspaper deadlines—demanded immediate attention.

As publisher of the *Gazette*, Ben endorsed the importance of freedom of the press and pledged the newspaper would publish reports about current affairs in an even-handed manner. While men may "differ in opinion, both sides ought equally to have the advantage of being heard by the public. When truth and error have fair play, the former is always an overmatch for the latter," he declared in his June 1731 "Apology for Printers."[4] Ben's news stories consequently claimed to represent both sides of an issue.

Still he managed to find a way to express his opinion. In an echo of the fictitious voices he once created in the *New England Courant*, Ben created new satirical characters with telling names like Anthony Afterwit, Celia Singleton, and Alice Addertongue, who mocked political intrigues and social frivolities. Still that did not satisfy Ben's ambitions. A businessman as well as a printer, he longed to reach a wider audience, one that would amuse and educate the ordinary man and simultaneously turn a handsome profit.

Before long Ben settled upon a solution: an almanac. To the average colonist, almanacs were important reference books. Six were already in print in Philadelphia, two of which Ben already published in his shop. Within them were calendars, holidays, weather predictions, phases of the moon, tides, astronomical events, and recipes. Typically they were monotonous pages of lists mixed with bits of folk wisdom. By late 1732, just as Deborah was about to give birth, Ben had created his own version filled with humor, homilies, and traditional information. Featuring a folksy fictional editor called Richard Saunders, Ben's new publication was called *Poor Richard's Almanack.*

The first edition arrived in Deborah's stationery store in late December 1732. Almost immediately sales skyrocketed as people discovered the *Almanack* contained humor, introduced by Saunders's tale of conflict with his shrewish wife. "I write almanacs with no other view than that of the public good," Ben's fictitious narrator announced. "The plain truth of the matter, I am excessive poor, and my wife, good woman, is, I tell her, excessive proud; she cannot bear, she says, to sit spinning in her shift . . . while I do nothing but gaze at the stars."[5]

Saunders's indolence had enraged his wife, Bridget, he humbly admitted to readers. In fact, she "has threatened more than once to burn all my books and rattling-traps (as she calls my instruments) if I do not make some profitable use of them for the good of my family."[6] While a dramatic contrast to the Franklins' companionable marriage, Bridget's reference to Saunders's "rattling-traps" may have been inspired by Deborah's view of Ben's knack for invention.

Today *Poor Richard's Almanack* is best remembered for its witty, penny-pinching proverbs. Readers usually assume Ben wrote them, even though he admitted many were borrowed "from the wisdom of many ages and nations."[7] The result was a blend of English proverbs, folklore, ditties, and phrases from authors such as Dryden, Pope, La Rochefoucauld, and Rabelais. Some were quoted verbatim; others Ben's sharp quill transformed into pithy pronouncements on prudence, thrift, and human folly. Priced at a modest three shillings each, the "Poor Dicks" as Deborah dubbed them, became the Franklins' best sellers.[8] The series became so popular that Ben's press could barely keep them in print. Soon sales reached ten thousand copies per year.

The 1733 version of the *Almanack* opened with Saunders's continuing saga of his marriage. "The purchase of my Almanacks, has made my circumstances much more easy in the world. . . . My wife has been able to get a pot of her own, and is no longer obliged to borrow one from a neighbor;

nor have we ever since been without something of our own to put it in. She has also got a pair of shoes, two new shifts and a new warm petticoat."[9]

Saunders added that he too had benefited from the profits. In fact, he gloated, he even "bought a second-hand coat, [one] so good, that I am now not ashamed to go to town." Best of all, Bridget's "temper [which is] so much more pacific than it used to be, that I . . . have slept more and more quietly within this last year, than in the three foregoing years put together."[10] Ben's readers loved it. In an era when women were often belittled for their ignorance, shrewishness, and vanity, what could delight male readers more than mocking a woman's fondness for finery while her husband celebrated the purchase of a secondhand coat?

In contrast to Ben's *Almanack*, other stories appeared in the *Gazette* that defended women. Did Ben publish these to avoid being labeled a misogynist? Or was it a rationalization for the inevitable conflicts in marriage? Superficially at least, the publication of "A Scolding Wife" in the July 5, 1733, *Gazette* reflected the latter and Ben's acceptance of a strong-willed, if well-meaning, spouse like Deborah.

Despite the "inconvenience" of a wife's outspoken manner, he admitted "she has conveniences enough to make it . . . a happiness. For I speak from experience, (as well as a long course of observation) women of that character have generally sound and healthy constitutions, produce a vigorous offspring, are active in the business of the family, special good housewives, and very careful of their husbands' interest. As to the noise attending all this, tis but a trifle when a man is used to it and observes that it is only a mere habit . . . in which all is well meant, and ought to be well taken."[11] Husbands should consequently realize that a wife's good intentions were more important than her sharp tongue.

By the same token several maxims within Ben's 1733 *Almanack* reminded readers to be grateful for a cheerful mate. "From a cross neighbor and a sullen wife, a pointless needle and a broken knife . . . From each of these, Good Lord, deliver me."[12] Nevertheless, a husband's tolerance of his wife's opinions did not imply that she should rule. After all, "I know not which lives more unnatural lives / obeying husbands, or commanding wives."[13]

Then, in what may have been an oblique rationale for Deborah's ordinary appearance, the *Almanack* insisted that plain women were better wives than beautiful ones. "You cannot pluck roses without fear of thorns / Nor enjoy a fair wife without the danger of horns," Ben wrote.[14]

Here and there the *Almanack* poked fun at domineering or vain women but overall praised them. Many of the maxims insisted that what counted in life was marriage to a good woman—clearly a reflection of Ben's personal happiness at that time. "A little house well filled, a little field well tilled / and a little wife well willed, are great riches."[15] Still, that "little wife well willed," Ben observed, resulted from her husband's amiable behavior. "Good wives and good plantations are made by good husbands."[16]

Beyond the advice offered readers in the *Almanack*, Ben covered daily events in the *Gazette*. The winter before he married Deborah, his newspaper warned readers about a smallpox epidemic in Boston that killed nearly a third of the sufferers. In that story Ben noted that those who survived had been inoculated. Primitive by contemporary standards, the process placed live smallpox virus into the bloodstream of a healthy individual. To do that, fluid was taken from the pox of a sufferer and scratched into the arm or thigh of the inoculant.

Contemporary smallpox inoculations contain the cells of dead viruses; in the colonial era physicians had no choice but to use live virus. Several days of illness usually followed, but most inoculants survived and achieved permanent immunity. In the 1730s, however, many Philadelphians were superstitious and avoided inoculation. Some considered it more dangerous than the disease itself. Others thought it unnatural, against God's will, and even the work of the devil.

Ben, who embraced the scientific advances of the Enlightenment, repeatedly tried to educate the city's residents. Consequently, when smallpox swept through Philadelphia in March 1731, his *Gazette* announced, "The practice of inoculation for the smallpox begins to grow among us. How groundless all those extravagant reports are, that have been spread through the province to the contrary."[17] To dispel those reports, Ben cited a respected English journal that supported inoculation. By July the epidemic had run its course but had killed nearly three hundred residents.

In September 1736, when smallpox again raged through Philadelphia, Ben resumed his campaign. By then he, Deborah, and Billy were apparently already inoculated. Not, however, little Franky, who was then sick with the "flux," or dysentery, with its fevers, bloody diarrhea, abdominal cramps, and malaise. Weeks passed as Deborah and Ben worried over Franky's failure to rally. In mid-November the child developed a high fever followed by the ominous sores of the "pox." On the twenty-first Francis Folger Franklin died, just a few weeks after his fourth birthday.

Deborah must have been heartbroken. Once again her reaction was not recorded in Ben's *Autobiography,* but neighbors reported she displayed Franky's portrait prominently in the Franklin home for the rest of her life. Ben was plunged into grief. "In 1736 I lost one of my sons, a fine boy of 4 years old by the smallpox taken in the common way. I long regretted bitterly and still regret that I had not given it to him by inoculation. This I mention for the sake of parents, who omit that operation on the supposition that they should never forgive themselves if a child died under it," Ben observed in his *Autobiography.* Whatever decision was made, Ben added, "the regret may be same either way, and that therefore the safer should be chosen."[18]

Decades later, his younger and favorite sister, Jane Franklin Mecom, wrote to him in London about his young grandsons in Philadelphia. Wistfully Ben replied that her letter brought "afresh to my mind the idea of my son Franky, now dead thirty-six years, whom I have seldom seen equal in everything, and whom to this day I cannot think of without a sigh."[19]

Despite Ben's earlier support for inoculation, many Philadelphians remained superstitious. Two months after Franky's death, rumors spread around the city that Ben had secretly inoculated Franky and thus caused his death. Enraged, the publisher's December 30 *Gazette* read, "I do hereby sincerely declare, that he was not inoculated, but received the distemper in the common way of infection. . . . Inoculation was a safe and beneficial practice."[20]

Historians usually accepted Ben's statement as truth. More recently, author Stephen Coss's article in the September 2017 *Smithsonian* doubted that. Instead he laid the blame on Deborah for Franky's death. Coss maintained that Deborah was an ignorant woman, one so overly protective of Franky in an effort to keep Ben tied to her that she refused to allow the boy's inoculation. According to Coss's theory, Franky's death thus accounted for Ben's later coolness toward his wife. "Whether he blamed Deborah, or blamed himself for listening to her, the hard feelings relating to the death of their beloved son . . . appear to have ravaged their relationship," Coss argued.[21]

Ben's writing about the first decade of his marriage refute Coss's misogynist assumptions. First, it seems highly unlikely that Deborah would have rebelled against Ben's decision to inoculate Franky. Throughout her life, she remained fervently devoted to her husband. Nor would she have forgotten Ben's "Rules and Maxims for Promoting Matrimonial Happiness," with its insistence upon obedience.

Second, Ben's comments about Deborah during the first decade of his marriage suggest he was happily married. Decades later from England, where he was writing his *Autobiography*, he attributed much of his financial success to being "once lucky enough to find in a wife" a frugal woman "who thereby became a fortune to me."[22]

This was not merely nostalgia. Ben trusted Deborah from the first years of their marriage. In fact, he was so impressed with her thrift, her business sense, and her impeccable accounts in the Franklin ledger books that on August 30, 1733, he granted Deborah power of attorney in his absence, a privilege rarely accorded to eighteenth-century women. Once a woman married, the concept of coverture, or male ownership of property, thus transferred her property and financial rights to her husband. Sometimes widows regained those rights, as had Deborah's widowed mother. But since Ben planned to travel in what were always risky excursions, he assigned Deborah the temporary rights given to widows.

> Know all men by these presents, that I *Benjamin Franklin of the City of Philadelphia in Pennsylvania, Printer* have constituted, made and appointed my trusty and loving Friend [Friend *struck out*] *Wife Deborah Franklin to be* my true and lawful attorney, for me and in my name and stead to ask, demand, sue for, levy, recover and receive all . . . sums of money, debts, rents, goods, wares, dues, accounts . . . whatsoever by *any Persons whatsoever.*[23]

Ben assigned Deborah power of attorney just before his trip to Boston to visit relatives. From there he rode to Newport, Rhode Island, to visit his ailing brother James, who, having moved there years earlier with his wife and five children, had established a successful printing house. Despite the long-standing bitterness between James and Ben, they had already reconciled. Now, learning that his brother was "fast declining" from an illness, Ben appeared at his bedside. "Our former differences were forgotten and our meeting . . . cordial and affectionate," Ben recalled in his *Autobiography*.[24] Sensing he was gravely ill, James asked Ben to bring his ten-year-old son to Philadelphia and train him as a printer. For several years James Franklin Jr. lived in the Franklin household under Deborah's care until he was old enough to apprentice with Ben.

Soon after James's death in February 1735, his grieving widow, Ann Smith Franklin, vowed to honor James's legacy. With advice and financial support from Ben, she assumed management of James's publishing house, winning her brother-in-law's admiration as she continued to publish books, almanacs, pamphlets, and legal notices. Around that time an anonymous reader of the *Gazette* wrote a scathing letter about the folly of marriage. It was, the disgruntled man declared, "mighty silly for a single man to change his state; for as soon as his wishes are crowned his expected bliss dissolves into cares in bondage. . . . Only fools in life wed, for every woman is a tyrant."[25]

The comment infuriated Ben. Regardless of his sly creation of Richard Saunders and satirical stories about his wife in the *Almanack*, Ben's appreciation of marriage was real. Mindful of the problems he once faced as a bachelor and the benefits of Deborah and his sister-in-law Anne's devotion to their husbands, he rose to the defense of married women. "Nor is it true that *as soon as a man weds, his expected bliss dissolves into slavish cares and bondage.* . . . If there be any bondage in the case, 'tis the woman enters into it, and not the man," Ben retorted.[26]

I and thousands more know very well that we could never thrive till we were married; and have done well ever since; What we get, the women save; a man being fixed in life minds his business better and more steadily . . . the idleness and negligence of men is more frequently fatal to families, than the extravagance of women. Nor does a man *lose his liberty* but increase[s] it . . . having a wife, that he can confide in, he may with much more freedom be abroad [away from home], and for a longer time; thus the business goes on comfortably, and the good couple relieve one another by turns, like a faithful pair of doves.[27]

In October 1737 Ben was appointed the postmaster of Philadelphia after his rival, the printer Andrew Bradford, was dismissed. The position was an honor, reflecting his favor with colonial authorities. The compensation was modest but inevitably brought new customers to Deborah's shop and Ben's printing office. Postal service in colonial America was inefficient; postage was not prepaid and required the postmaster's extension of credit to the senders. Once those letters were received, bills were sent to the post office, requiring Ben and Deborah to search through their books to locate the sender for billing. As a busy publisher, clerk of the Assembly, and civic innovator, Ben depended upon Deborah to assume many of the more thorny postal tasks. Among them was calculating the changing values of "Barbados Currency," "sterling value," and other intercolonial money.[28]

Within a few years Ben's pride in his wife and the harmonious life they shared inspired a celebratory poem. Nothing is known about the details of his 1742 presentation to the Junto, but it was so well regarded that it was preserved.

I SING MY PLAIN COUNTRY JOAN

Of their Chloes and Phillisses Poets may prate
    I sing my plain Country Joan
Now twelve Years my Wife, still the Joy of my Life
    Blest Day that I made her my own.
      My dear Friends
    Blest Day that I made her my own.

Not a Word of her Face, her Shape, or her Eyes,
    Of Flames or of Darts shall you hear;

Tho' I Beauty admire 'tis Virtue I prize,
   That fades not in seventy Years,
      My dear Friends

In Health a Companion delightfull and dear,
   Still easy, engaging, and Free,
In Sickness no less than the faithfullest Nurse
   As tender as tender can be,
      My dear Friends

In Peace and good Order, my Household she keeps
   Right Careful to save what I gain
Yet chearfully spends, and smiles on the Friends
   I've the Pleasures to entertain
      My dear Friends

She defends my good Name ever where I'm to blame,
   Friend firmer was ne'er to Man giv'n,
Her Compassionate Breast, feels for all the Distrest,
   Which draws down the Blessing from Heav'n,
      My dear Friends

Am I laden with Care, she takes off a large Share,
   That the Burthen ne'er makes [me] to reel,
Does good Fortune arrive, the Joy of my Wife,
   Quite Doubles the Pleasures I feel,
      My dear Friends

In Raptures the giddy Rake talks of his Fair,
   Enjoyment shall make him Despise,
I speak my cool sence, that long Experience,
   And Enjoyment have chang'd in no wise,
      My dear Friends

[Some Faults we have all, and so may my Joan,
    But then they're exceedingly small;
And now I'm us'd to 'em, they're just like my own,
    I scarcely can see 'em at all,
        My dear Friends,
    I scarcely can see them at all.]

Were the fairest young Princess, with Million in Purse
    To be had in Exchange for my Joan,
She could not be a better Wife, might be a Worse,
    So I'd stick to my Joggy alone
        My dear Friends
    I'd cling to my lovely ould Joan.[29]

A happy marriage, wealth, and political influence were benefits Ben enjoyed at the time he presented "I Sing My Plain Country Joan." If, as Ben suggested, time cooled passion in marriage, its prudential benefits more than compensated. Only one thing was missing: the birth of another child. Yet by then a decade had passed since Deborah had delivered their only son, Franky.

"In the Dark, All Cats Are Grey"

ON SEPTEMBER 11, 1743, eleven years after Franky's birth, Deborah delivered a second child. Named Sarah after her maternal grandmother, the Franklins called her Sally. Ben's delight in Franky and the high birth rate among other colonial couples suggest Deborah's long years of childlessness were not intentional. One hint that Deborah may have become pregnant between the birth of her two children was Ben's comment in the 1735 *Almanack*: "A ship under sail and a big-bellied woman / are the handsomest two things that can be seen in common."[1] After that entry, Ben made no other references to pregnant women. Perhaps Deborah suffered a miscarriage or a stillbirth or had other fertility problems.

Her barrenness must have been puzzling. Deborah's mother had delivered seven children, and Ben's mother, Abiah, ten. From the earliest days of the Franklin marriage, Ben consequently assumed his wife would be similarly fertile. As a newlywed, he even announced in the *Gazette* that one of the advantages of "scolding wives" was their "generally sound and healthy constitutions" enabling them to "produce vigorous offspring."[2] Yet for all Deborah's feisty spirit, Sally was the Franklins' only living child.

Having cared for Billy, who by then was a restless thirteen-year-old, Deborah was thrilled to have a daughter upon whom to dote. Ben, too, was pleased but probably spent little time with little Sally. As his November 4 letter to New York physician, politician, and natural scientist Cadwallader

Colden revealed, "My long absence from home in the summer, put my business so much behind-hand that I have been in a continual hurry ever since."[3]

Sally's arrival was also simultaneous with Ben's interest in electricity. During his stay in Boston that summer he had attended Dr. Archibald Spencer's demonstration on electricity. During his lecture the showman suspended a boy on silken cords attached to the ceiling, then rubbed a glass and produced sparks in his hands. The stunt fascinated Ben so much that when Dr. Spencer arrived in Philadelphia, he advertised his appearance in the *Gazette* and sold tickets in his shop.

To Deborah, Ben's enthusiasm could not have been a surprise, for he was always fascinated by scientific discoveries. Not only did he read about them in books, but he also kept journals filled with observations on the flow of air, tides and water, weather, the behavior of animals, and the growth of plants. Ben also had a keen interest in invention. By the harsh winter of 1740 he was already experimenting with a cast-iron stove. When placed in the middle of a room, the vents of his new "furnace" allowed hot air to flow freely, circulate, and provide even warmth.

Was Deborah's health, or concerns about it, the source of Ben's inspiration? Quite possibly, since his 1744 advertisement claimed his stove reduced women's susceptibility to illnesses from the inefficient heat of conventional fireplaces. In it Ben observed that women tended to "get colds in the head, rheums [runny eyes and nose] and defluctions [chest disturbances]." In addition, the "great and bright" flames from conventional fireplaces could damage "the eyes, dry and shrivel the skin and bring on early the appearance of old age."[4] Was Ben referring to the fading beauty of women as they aged or specifically referring to the nearly forty-year-old Deborah?

The stove's efficiency, Ben claimed, was a result of his "own experience and that of his family and friends, who have used warm rooms for these four winters past" and were "less liable to take cold."[5] By 1744, the "Pennsylvania Fire-Place" was selling so rapidly that the governor offered Ben a patent. Insisting that inventors "should be glad of an opportunity to serve others," Ben dismissed the offer so that the stove would be less expensive and easily available.[6]

Whatever warmth Deborah enjoyed from the new stove after Sally's birth was soon displaced by the cooler air of Ben's preoccupation with other projects. If she noticed, it may not have bothered her because she too was very busy: caring for Sally, managing the store, assisting in the post office, weaving cloth for clothes, and overseeing the Franklin household. To do that required a strong woman with a resilient spirit, one sometimes too spirited for those who disagreed with her.

One of those people was Deborah's next-door neighbor and cousin by marriage, James Read Jr. By August 1745 the newly wed attorney complained about Deborah's temper. To that, Ben drolly observed that as an attorney, his nephew should pick a "proper court" more sensibly. "Don't you know that all wives are in the right? It may be you don't, for you are yet but a young husband . . . I advise you not to bring it to trial; for if you do, you'll certainly be cast [found invalid]."[7] A decade later twenty-one-year-old visiting clerk Daniel Fisher noted that on one occasion when Deborah grew angry, she burst into "the foulest terms I ever heard from a gentlewoman."[8] After a neighbor, Sara Broughton, quarreled with Deborah over money, she complained to Ben, comparing his wife to a "hedgehog" who "shot a great many quills." Writing from London, Ben dismissed it as a "silly complaint."[9] As he once advised readers of the *Almanack*, "Keep your eyes open before marriage, half-closed afterwards."[10]

Deborah too tried to keep her eyes "half-closed" over things that annoyed her about Ben. One was his indulgence of the teenage Billy, who tried to run off to sea only to be "fetched" at the last moment by Ben from a privateer on the Delaware. After the youth drifted aimlessly at home, Ben finally urged Billy to enlist as an ensign in the British army during King George's War. Another issue that rankled Deborah was the incessant stream of admirers who appeared at the Franklin home to seek Ben's advice and interfered with his work. "All the world claimed a privilege of troubling her Pappy [Ben] with all their calamities and distresses," Deborah once complained to Daniel Fisher.[11]

In contrast to her domestic duties and business assistance was Ben's rising prominence as a publisher and civic innovator. Perhaps her behind-the-scenes role explains the picture several historians drew of Deborah as ignorant, only modestly intelligent, and provincial. Biographer Ormond Seavey described Ben's long travels in England and Europe as a foreign minister as an "escape from his wife, the shrill, dumpy and semi-literate Deborah."[12] Daniel T. Morgan found her "neither educated nor interesting."[13] Despite Deborah's contributions to Ben's economic, social, and political ascendancy in Philadelphia, historian Paul W. Conner described Deborah as "not the sort that the wives of Franklin's more select acquaintances would welcome."[14]

But as Jennifer Reed Fry observed in her scholarly article "Extraordinary Freedom and Great Humility": "No individual has suffered more acutely than Deborah Read Rogers . . . whose activities have been all but obliterated by her husband's considerable shadow . . . [and] portrayed (her) as servile rather than as an active contributor to the success of Benjamin's political career and the Franklin household."[15] Nevertheless, as recently as 2017 Stephen Coss once again characterized Deborah as Ben's "poor, uneducated wife" and one so desperate to keep him tied to her through Franky that she insisted the child's "inoculation was unacceptable."[16]

The condemnation of someone who lacks an education or has a provincial worldview is hardly a measure of IQ. Contemporary research suggests at least eight kinds of intelligence, among them the ability to be logical, mathematical, and to converse successfully with people, traits that Deborah—as a saleswoman, shopkeeper, bookkeeper, nurse, and household manager—exemplified. She was also a shrewd businesswoman. "I would not have given above half he has [paid] for them," she once scoffed at the price an acquaintance paid to buy several homes.[17] Even her penny-wise husband acknowledged Deborah's capability. "As Mrs. Franklin has had a great deal of experience in the management of the post office, I depend upon your paying considerable attention to her advice in that matter," Ben insisted to William Dunlap, who assumed his duties as the colonies' postmaster general before his 1757 trip to London.[18]

Deborah was not brilliant like Ben but, as her later letters reveal, she was a socially savvy and capable woman far more instrumental to her husband's success than scholars and historians have traditionally described her. As clerk Daniel Fisher observed, Deborah's assumption of responsibilities freed Ben for other pursuits; that in turn gave her "extraordinary freedom" and confidence compared to other women. Simultaneous with her commercial skills and work in Ben's post office, Deborah remained respectful of others and radiated "great humility."[19]

Despite Ben's wealth, stature as publisher of the *Gazette*, championing of civic causes, and friendships with highly placed men, she continued to behave before those of higher status as a conventionally modest woman. One morning when Fisher—who temporarily boarded with the Franklins' neighbor, the silversmith Samuel Soumain—walked downstairs, he saw a "gentlewoman" sitting on one of the bottom steps. Hearing Fisher's footsteps above, Deborah immediately rose and sat on the floor. Regardless of Mr. Soumain and his wife's offer of a chair, Ben's stubborn wife refused, and did so "the longer for their entreaty."[20]

By the early 1740s, as the Franklins achieved financial success, their interests diverged even more. Deborah remained focused on family and finances as Ben turned increasingly outward to social and civic matters. Through his success as a publisher—owner of intercolonial editions of the *Gazette*, printing houses, and paper mills—Ben had become a wealthy man whose influential network made him an eighteenth-century version of a media mogul. Yet, while often remembered for his lectures on money and thrift, Ben was deeply interested in the public welfare. From his perspective, wealth was a means to improve society and, specifically, to transform Philadelphia into North America's leading urban center.

An international struggle soon delayed those plans. For nearly a decade England and France had engaged in the War of the Austrian Succession, but by the time Ben was promoting his stove, the conflict between France and England had erupted in North America in what the colonists bitterly dubbed King George's War. At issue were trade and transportation routes on waterways from the Atlantic to the Mississippi. By early 1747, express riders had arrived from the eastern part of Pennsylvania to warn of an attack upon Philadelphia. As a well-informed journalist and the clerk of the Assembly, Ben urged the legislators to act. Most, however, were wealthy pacifist Quakers who refused to engage in war and left Philadelphia defenseless.

Fearing for his family and his beloved city, Ben dashed off and distributed two thousand copies of his pamphlet "Plain Truth" to "we . . . the middling people . . . the tradesmen, shopkeepers and farmers of this province and city," to rouse them to action. "On the first alarm, *terror* will spread over all. . . . Those that are reputed rich, will flee. . . . The man that has a wife and children, will find them hanging on his neck, beseeching him with tears to quit the city, and save his life. . . . All will run into confusion, amidst cries and lamentations. . . . *Sacking* the city will be the first, and *Burning* it, in all probability, the last act of the enemy."[21] To prevent this destruction, Ben's pamphlet urged the formation of a citizens' militia.

Across the colony men gathered in groups, forming military units and organizing them under an association of militias. In a departure from traditional English custom, which allowed only elite men to serve as officers, Pennsylvania's ordinary citizens elected officers from their ranks. The militias also declared fast days and funded cannons and other military equipment through lotteries. Refusing the title of colonel of the Philadelphia militia, Ben insisted upon serving as a common soldier. By early August 1748, ten thousand militiamen had finally repulsed the attack and ended the conflict.

Once peace was restored, the association disbanded. However, its emergence as a military force had enraged Pennsylvania's autocratic "proprietor," Thomas Penn. Despite his residency in London, Penn and his family still owned most of Pennsylvania's unsettled land through the 1681 charter granted to his father, William Penn. To Thomas, Ben's upstart citizen militia did "much mischief" to authority. "This Association is founded on a contempt to government and cannot end in anything but anarchy and confusion," he warned.[22] By defying Penn's tyrannical rule and taking the matters into their own hands, the citizen militias had usurped the role of the authorities. "When ordinary men . . . know they may act . . . in a body and a military manner, and independent of this government, why should they not act against it?" Franklin, he concluded, was a "very dangerous man" but then conceded that since he was "a sort of tribune of the people," he must be treated "with regard."[23]

Regardless of Penn's resentments, Ben resumed plans to make Philadelphia the leading city of the colonies. After a failed attempt to win support for a college, he sought other ways to stimulate interest in the pursuit of intellectual thought. As postmaster of Philadelphia, Ben received newspapers from other colonies before he distributed them to readers, thus becoming the first to learn about the latest ideas and innovations. Already he exchanged ideas with educated men from other colonies, but bad roads, storms, and inefficient mail delivery slowed the process. Thanks to an idea from Pennsylvania botanist Richard Bartram, Ben proposed an intercolonial organization modeled upon the Junto, where "ingenious and curious men" might share knowledge of "natural secrets, arts and sciences."[24]

By 1743 his concept of a learned society had become a reality. Known as the American Philosophical Society, today the institute remains a leading forum for the exchange of ideas and intellectual inquiry among scholars, scientists, and researchers.

Ben then returned to the concept of founding a college. An institution for higher education was critical to the rise of a great city, he observed and advocated, "by wise men in all ages, as the surest foundation of the happiness." Studies in that college must not be merely theoretical but should focus upon the "most *useful*" subjects so that graduates could "serve mankind, one's country, friends, and family."[25] Ben's appeal soon attracted support, and in 1749 the first students arrived for classes at the Philadelphia Academy, forerunner of the University of Pennsylvania.

Ben then applied himself to other civic improvements: establishment of a hospital, a constable patrol, a fire corps, street lighting, and paved streets.

Coupled with his urban accomplishments was Ben's prurient interest in the opposite sex. In June 1745 his letter "Advice to a Young Man on Choosing a Mistress" (or "Old Mistress Apologue," as it was later blandly titled) casts doubt on his faithfulness to Deborah. For generations historians kept that letter secret, fearing the subject would taint the reputation of the founding father. Then and today no one knows to whom Ben addressed it or even when he wrote it. It was not until 1926 that Dr. Phillips Russell included it in his biography of Franklin.

The first lines were utterly proper: "I know of no medicine fit to diminish the violent natural inclinations you mention; and if I did, I think I should not communicate it to you. Marriage is the proper remedy. It is the most natural state of man, and therefore the state in which you are most likely to find solid happiness." But, Ben added, "if you will not take this counsel, and persist in thinking a commerce with the sex inevitable, then I repeat my former advice, that in all your amours you should *prefer old Women to young ones.*"[26]

To support his odd statement, Ben listed eight reasons to support his theory. Older women were more experienced in the ways of the world, were more knowledgeable, and were better conversationalists. Moreover, "when women cease to be handsome, they study to be good . . . are the most tender and useful of all friends when you are sick . . . hence there is hardly such a thing to be found as an old woman who is not a good woman." Nor were older women likely to become pregnant, which inevitably resulted in "much inconvenience."[27] Older women were also more discreet than younger ones on affairs and less likely to wreck their lovers' health and finances during it.

Admittedly, an older woman's face, neck, and breasts were more wrinkled than a younger woman's. However, Ben slyly observed, "the lower parts continuing to the last as plump as ever. Regarding only what is below the girdle, it is impossible of two women to know an old from a young one. And as in the dark all cats are grey, the pleasure of corporal enjoyment with an old woman is at least equal, and frequently superior."[28]

Furthermore, the corruption of a virgin was unwise, for it might later trouble her lover, while intimacy with an older woman avoided such problems. Not only did an affair make an older woman happy but inevitably she was "so grateful."[29]

Much ink has been spilled over how Ben acquired that knowledge. Theories abound about the inspiration for the letter. Was the future founding father simply imitating other bawdy writings of the day? Was "Old Mistress Apologue," as it was discreetly cataloged in Franklin's letters, a reflection of his sexual encounters as a bachelor? Or was it based on Ben's affairs with older women while married to Deborah?

That was not Ben's only writing about sexuality in the 1740s. Some historians attributed his interest to the angst of middle age. Others believe Ben was so disgusted at the insults he received for siring a child born outside of marriage that he felt compelled to defend free love. The result was "The Speech of Miss Polly Baker" of 1745–46, which pleaded for a more humanistic attitude toward the consequences of illicit sex.

Written in still another fictitious voice, Ben's Polly faced a panel of stern male judges who were trying her for the "sin" of bearing another child out of wedlock.

> This is the fifth time gentlemen, that I have been dragged before our court on the same account. . . . I think this law by which I am punished is both unreasonable . . . and particularly severe with regards to me, who have always lived an inoffensive life. I have brought five fine children into the world, at the risk of my life; I have maintained them well by my own industry, without burdening the township, and should have done it better if it had not been for the heavy charges and fines I have paid. Can it be a crime . . . to add to the number of the king's subjects in a new country that really wants its people?[30]

In a final ironic twist in Ben's satirical tale, one of Polly's stern judges decides to marry her.

In 1747 "The Speech of Miss Polly Baker" was published in England and in North America, where readers assumed it was the story of a real woman. Did Deborah know about it? Almost certainly not. Ben never admitted to anyone he had authored it, even though the style and use of a pseudonym confirmed him as the same freethinker who once defended prostitutes and scorned hypocrisies in his brother's *Courant*.

In 1748, forty-two-year-old Ben announced his retirement. It was not to be a life of leisure, he assured his pious mother, Abiah, but one dedicated to social improvements. "I would rather have it said 'he lived usefully' than 'he died rich.'"[31] Ben's financial success also made life more comfortable for Deborah. While the Franklins had employed a maid since the mid-1730s, Ben had purchased a carriage in 1747 primarily for his wife. Ben's income was substantial—650 pounds a year as guaranteed income for the next eighteen years—from a buyout arrangement he made with his foreman, David Hall, the new manager of Ben's printing company. In

1748 Ben and Deborah moved to a larger house on Second Street, not far from the clatter of horse-drawn carts, bleating sheep, and the bustle at the Market Street stalls.

In recognition of Ben's rise from lowly tradesman to prominent citizen, his brother John commissioned visiting artist Robert Feke of Boston to paint his portrait. To some historians his stiff depiction in a velvet coat, ruffles, and a wig suggested Ben's aspirations to join Philadelphia's elite, but his roots were those of a humble tradesman—roots he never forgot. Quite deliberately, he wore a short brown wig, not one in the traditionally white or grey hues of a professional man or a gentleman. Compared to those of higher-status men, as biographer Walter Isaacson observed, Ben's portrait was devoid of "social ostentation."[32]

No portrait exists of Deborah from this period, but a newspaper story indicates she was now dressing quite fashionably. In November 1750, after a thief broke into the Franklin home, the *Gazette* carried a story asking readers to notify the Franklins if they came upon the stolen goods. Among them were Deborah's long scarlet cloak with a double cape, a cotton gown brocaded with colorful flowers, and a double necklace of gold beads.

By then, too, the Franklins' African American slaves, Peter and Jemima, may have helped with chores and with the flow of relatives and other visitors and admirers whom Deborah constantly entertained. While his ownership of slaves may surprise modern readers who associate Ben with support for civil liberties, only later in life did he embrace the idea of abolition. Once again, Deborah's reaction is not known, but apparently she looked to the household slaves to relieve her of some of the time-consuming chores of colonial housekeeping. The slaves' help left her free to assist Ben in the post office. That in turn left Ben free to pursue his interests in scientific experiments. As "assistant postmistress," Deborah worked long hours and became a familiar and respected face to Philadelphians young and old, rich and poor, who visited the post office. At this writing the American Philosophical Society is featuring a multiyear digital initiative entitled "Franklin's Post Office Ledgers," whose margins reveal a number of notes in Deborah's hand.

Like many contemporary men who retire after years of toil, Ben was filled with ideas for new projects. In September 1748 he wrote to his friend Cadwallader Colden, a physician, natural scientist, and acting governor of New York, and assured him, "I too am taking the proper measures for obtaining leisure to enjoy life and my friends more than heretofore . . . and hope soon to be quite a master of my own time." Above all, he cherished the chance "to read, study and make experiments."[33]

At the top of Ben's list was electricity. A year before his retirement, Peter Collinson, an English botanist and member of the Royal Society, sent Philadelphia's Library Company a glass tube with instructions on how to generate electricity. Before long Ben also learned about the Leyden jar, fashioned by Dutch scientist Pieter van Musschenbroek. By spinning a glass jar lined with metal on the interior and exterior, and topped by a metal tip, the Dutchman produced an electric charge. Intrigued, Ben began experimenting even before his official retirement.

In an echo of Richard Saunders's description of his wife, who jeered at his "rattling-traps," Ben used some of Deborah's household items for his experiments. Among them were a salt cellar, thimbles, silken thread, a vinegar cruet, a cake of wax, a pump handle, and the gold leaf from a bound book. If Deborah was curious, she did not interfere—for electricity was a mysterious force to be feared.

To Ben the mystery had to be solved and tamed through experimentation. First, using one of Deborah's bottles, he lined the inside and outside of the mouth with iron strips. Then, after suspending a small cork ball from silken threads he hung from the ceiling, he electrified the bottle so that the ball was "repelled to the distance of 4 or 5 inches." After touching a long metal piece to the bottle, "the repellency is instantly destroyed, and the cork flies to it," he wrote to Collinson.[34]

After two years of trial and error, Ben invited his friends to the banks of the Schuylkill to illustrate his success by electrocuting a turkey, then the only known "practical" use for electricity. That experiment went well, but another one nearly killed him. In a letter to his brother John, Ben described what happened. Just as he was "about to kill a turkey from the shock of two large glass jars, containing as much electrical fire as forty common phials, I inadvertently took the whole through my own arms and body." Nearby friends reported a "great flash" and heard a sound like a pistol shot. Later Ben admitted he remembered nothing, "my senses being gone . . . nor did I feel the stroke on my hands." To him, it felt like "a universal blow through my body from head to foot." The first thing he noticed was "a violent quick shaking of my body, which gradually remitting, my senses as gradually returned."[35]

Undoubtedly that increased Deborah's fears about Ben's electricity experiments, although she knew her disapproval would not prevent future tinkering. Subsequently, though, Ben proceeded more cautiously, using intuition, observation, and systematic trial and error. By early 1750 he wrote Collinson about his theory that electricity was a universal force commonly observed during thunder and lightning storms.

The English scientist was impressed. "Your very curious pieces relating to electricity and thunder-gusts have been read before the society and have been deservedly admired." Consequently he was collecting "all these tracts . . . with intention to put them into some printer's hand to be communicated to the public."[36] By 1751 Collinson published Ben's eighty-six-page booklet, "Experiments and Observations on Electricity," and presented it to the Royal Society. Despite the clarity of Ben's theory, the Society did not respond.

Across the channel on May 10, 1752, physicist Thomas-Francis d'Alibard erected a forty-foot iron rod near Paris in Marly-la-Ville. When lightning struck the top of the rod, the physicist drew sparks from its base and proved Ben's theory. The confirmation was a thunderclap that jolted the scientists of western Europe. "All Europe is in agitation on verifying electrical experiments. . . . All commends the thought of the inventor," Collinson wrote Ben that September.[37]

Deborah's reaction, like other details during this period in her life, has not been preserved, but by then she probably knew that in June Ben had already confirmed his theory. Because the steeple of Christ Church, the tallest structure in Philadelphia, was still incomplete, her husband had resorted to using a kite. Fearing ridicule if his experiment failed, Ben waited for a rainy evening. Then, with help from his twenty-two-year-old son, Billy, he flew the kite over a dark cloud. At first nothing happened. Several moments later, though, loose threads from the kite's silk string stood on end. A spark then jumped from the string to the key attached to a string in Ben's hand and proved his theory.

Ben kept his discovery private that summer. Even in October, when he published a report on the "kite experiment" in the *Gazette*, he did not admit he had conducted it. Instead Ben announced, "Frequent mention is made in the newspapers from Europe, of the success of the Philadelphia experiment for drawing the electric fire from clouds by means of pointed rods of iron erected on high buildings . . . [and now] the same experiment has succeeded in Philadelphia, though made in a different and more easy manner, which anyone may try."[38] His story then explained how readers could use a kite to test the theory.

That same month, Ben decided to find a practical purpose for electricity. Gamely, if with little regard for Deborah's trepidation, he installed the first lightning rod on the roof of the Franklin home. Whatever doubts she had vanished during the next thunderstorm, when the rod repulsed the lightning. Who was she, after all, to doubt her husband? Ben was internationally acclaimed; scientists across Europe were awed. News about his experiments attracted still more visitors to the Franklin home. Too many. In an effort to encourage people to install lightning rods themselves, Ben's 1753 edition of the *Almanack* explained how, thereby eliminating "mischief by thunder and lightning."[39]

The one in the Franklin home, however, was not only a model lightning rod but also an important research tool. After the initial experiment, Ben attached a wire to the rod, which was threaded through a small opening in the roof and hung down the staircase near the Franklins' bedroom. At the bottom of the stairs, the wire was divided, its two ends "separated about six inches, a little bell on each end." Between the bells was a "little brass ball [which was] suspended by a silk thread to strike the bells when the clouds passed with electricity in them."[40]

One night Ben awoke to a loud crack, dashed out of bed, and thrust open the bedroom door. "Instead of vibrating as usual between the bells," the brass ball "was repelled and kept at a distance from both, while the fire [electricity] passed . . . sometimes in a continued dense, white stream . . . whereby the whole staircase was enlightened as with sunshine."[41]

Deborah must have awakened too but probably remained in the bedroom, frightened by the noise and bright light. For years the experiment was repeated in the Franklin home, creating shrill ringing that disturbed her. Still it remained, even when Ben moved to London. From there he wrote Deborah, "If the ringing frighten[s] you, tie a piece of wire from one of the bells to the other, and that will conduct the lightning without ringing or snapping but silently." Nevertheless, Ben preferred that she leave them alone. "I think it best the bells should be at liberty to ring, that you may know when the wire is electrified . . . if you are afraid, may keep at a distance."[42]

Ben's electricity alarm consequently remained a fixture in the Franklin home.

5

"Kisses in the Wind"

"I AM ORDERED BY my master to write for some books for Sally Franklin," Deborah wrote the wife of Ben's English publisher friend, William Strahan, on Christmas Eve 1751. Included on her list were dictionaries, philosophical treatises, and fables. Most were inappropriate for eight-year-old Sally, but Ben requested them because he wanted his daughter to learn about economy and thrift by selling them in Deborah's store.[1]

To the Franklins, the blue-eyed, blonde-haired Sally seemed every bit as promising as their deceased son, Franky. When she was three, Ben bragged to his elderly mother, Abiah, "Your granddaughter is the greatest lover of books of any child that I ever knew."[2] Two years later Ben again praised Sally for being "extremely industrious with her needle and delights in books. . . . I have hopes that she will prove an ingenious, sensible, notable and worthy woman."[3]

In 1749 he wrote to Strahan that Sally "discovers daily the seeds and tokens of industry and economy, and, in short, of every female virtue."[4] By then he and Strahan had agreed upon a future marriage between Sally and the Englishman's son. To contemporary readers the idea may sound outrageous, but Ben was so determined on the match that he wrote Strahan, "I am glad to hear so good a character of my [future] son-in-law. Please to acquaint him that his spouse (Sally) grows finely . . . [and has] the best disposition in the world."[5] Deborah was horrified. Not only was it customary in America for men and women to make their own decisions about whom to marry, but Sally was Deborah's only daughter, upon whom she doted. The thought of Sally living abroad without her was unbearable. More than likely Deborah had protested. Soon afterward Ben dismissed the idea of wedding Sally to Strahan's son.

Paradoxically, Ben's belief in personal independence clashed sharply with his attitude toward his family. Years later, when Billy was grown, Ben expected him to marry his Philadelphia sweetheart, but the young man rebelled. Later in life Ben had no better luck arranging marriages for one of his grandsons. The only person who consistently obeyed him was Deborah. "There are three faithful friends, an old wife, an old dog and ready money," Ben's *Almanack* observed.[6]

By 1751, with Ben's "old wife" and "ready money" in place, he devoted himself to campaigning for election to the Assembly—and won. Once in office as a legislator, he proposed paving the streets and installing lamps to illuminate the streets of Philadelphia at night. In contrast to the refinements those improvements implied, hostilities broke out in the raw backwoods country of western Pennsylvania between the French, their tribal allies, and settlers. By July of 1753 reports of the violence had become so alarming that the Assembly dispatched Ben and two others to make peace. After a month of fruitless negotiations, they and the discouraged Ben returned to Philadelphia.

Suddenly news came from England that George II had appointed Ben the deputy postmaster general for the Colonies. His fellow deputy was William Hunter, editor of the *Virginia Gazette*. Since nepotism was considered the privilege of powerful men, Ben promptly appointed relatives and friends to postmaster positions in other colonies. Nor did he forget his son Billy, who assumed his father's position as postmaster in Philadelphia.

Deborah must have winced; for eleven years she had assisted Ben in the post office and kept the mails running smoothly. How well would Billy run the post office in Ben's place? Would she, a seasoned postal assistant and his estranged stepmother, be expected to do his bidding?

History has not preserved the details, but apparently their work together did not go well. One day, as Deborah visited with Daniel Fisher, a handsome young man passed by the Franklin door. "Mr. Fisher, there goes the greatest villain upon the earth," Deborah exclaimed, indicating Billy. "This greatly confounded and perplexed me but did not hinder her from pursuing her invectives in the foulest terms I ever heard from a gentlewoman," Fisher recalled.[7]

Even Ben was upset with Billy. When the youth was nineteen, Ben had confided to his mother, Abiah, that his son was tall, proper, and "much of a beau" but had "acquired a habit of idleness" in the army. Disturbing too was Billy's fondness for luxury, high living, and an assumption he would live off his father's wealth. Ben finally set him straight. "I assured him that I intend to spend what little I have, myself," he wrote to Abiah.[8] Moreover, Ben expected Billy to become an upright citizen, who, like him, would make significant contributions to society. To foster that, he insisted that Billy "read law" with young Philadelphia attorney Joseph Galloway. He also asked his friend Strahan to enroll Billy for future training in London's prestigious law school, the Inns of Court.

Ever since his youthful visit to London, Ben had admired British institutions, among them their efficient postal system. In contrast, colonial America's mail delivery was primitive. Letters and packages were often delayed, miscarried, or lost. As deputy postmaster general of the colonies, Ben improved the unreliable system by hiring overnight mail carriers, initiating home delivery, and creating a dead-letter office. Knowing his innovations would work only if every colonial post office adopted those standards, Ben left Philadelphia in late 1754 to inspect post offices in New York and Massachusetts. While in Boston he lived at the home of his brother John in Cornhill, today part of Washington Street. There he was struck by what the French called a *coupe de feu*, or thunderbolt of passion. Her name was Catharine Ray, an attractive young woman from Block Island, who was visiting her sister, Judith Ray Hubbart, married to John's stepson.

The attraction between forty-eight-year-old Ben and twenty-three-year-old Katy (as he called her) was classic, fraught with tension. The petite high-colored brunette was pretty, playful, and so intrigued by the famous publisher-scientist that she spent hours talking, teasing, and flirting with him. To demonstrate her domestic skills, Katy made Ben a batch of sugar plums. He told her they were "sweeter" because they were made by her hands. During one of the parlor games they played, Ben guessed Katy's thoughts, leading her to declare him a "conjurer."[9]

A week later, when Katy prepared to visit relatives in Rhode Island, Ben offered to escort her. Accompanying them part of the way was her relative Elizabeth "Betsy" Hubbart and a post rider. To their families, Ben's invitation seemed a courtly gesture offered to protect a vulnerable young woman from the dangers of solitary travel. But to the infatuated couple, the trip provided a delightful opportunity to spend more time together.

On a chill December 30, 1754, Ben, Katy, Betsy, and a Mr. Post (perhaps the driver) left in a carriage. During the journey as they climbed an icy hill, the poorly shod horses slipped and fell. At an undetermined point in that trip, the carriage delivered Betsy to her destination, leaving Ben and Katy alone with their driver. Even in good weather, the seventy-mile trip between Boston and Rhode Island took two days by carriage, according to Rhode Island historian William Greene Roelker. More than likely that meant Ben and Katy were obliged to stay at least one night at a roadside tavern. Perhaps the innkeeper wondered at the unconventional arrival of the balding middle-aged man and the comely young woman and rented them a room—or possibly just a bed, if his hostelry was already full. To the ongoing frustration of historians, neither Ben nor Katy recorded where they slept that night.

Instead, and apparently intentionally, Ben and Katy preserved only scraps of their flirtatious conversation along the road. After arriving in Newport, they traveled on to nearby Westerly. In the course of their long conversations, each mentioned their plans for the future. That in turn inspired Ben's lecture that when Katy wed, she must "practice addition to your husband's estate, by industry and frugality; subtraction of all unnecessary expenses"; and "multiplication." As to the last of those skills, Ben later reminded her "I would gladly have taught you that myself, but you . . . wouldn't learn."[10]

Despite Katy's rejection of Ben's lesson in "multiplication," they remained enthralled. Suddenly the spell was broken when Katy received a letter from Block Island announcing her father was seriously ill. Anxiously, Ben escorted her to the shore and watched her sail away. "Too much was hazarded when I saw you put off to sea in that little skiff, tossed by every wave. . . . I stood on the shore and looked after you till I could no longer distinguish you even with my glass. Then I returned to your sister's, praying for your safe passage," he later wrote.[11]

On March 1, after lingering in New England for nearly two months, Ben returned to Philadelphia. There he received Katy's letter, one apparently so emotional that it later "disappeared" from Ben's correspondence. Four days later he wrote that after Katy's return to Block Island he "left New England slowly, and with great reluctance." He delayed, Ben claimed, because of the fond memories of his youth and receiving "many fresh marks of the people's goodness and benevolence." Indeed, "I almost forgot I had a home, till I was more than half-way towards it."[12]

Ben almost forgot he had a home? For a man whose life was rooted in pragmatic decisions, the comment seems extraordinary. Was the future founding father so smitten with Katy that he momentarily "forgot" about Deborah, his family, and his beloved Philadelphia? If so, and only because Katy would not learn "multiplication," it seemed that prudence had rescued Ben from passion.

By the time he replied to Katy's letter in early March he had recovered his balance, returned to his "practical" marriage with Deborah, and reaffirmed its importance. "I drove on violently and made such long stretches that a very few days brought me to my own house and to the arms of my good old wife and children, where I remain thanks to God, at present well and happy."[13] Afterward, however, Ben continued to think about Katy and worried he might never hear from her again. Then, to his relief, her letter arrived.

"Persons subject to the hyp [melancholia] complain of the North East wind as increasing their malady," Ben replied. "But since you promised to send me kisses in that wind, and I find you as good as your word 'tis to me the gayest wind that flows, and gives me the best spirits." Despite the return of his "best spirits," Ben still resented Katy's refusal to be intimate. He was writing, he added, "during a Northeast storm of snow, the greatest we have had this winter. Your favors come with the snowy fleeces which are as pure as your virgin innocence, white as your lovely bosom—and as cold." Then, catching his slip, Ben recast their infatuation as a harmless flirtation and himself as a fond father figure. "Let it warm towards some worthy young man, and may Heaven bless you both with every kind of happiness."[14]

Katy's next letter of March 31 (which has also "disappeared") accepted Ben's new role as an adviser in regard to her suitors. Within it, she fretted about revealing too much. In reply Ben assured her of his confidentiality. "You may write freely everything you think fit, without the least apprehension of any person's seeing your letters but myself. You have complimented me so much in those I have already received, that I could not show them without being justly thought a vain coxcomb. . . . I know very well that the most innocent expressions of warm friendship, and even those of mere civility and complaisance between persons of different sexes, are liable to be misinterpreted by suspicious minds." For that reason, "though you say more I say less than I think, and end this letter coolly in the plain common form, with only Dear Miss."[15]

On April 28 Katy wrote again, not realizing Ben was touring post offices in the South. By late June her next letter complained about his silence. It "gives me a vast deal of uneasiness and occasioned many tears, for surely I . . . wrote too much and you are affronted." Admittedly, she "said a thousand things that nothing should have tempted me to [have] said to anybody else for I knew they would be safe with you. I'll only beg the favor of one question. What is become of my letters? Tell me you are well and forgive me and love me one thousandth part so well as I do you and then I will be contented." In closing, Katy conveyed "My proper respects to Mrs. Franklin and Daughter. Pray take care of your health and accept the sugar plums, they are every one sweetened as you used to like."[16]

Ben's September 11 reply blamed his delay upon his southern journey and his many political duties. As a legislator, he was busy providing "general services to the country, and to the army, for which both have thanked me and say they love me. They *say so,* as you used to do," Ben slyly added. "I ran in debt to you three or four letters, and as I did not pay, you would not trust me any more. . . . But believe me, I am honest and though I should never make equal returns you shall see I'll keep fair accounts."[17]

Despite his paternal tone, Ben could not resist adding that Katy's newsy letters reminded him of "those hours and miles that we talked away so agreeably . . . in a winter journey, a wrong road and soaking shower." Had she "continued ever since in that monastery [Block Island] or have broke into the world again, doing pretty mischief? . . . and what the state of your heart is at this instant?"[18]

The "general services" Ben mentioned were more complex than he had time to explain. During his southern postal tour that spring, he met with General Edward Braddock in Maryland, who had arrived with four regiments from England to repulse new French and tribal attacks upon the settlers at Pennsylvania's frontier along the Ohio River. Billy had accompanied his father on that journey; together they helped Braddock acquire wagons and horses from civilians, paid from tax money for their equipment and animals.

Deborah, meanwhile, was left to manage the Philadelphia and intercolonial post offices, the Franklin finances, and Ben's mail. In his absence she even wrote to his English friend Peter Collinson, a Fellow of the Royal Society, to excuse Ben's delayed letters: "My husband is now in the back counties, contracting . . . wagons and horses for the army, which though so much out of his way, he was obliged to undertake" to prevent "inconveniencies that might have attended so many raw hands [soldiers] sent us from Europe."[19] Ultimately those "inconveniences" ended tragically when Braddock, ignoring Ben's warnings about surprise attacks, advanced into enemy territory, was ambushed, and died.

Before Ben's departure that spring, he casually mentioned Katy to Deborah. Naively, the matron welcomed the plums and cheese that the young woman sent from Block Island. "Mrs. Franklin was very proud, that a young lady should have so much regard for her old husband, as to send him such a present," Ben wrote Katy in September. "We talk of you every time it comes to table; she is sure you are a sensible girl and a notable housewife, and talks of bequeathing me to you as a legacy. But I ought to wish you a better [husband], and hope she will live these 100 years; for we are grown old together, and if she has any faults I am so used to them that I don't perceive them. . . . Sally says, 'Papa, my love to Miss Katy.' If it was not quite unreasonable I should desire you to write to me every post, whether you hear from me or no."[20]

Franklin biographers Claude-Anne Lopez (who spent years transcribing Ben's letters at Yale University and wrote two books about his private life) and Walter Isaacson claimed Ben's flirtation was no more than a pleasant diversion, enjoyed for the thrill of the chase rather than any realistic hope for its consummation. I question that. Ben's tone, the occasional slips in his letters, and his dismay after Katy's abrupt departure belie that theory. While prudence ultimately prevailed, the middle-aged Ben was still so vulnerable to passion that he could not forget Katy.

In October 1755, after learning she had returned to Boston, he wrote Katy that he imagined she was still "gay and lovely as usual." In the next sentence Ben caught himself again and, adopting a paternal tone, warned her about her fondness for flirtations. "Kill no more pigeons than you can eat," Ben advised. When "I have again the pleasure of seeing you" he expected her to be married. Then he would find her, "like my grape vine surrounded with clusters, plump, juicy, blushing pretty little rogues, like their Mama. Adieu. The bell rings and I must go among the grave ones, and talk politics. P.S. The plums came safe, and were so sweet from the cause you mentioned, that I could scarce taste the sugar."[21]

By then Ben's duty to "talk politics" concerned the Assembly's tense relation to Thomas Penn, the autocratic, absentee "proprietor" of the Colony of Pennsylvania, who still owned thousands of acres of fertile lands along the Ohio. From London, Penn and his family continued to veto tax requests from the Pennsylvania Assembly for funds to support British soldiers and end the French and Indian Wars. Social rivalries within the colony complicated the stalemate. On one side the Assembly's Quaker and German majority demanded that Penn pay taxes. In contrast the proprietor's wealthy supporters disapproved, and Pennsylvania's feckless Governor Robert Hunter Morris wavered. In short, nothing was done as French and tribal violence increased on the frontier.

By mid-November a report of a brutal Native American attack upon Tulpehocken, north of Reading, sent shock waves through the Assembly.

Ben consequently rallied members of the Assembly, including some Quakers, to support a bill for a new citizens' militia. Morris confided to Penn that the bill would do little to protect the province, but he approved it to avoid the threatened arrival of a backwoods mob in Philadelphia and resultant public censure. By early December, Ben, former lieutenant governor James Hamilton, and Joseph Fox were appointed commissioners to order a defense. After learning about the printer's leadership, Penn reiterated his opinion that Ben was a "dangerous man," a rabble rouser who influenced the public and threatened Penn's rights as proprietor of Pennsylvania's unsettled land.[22]

Ben was not intimidated. "The proprietors are greatly incensed at some parts of my late conduct. I am not much concerned," he wrote Collinson. "I have not the least inclination to be in their good graces. . . . I have some natural dislike to persons who so far *Love Money,* as to be *unjust* for its sake . . . from a regard to the public good. I may be mistaken in what is that public good; but at least I mean well."[23]

On December 18 Ben traveled with Billy, his fellow commissioners, and fifty men toward Bethlehem near Easton to organize defenses on the frontier. The devastation was so horrific that the commissioners ordered a garrison built at Easton. In Philadelphia Deborah was again left to manage Ben's affairs. For months before he left, she unhappily observed that her husband seemed preoccupied and distant. In fact, Deborah fretted, he seemed more interested in Billy than anyone else. Ben, Deborah complained to visiting clerk Daniel Fisher, had "too great an esteem for his son in prejudice of herself and her daughter."[24]

Still, Deborah worried so much about Ben during his travels to the frontier that she sent him barrels of cooked food, especially to honor his fiftieth birthday on January 6, 1756. After arriving at Gnadenhutten on January 18, where Ben and his fellow commissioners discovered "the houses burnt [and] the inhabitants butchered in the most shocking manner," they ordered construction of Fort Allen.[25]

On Sunday the 25th, as Ben and his men built a stockade, he wrote Deborah: "We have enjoyed your roast beef, and this day began on the roast veal; all agree that they are both the best that ever were of the kind. . . . The apples are extremely welcome . . . the minced pies are not yet come to hand, but suppose we shall find them among the things expected up from Bethlehem."[26] Five days later Ben acknowledged Deborah's kindness again. "Billy presents his duty to you, and love to his sister: all the gentlemen their compliments, they drink your health at every meal, having always something on the table to put them in mind of you."[27]

Gradually, as Ben's life diverged from hers, Deborah was developing an identity of her own. The same Sunday of Ben's letter, after attending services at Christ Church, Deborah invited to dinner Charlotte Brown, the matron of the British army's General Hospital. Impressed with Deborah's graciousness, Brown's comments revealed that Ben's wife was one of Philadelphia's prominent seven women who had welcomed her in October. She was also one of the most gracious. As Charlotte observed just before a meeting, Deborah "sent her Chaise for me and I was receiv'd with great pleasure."[28]

Later that night, when Charlotte prepared to return to her lodgings, Deborah "did me the favor to drive me home herself." On February 15, when Charlotte prepared to leave for New York, she "took Leave of Mrs. Franklin who was so kind as to give me Letters [of introduction] . . . [then] waited on me to the Boat."[29] Despite earlier reports of Deborah's temper and servile status, there was another side to Ben's wife. Perhaps time and a growing awareness of her own talents had mellowed Deborah, transforming her into a woman of charm and influence, not only as Ben's "deputy husband" but as an independent political force as well.

In April 1756, after a two-month return to Philadelphia from the frontier, Ben and his son left home again, this time to inspect southern post offices. Still the war dragged on. During the summer of 1756 the French captured the British fort at Oswego on Lake Ontario. In November their tribal allies conquered Fort Allen southwest of Fort Duquesne, leaving central Pennsylvania vulnerable to invasion. By early 1757, the Assembly became so alarmed they decided to petition the British king to demand Penn pay taxes on his unsettled lands.

The legislators chose Ben as their colonial agent. Honored, he agreed to serve, assuming that Deborah would join him in London. But she refused.

Historians cannot explain why with any certainty. Some believe she was traumatized by memories of the 1711 transatlantic crossing that brought her as a child and her family to Pennsylvania. The most misogynist theorized that Deborah was so ashamed of her ignorance and provincial manners that she felt herself no match for the polished men and women Ben would meet in London. Years later, her response to Strahan's invitation confirmed her fear of crossing the ocean. Deborah's reluctance was not entirely unreasonable. Even in the mid-eighteenth century, transatlantic voyages were notoriously difficult, crowded and uncomfortable, and inevitably vulnerable to the ever-present threat of disease, piracy, and shipwreck.

Still, Ben was stunned. Undoubtedly he appealed to reason, reminding Deborah that the packets, or mail boats, regularly sailed between England and America without mishaps. Hundreds of passengers also crossed the Atlantic safely every year in privateers and other vessels. If Deborah would not go because she was afraid to leave Philadelphia to live in a foreign land, Ben assured her that his assignment would last only six months, after which they would return to Philadelphia. Still Deborah refused: She would not sail with Ben to England.

To Ben, his wife's insistence upon staying in Philadelphia seemed unfair, even unloving. Would another, bolder, more adventurous woman have done the same? Frustrated, Ben dashed off a last-minute letter to Katy. "Being about to leave America for some time, I could not go without taking leave of my dear friend. I received your favor [letter] of the 8th of November, and am ashamed that I have suffered it to remain so long answered, especially as now, through shortness of time, I cannot chat . . . in any manner agreeably. I can only wish you well and happy" he wrote on March 3. "Present my best compliments to your good mamma, brother and sister . . . in short, to all that love me. I should have said all that love you, but that would be giving you too much trouble."[30]

Ultimately it was not Katy who threatened the Franklin marriage, but Deborah. Her insistence on remaining in Philadelphia was the worst mistake of her life.

6

The Ghost Wife

"A MAN IN A PASSION RIDES A MAD HORSE," Ben's *Almanack* once warned his readers.[1] Yet, by the time the horses hitched to his carriage were leaving Philadelphia, Ben's anger with Deborah had cooled. By early April 1757 he even saw an advantage in her decision to remain at home. From Trenton, Ben wrote Deborah that he was starting "this long voyage more cheerfully, as I can rely on your prudence in the management of my affairs and education of my dear child."[2]

In reality she had already proven her "prudence" by managing Ben's affairs during his travels to the frontier and his postal tours. Ben was not only grateful but now trusted Deborah implicitly. On April 4, he reminded William Dunlap, the postmaster to the colonies, to heed Deborah's advice. "As Mrs. Franklin has had a great deal of experience in the management of the Post Office, I depend on your paying considerable attention to her advice in that matter."[3] All postal accounts should thus be payable to Deborah. As he was departing the following morning, April 5, Ben assigned power of attorney for the second time in his marriage to his "trusty and loving friend and wife Deborah Franklin . . . as I myself might or could do, if I was personally present."[4]

Tearfully, Deborah watched him ride away, this time with Billy and two slaves, one of them named Peter (probably the son of the Franklins' slaves Peter and Jemima). Deborah expected she would not see her beloved

67

husband for at least six months. As Ben traveled north, he learned that Lord Loudoun, Britain's North American commander in chief, had suddenly closed the port of New York. Loudoun had done so while assembling a large fleet to rout the French in Louisburg, Nova Scotia. The delay meant Ben would remain at the Woodbridge, New Jersey, home of his publishing partner, James Parker.

After discovering her husband was delayed in New Jersey, Deborah and fourteen-year-old Sally rode to join him. The spring journey through wooded hills, the fast-flowing waters of the Woodbridge River, and the nearby clay pits were new to Deborah, who seldom left Philadelphia. As the happily reunited Franklins waited for news, Ben led them, the Parkers, and other friends to see the Passaic River's seventy-seven-foot waterfall (today Paterson Great Falls National Historical Park). Subsequently they toured the Schuyler Copper Mine, where a steam-powered pump drained water from a hundred-foot shaft.

By late May, when news arrived that Loudoun would soon open the New York harbor, Ben left Woodbridge planning to sail on one of the packet ships that regularly voyaged between North America and Great Britain. "One would imagine that I was now on the very point of departing for Europe," Ben wrote, but again his trip was delayed. Finally, Loudoun announced the fleet was ready to depart but insisted the packet boats sail from New York with the British fleet. "But when that will be is yet uncertain," Ben sourly wrote Deborah. Consequently, "I leave it to yourself, whether to go home directly or stay a little longer." Worried about the unattended business waiting for her in Philadelphia, he warned Deborah the "longer [your] absence from home [you] will be attended with some inconvenience."[5]

He had no reason to worry. Deborah continued to manage the post office as Dunlap learned his new responsibilities. While doing so, she chafed at Lord Loudoun's orders for royal mail to be delivered within three hours after arrival at the post office. To do that disrupted the postal rider delivery service and created a deficit for the mail service. Overlooking Loudoun's high position, Ben's wife felt confident enough to complain. After acknowledging compliance with his orders, she wrote: "I therefore hope our Lordship will order the Posts for the future to be regularly discharged from New

York. And I shall be glad to know how the charges of expresses may be defrayed."[6]

To that, Lord Loudoun replied that he "never meant or intended to offend anyone, much less Mrs. Franklin" but explained that as a royal appointee with the "Privileges of a Peer" he could not change the rules, since that would weaken his authority.[7] While their subsequent correspondence has been lost, historian Jennifer Reed Fry observed that the interchange revealed Deborah's political savvy and growing confidence as assistant postmistress.

By mid-June, Ben's packet boat had followed the royal fleet as far north as Halifax before sailing toward the British Isles. As Deborah had feared, the Atlantic crossing was perilous. Not only did French privateers chase Ben's ship, but as it neared Falmouth, England, the vessel barely missed the shoals. For six weeks Deborah waited anxiously in Philadelphia for his letter. By July she was so nervous—and perhaps overworked—that she developed a cold and fever, becoming so ill she could hardly "bear the least thing in the world."[8]

Shortly after July 17, when Ben's ship landed, he wrote Deborah that he was so grateful for his survival that, despite his usual distaste for formal religion, he attended church with the other passengers. After a brief stay with William Strahan, publisher and co-owner of the *London Chronicle*, Ben rented four rooms for himself, Billy, and their slaves in a Georgian townhouse at 7 Craven Street (now number 36). Located in central London near Trafalgar Square, Ben's new home was a four-story middle-class residence owned by the widowed Margaret Rooke Stevenson, whose husband, the merchant Addinell Stevenson, had died a decade or so earlier. Ben's landlady was born the same year as Ben. A warm, sociable woman with a forthright but prickly personality, she enjoyed concerts, theater, dinner parties, and card games. Margaret also had a daughter, eighteen-year-old Mary, known as Polly, who lived near London as a companion to a wealthy elderly aunt and several relatives. To supplement Margaret's income, she often rented spare rooms in her townhouse to travelers.

Beyond that, few details are known about Margaret except that she was instantly charmed by Ben. "Mrs. Stevenson," as he referred to her in his letters to Deborah, soon became more than a disinterested landlady who performed tasks expected of a wife—cooking, attending to Ben's wardrobe, and acquainting him with English customs. After scrutinizing his provincial clothes, Margaret urged Ben to buy English suits, shoes, and a wig. Nevertheless, his first letter from London avoided mentioning Margaret's name. He simply referred to her as the "good lady of the house who kindly nursed me" when he became ill that autumn.[9] Historical accounts of landladies caring for sick tenants are rare, but Margaret was so fond of Ben that she attended to him.

How intimate the two of them became has continued to tantalize historians. Billy began legal studies at the Inns of Court and gallivanted around town in his free time, so Ben and Margaret were often left alone. Their closeness and Ben's later references to the Stevensons as his English "family" suggests that he and Margaret enjoyed more than a fond friendship.

As colonial agent for the Colony of Pennsylvania, Ben's first assignment before presenting a petition to the king was to persuade Penn to pay taxes on his unsettled colonial lands. By mid-August Ben had arranged a visit with fifty-six-year-old Thomas Penn at his handsome townhouse. His younger brother, Richard Penn, was also present. Both men greeted Ben politely but regarded him with suspicion. In contrast to their late father, William Penn, founder of Pennsylvania, the brothers lived as aristocrats with little sympathy for the colony. "The Proprietors justified their conduct as well as they could, and I, the Assembly's. We now appeared very wide, and so far from each other in our opinions, as to discourage all hope of agreement," Ben recalled in his *Autobiography*.[10]

During that meeting the Penns asked Ben to commit the colony's grievance to paper. The colonial agent did so promptly; two days later, he sent them his list, the "Heads of Complaint." Coldly, the Penns delegated that document to their lawyer, Ferdinand John Paris. That too was unfortunate for Ben, who considered the attorney a "proud angry man" with whom he had previously exchanged contentious letters on behalf of the Assembly.[11]

Deborah, meanwhile, had received only one letter after Ben's arrival in Falmouth and remained in suspense. Adding to her anxiety was his letter of early September explaining he had become ill with a severe respiratory infection. After that Ben's letters ceased, leaving Deborah to wonder why.

Perhaps to ease her alarm, she wrote regularly, timing her letters to the departures of the packet ships. After three long months Deborah finally heard again from Ben, who excused his lapse on his illnesses. "I have now before me, your letters of July 17, July 31, August 11, August 21, September 4, September 19, October 1 and October 9. I thank you for writing to me so frequently and full," Ben wrote on November 22.[12]

"The 2nd of September I wrote to you that I had . . . a violent cold and something of a fever, but that it was almost gone. However it was not long before I had another severe cold . . . attended by a great pain in my head . . . [making me] a little delirious." Having been bled, as was then the conventional medical practice for disease, and given "bark" or quinine to reduce his fever, Ben spent weeks in bed before becoming well enough to sit up and write.[13]

His illness was probably compounded by London's foggy air and coal-burning fireplaces and stoves. "The whole town is one great smoky house and every street a chimney, the air full of floating sea coal soot . . . you never get a sweet breath of what is pure, without riding for it into the country," Ben observed several months later.[14]

Added to Deborah's worries was Ben's silence about his meeting with the Penns. Instead he simply instructed her to ignore rumors that his negotiations had failed. "While spread by my enemies to my disadvantage . . . let none of them trouble you . . . though I may perhaps not be able to obtain for the people what they wish . . . no interest shall induce me to betray the trust they have reposed in me."[15]

In London the months passed, but Ben heard nothing from the Penns. Frustrated, he wrote to Pennsylvania Assembly member Joseph Galloway to urge the legislators to assert their rights. The Penns' refusal to consider his plea was outrageous. In fact, Ben added in an unusual show of pique, they should be "gibbeted up as they deserve, to rot and stink in the nostrils of posterity."[16]

Despite his disgust with the Penns, Ben befriended many of London's intellectual, literary, and scientific men. Among his closest friends were William Strahan, Peter Collinson, the royal physician Dr. John Fothergill (who became Ben's personal physician), and Sir John Pringle, a Scottish professor of moral philosophy. Through Strahan and Collinson, Ben met other learned men at London's coffeehouses, where they discussed books, science, and current events. He also joined a group of pro-American Englishmen at the Honest Whig Club and played cribbage with others.

Within Ben's first few months in London he had become so popular that his friend Strahan wrote Deborah an alarming letter:

> For my own part, I never saw a man who was, in every respect, so perfectly agreeable to me . . . Now madam as I know the ladies here consider him in exactly the same light I do. I think you should come over, with all convenient speed to look after your interest; not but that I think him as faithful to his Joan, as any man breathing, but who knows what repeated and strong temptation, may in time, and while he is at so great a distance from you accomplish.[17]

Strahan then became more blunt:

> I cannot take leave of you without informing you that Mr. F. has the good fortune to lodge with a very discreet good gentlewoman, who is particularly careful of him, who attended him during a very severe cold . . . with an assiduity, concern, and tenderness, which perhaps only yourself could equal: so that I don't think you could have a better substitute till you come over, to take him under your own protection.[18]

Deborah's answer, like all her correspondence from that era, has not been preserved. One hint of her response came from Strahan's letter to a friend reporting that Deborah wrote she refused to cross the ocean. If Strahan's letter had upset her—as surely it must have—she ultimately dismissed his warning. Either out of trust or high ideals, Deborah assumed her twenty-seven-year marriage to Ben was secure, that her husband was faithful and his trip only a temporary separation. The few letters she received from him were always affectionate. Typically, he began with the salutation "My Dear Child"—the Franklins' apparent equivalent of current endearments like "baby" or "sweetie"—and concluded with "Your loving husband."

Reassuring, too, were the gifts Ben sent from London. "Had I been well," he added to his November 22 letter, he "intended to have gone round among the shops, and bought some pretty things for you and my dear good Sally (whose little hands you say eased your headache) to send by this ship, but I must now defer it to the next, having only got a crimson satin cloak for you, the newest fashion, and the black-silk for Sally."[19]

Historians and scholars have debated the sincerity of Strahan's letter and wondered if he wrote to Deborah after she received a letter from Ben of January 14, 1758. "Strahan has offered to lay me a considerable wager, that a letter he . . . wrote to you, will bring you immediately over here but I tell him I will not pick his pocket, for I am sure there is no inducement strong enough to prevail with you to cross the seas," Ben wrote.[20] If, as his comment suggested, Strahan's letter was no more than a mischievous challenge between two friends, it seems an incredibly insensitive joke to have played upon Ben's lonely, hardworking wife. Or was it Ben's way to mitigate the warning Strahan had written to Deborah?

Yet the tone of Strahan's letter suggests he was sincere, that he was more worried about Ben's vulnerability to women than his American friend could admit to himself. If, on the other hand, Strahan privately proposed a bet to Ben after his letter was sent, and Deborah agreed to sail, the Englishman would have won the contest.

Additional proof for Strahan's sincerity is reflected in his letter to Ben's Philadelphia partner, David Hall. After asking Hall to send Deborah his regards, he added, "Tell her I am sorry she dreads the sea so much that she cannot prevail upon herself to come to this fine place. . . . There are many ladies here that would make no objections to sailing twice as far after him; but there is no overcoming prejudices of that kind."[21]

By then or soon afterward, Strahan knew that Ben and Margaret were living at Craven Street as a couple. Together they attended concerts, plays, lectures, and parties with friends; together, too, they accepted invitations to dinners and hosted their own at Craven Street. Their relationship was a given to others: No questions were asked. Discreetly, Ben's first letters to Deborah minimized his relationship with Margaret. Instead, he filled his letters with reports about his health and complaints about London's expense, filth, and the inconvenience of living there.

Despite those complaints, Ben enjoyed London so much that he evolved from a thrifty, plain-living printer into a fashionably dressed gentleman who appreciated the English lifestyle, furnishings, and household goods. The presents he sent Deborah in February 1758 reflected his new attitude. Among the gifts she received were fine china, salt ladles, candle snuffers, upholstery fabric, and "six coarse diaper breakfast cloths . . . to spread on the tea table, for nobody breakfasts here on a naked table." He also sent Deborah seven yards of blue cotton to make a dress and sixteen yards of better material, fancy flowered "tissue," to make a more formal gown. The last of these, Ben gingerly explained, was a favorite of his landlady, "Mrs. Stevenson," who sent her "compliments" to Deborah.[22]

Another affectionate if amusing gift was a "large, fine, jug for beer . . . I fell in love with it at first sight; for I thought it looked like a fat, jolly dame, clean and tidy, with a neat blue and white calico gown . . . good natured and lovely, and put me in mind of—Somebody."[23] Obviously, that "somebody" was Deborah. Why then should she worry about a rival? No man would be so thoughtful if he was tempted to stray.

In that same letter Ben assured Deborah she meant more to him than anyone else. While the "friendship I meet with from persons of worth, and the conversation of ingenious men, give me no small pleasure . . . domestic comforts afford the most solid satisfaction. . . . My uneasiness being absent from my family and longing desire to be with them, make me often sigh in the midst of cheerful company."[24]

He admitted that Mrs. Stevenson took "great care of my health and is very diligent when I am in any way indisposed." Nevertheless, "I have a thousand times wished you were with me. . . . There is a great difference in sickness between being nursed with that tender attention which proceeds from sincere love."[25]

Who could argue with that? Certainly not Deborah, toiling three thousand miles away at the colonial postmaster general's office, overseeing purchases and sales for Ben's wholesale paper trade, corresponding with his publishing partnerships, paying bills, handling debtor's letters, and dealing with countless other details in her husband's publishing empire.

In the summer of 1758, as Ben waited for the Penns' response, he escaped London's foul air by traveling through the English countryside with Billy. Twice they stopped at Cambridge, first when Ben conducted experiments on evaporation with chemist John Hadley, and then to attend commencement. Later Ben and Billy visited the Franklins' ancestral home in Ecton, Northamptonshire, sixty miles northwest of London.

From there they rode to Birmingham, where they met Deborah's relatives. Several of them still remembered her mother, Sarah, before she and her husband emigrated to Pennsylvania. One of them, a Mrs. Salt, a "jolly lively dame, both Billy and myself agreed that she was extremely like you, her whole face has the same turn and exactly the same little blue Birmingham eyes." Later they met still other members of the Read family, whom Ben described as "industrious, ingenious working people and think themselves vastly happy that they live in dear old England."[26]

Ben had praised Deborah as a "jolly lively dame," but her reality in Philadelphia was far less merry. Faced with constant demands from Ben's business affairs, the post office, the Franklin household, Sally's education, her sister-in-law Jane's needy son, and other relatives, Deborah juggled what seemed like an endless list of tasks. Even so, Ben expected her to help the needy and sick. "I need not tell you to assist Godmother in her difficulties, for I know you will think of it as agreeable to me, as it is to your own good disposition," he reminded her.[27]

Did Deborah really have such a "good disposition," or, as biographers Claude-Anne Lopez and Eugenia W. Herbert wondered, was she simply fulfilling the era's social expectations for women? Given the absence of Deborah's letters from this time, those biographers regretfully concluded "there is no flesh and blood Debbie for this period."[28]

Gradually, Deborah's distance from Ben, his friendships with learned men, admiration from scientists, social life with Margaret, and struggle against the Penns made her less relevant. To Ben she became a ghost wife, a fading memory of a dependable helpmate across the seas to whom he occasionally wrote. For the second time in her life Deborah lived as a woman apart, married to an absentee husband whom she longed to embrace in her arms instead of her dreams.

As Ben continued to wait for a decision from the Penns, he fumed over their long silence. During their earlier discussion he reminded them that William Penn's charter had assured those emigrating to Pennsylvania they would have the same rights as English subjects in Great Britain. To that Thomas had scoffed, "if they were deceived, it was their own fault," Ben angrily reported to Isaac Norris, the speaker of the Pennsylvania Assembly. "And that he said with a kind of triumphing laughing insolence, such as a low jockey might do when a purchaser complained that he had cheated him in a horse."[29] Somehow the comment was leaked back to the Penns through one of Ben's enemies.

Months later, attorney Paris reinforced Thomas Penn's comment. In November he archly informed the Pennsylvania Assembly that the royal charter "gives the power to make laws to the Proprietary" and that colonial legislators could only provide "advice and consent." Moreover, Paris acidly added, his clients did not consider Franklin among those "persons of candor," a slur that the Penns repeated to the legislators. If negotiations were to continue, they demanded a different agent. Soon afterward Thomas Penn even told Ben to his face that his family saw no reason to continue with him, since he had "acknowledged a want of power to conclude proper measures."[30]

Thus reprimanded, Ben wrote to the Assembly that if they wished to continue negotiations, "it will be necessary to recall me and appoint another person." Still believing there were other options, he added that he intended to persuade the British government to "take the province into its immediate care . . . if so, I think I could still do service," to transform Pennsylvania into an English Crown colony.[31]

Ben's idea was not altogether unrealistic. All but two other North American colonies were governed by Parliament through their Assemblies and their citizens accorded the same rights as residents of Great Britain. But to the Penns, the royal charter meant that only they, as proprietors, held sway over the Pennsylvania legislature. In 1760, after months of wrangling, the

Penns insisted their "unsurveyed wastelands" would remain tax-free. They did, however, make one concession. Land already settled by farmers would be taxed at no more "than the lowest rate" than those other settlers once paid.[32]

Who, then, could be called to the frontier to make those calculations, especially as land was still being settled there by farmers? Given the murky obstacles of the Penns' concession, Ben decided to remain in England. The best he could predict to Deborah about his return to Philadelphia was that he would "endeavor to return early next spring." More a hope than a promise, as flimsy as the silk fabrics that Ben sent from London, Deborah nevertheless clung desperately to it. As she waited, she dutifully exchanged presents, recipes, and expressions of regard with "Mrs. Stevenson."

Ironically, Margaret was similar to Deborah in many ways, a sociable, good-natured matron who was passionately devoted to Franklin. Like Deborah, she too spelled poorly and was so insecure about her writing that Ben often conveyed messages for her. In response to Deborah's gifts of dried venison, beef, and rashers of bacon, Ben reported that "Mrs. Stevenson thinks there never was so good in England."[33] Other messages were more perfunctory: "Mrs. Stevenson and her daughter desire me to present their respects and offer their services to you" and "Mrs. Stevenson and Miss desire their compliments to you and Sally."[34]

From London, meanwhile, Ben reminded Deborah it was her duty to ensure their teenage daughter became a responsible young woman. "My love to dear Sally. I confide in you the care of her and her education: I promise myself the pleasure of finding her much improved at my return," he sternly warned her in January 1758.[35]

Despite his expectations, Ben did little to encourage Sally's intellectual goals beyond having her trained to become a conventional colonial wife and mother. The talkative teenager still enjoyed books and was so fond of music that Ben promised to buy her a harpsichord. After Sally expressed interest in learning French, Ben hired a tutor just before his voyage. But after reading his daughter's first letter in French, he wrote Deborah he thought it "rather too good to be all her own composing. I supposed her master must have corrected it."[36] Not long after Sally read her father's comment, she abandoned her French lessons.

Ben kept urging Deborah to have their daughter study more and lead a moral and ethical life. "I hope Sally applies herself closely to her French and music, and that I shall find she has made great proficiency. . . . I only wish she was a little more careful of her spelling. I hope she continues to love going to church and would have her read over and over again the whole *Duty of Man* and *The Lady's Library*," he reiterated in his February 19 letter.[37]

Nor had Ben forgotten his earlier plan to have Sally married to Strahan's son. In March 1760, his letter to Deborah described Strahan's hopes that Ben would remain in England and that she would soon "remove hither with Sally." The Strahans, Ben observed, were a "very agreeable" family and their son a "sober, ingenious and industrious" young man who would make a fine husband for their daughter.[38]

Again and probably angrily, Deborah rejected the invitation. Soon Ben began writing less frequently. His wife's "invincible aversion to crossing the seas," as he bitterly described it, along with years of separation from her and Sally, made them less important to him.[39]

In their place was Ben's new "English family," Margaret Stevenson and her intellectually curious daughter, Polly. The one portrait of Polly is a pastel depicting her as a thin, finely featured young woman. Three years younger than Sally, Polly was well educated and imbued with a lively and gregarious spirit. So deeply did she admire Ben for his scientific knowledge that she often plied him with questions about natural phenomena as well as how ordinary things worked. Since Polly visited Craven Street only occasionally, Ben sent long answers to her questions. Among his explanations were letters on electricity, the flow of salt into estuarial rivers, the movements of tides, and how chimneys were built.

In contrast to the stern messages he directed to Sally, his letters to Polly were affectionate. "At length I have found an hour, in which I think I may chat with my dear good girl; free from interruption. The attention you have always shown to everything agreeable to me, demands my most grateful acknowledgments," Ben wrote in 1759 to reassure Polly that she did not impose on his time.[40]

Polly's letters, in turn, expressed an admiration bordering on awe. Nor was she shy about her feelings toward Ben. "I hope soon to have the pleasure of seeing you, or if I cannot have that happiness I shall take an opportunity of writing to you again. . . . Thanks for the charming letter I received yesterday . . . am always ready to lay hold of the privilege you give me," typified Polly's respectful replies.[41]

The warmth of those letters led some historians to suspect Ben was romantically involved with her, as he once had been with Catharine Ray. Yet that seems unlikely given his warm and probably intimate relation to her mother, Margaret. Chances are that Ben was simply enjoying her admiration and his role as an entertaining mentor to a worshipful young woman. Attentive as he was to Polly's intellectual questions, he also behaved as her surrogate father, sending notes, offering advice, and inviting her to social events with Margaret. One of his letters from 1762 sounds like that of any fond father diplomatically chastising an inattentive daughter: "Your good mama has just been saying to me that she wonders what can possibly be the reason she has not had a line from you for so long a time."[42]

How well Deborah gleaned the depth of the affection between Ben and Margaret is unknown. By 1760 she may have suspected something, for in one of her now-lost letters she apparently asked Ben about certain rumors from London. Annoyed, he promptly dismissed them and insisted Deborah should do so as well. "I am concerned that so much trouble should be given you by idle reports concerning me," Ben chastised her. "Be satisfied, my dear, that while I have my sense, and God vouchsafes my protection, I shall do nothing unworthy the character of an honest man, and one that loves his family."[43]

The stalemate with the Penns may explain Ben's vague comments about returning to Philadelphia, even though in March 1760 he suggested he would soon return. "I have now the pleasure to acquaint you, that our business draws near a conclusion, and that in less than a month, we shall have a hearing, after which I shall be able to fix a time for my return," he wrote Deborah that month.[44] Again, though, months passed without another reference to his return.

Meanwhile, Ben—who was addressed as "Doctor Franklin" after 1761, when the University of St. Andrews awarded him an honorary doctorate—spent his summers traveling with Billy. Among those trips were excursions to Liverpool, Coventry, Glasgow, Holland, Belgium, and France.

Since nothing was likely to change with the Penns, historians wonder why Ben lingered in London. According to one theory, he stayed to ensure his ambitions for Billy were fulfilled. By 1762, after his son had graduated from the Inns of Court as a barrister, Ben hoped he would marry Polly and unite their families. But at thirty-two Ben's son had exciting plans of his own. Not only was Billy appointed the new royal governor of New Jersey, but he also became engaged to Elizabeth Downes, the frail but personable English daughter of a wealthy Barbados planter.

Ben was deeply disappointed, so unhappy that he decided to leave England three weeks before the wedding. Still, after five years living abroad, returning to Philadelphia worried him. "I have in America connections of the most engaging kind . . . happy as I have been in the friendships contracted here, those promise me greater and more lasting felicity. But God only knows whether those promises shall be fulfilled," he admitted to Polly in June 1762.[45]

Two months later Ben wrote her again from a "wretched inn" in Portsmouth, admitting how much her friend is "afflicted, that he must, perhaps never again, see one for whom he has a sincere an affection so joined to so perfect an esteem." Once he hoped Polly would become his daughter-in-law, but now he could no longer "entertain such pleasing hopes . . . Adieu, my dearest child I will call you so; why should I not call you so, since I love you with all the tenderness, all the fondness of a father?"[46]

Twelve days later, still stalled in Portsmouth because of "contrary winds," Ben acknowledged to Strahan that while glad to be sailing soon, "it carries me still further from those I love." While "reason" dictated the sensibility "for the other side of the water," he admitted his "inclination will be for this side."[47]

Deborah waited in Philadelphia for the return of her beloved Ben. Life had been difficult without him, especially since her mother, Sarah, had died after falling into an open hearth. Properly, if rather coldly, Ben had expressed his sympathies in a March 24 letter: "I condole with you . . . on the death of our good mother, being extremely sensible of the distress and affliction it must have thrown you into. . . . Your comfort will be, that no care was wanting on your part towards her."

Ben then added a promise. "I am finishing all business here in order for my return, which will either be in the Virginia Fleet, or by the packet of May next. I am not determined which. I pray god grant us a happy meeting."[48]

After that one letter, Deborah did not hear from him again. Was he really coming home, and if so, when?

7

Home, but Not in His Heart

IN ANTICIPATION OF BEN'S RETURN in May, Deborah started a new ledger
listing the household purchases she had made since January. "I begin again
to keep an account of expenses," she scrawled at the top. Among them were
homespun thread, six pounds of brown sugar, twenty-five limes, a pound
of green tea, a homespun coverlet, Dutch fabric for pillowcases, a blue and
black silk for Sally, and a jet necklace for herself. Then, in an unprece-
dented burst of extravagance, Deborah spent six pounds, three shillings for
"goodies for my pappy."[1]

Still Ben did not appear. Nor did she receive a letter from him later that
spring, that summer, or even in early fall. What then had caused his delay?
As it happened, bad weather and French hostilities at sea had stalled his
return. It was not until November 1, 1763, that Ben arrived at the Franklin
home. He did that secretly, as he wrote Strahan, to avoid a celebration from
his admirers who would meet him with "500 Horse."[2] Instead, a surprised
and delighted Deborah and Sally welcomed him privately. "I had the great
happiness of finding my family well at my own house," Ben later wrote his
sister Jane.[3]

He insisted he was well "except a little touch of gout," which made him
limp, according to his friends. He assured Jane it was "no disease" at all."[4]
Of course it was. Then as today, gout begins as a painful swelling of a toe
or joint. If left untreated, gout can permanently damage a joint. Even in the
eighteenth century, doctors observed that rich meats, seafood, and beer and

83

wine seemed to exacerbate it, especially in older men. And by then, Ben was just two months shy of fifty-seven. His full head of brown hair had thinned, tiny lines had formed around his eyes, and he was becoming paunchy. Time had left its mark on Deborah, too, weakening her eyes, slowing her gait, and adding weight to her already round frame.

News of Ben's arrival quickly spread through Philadelphia, bringing dozens of visitors to the Franklin home. Suddenly Deborah had new obligations as a hostess; as Ben wrote Strahan, "my house has been full of a succession of them from morning to night ever since my arrival, congratulating me on my return."[5] For weeks Deborah, Sally, and the Franklins' household slaves attended to the admirers who clustered in the hall and parlor to pay their respects. That left Deborah so busy entertaining, as Ben explained to his sister Jane, that her correspondence was delayed "at present [so] short of time."[6]

Ben, meanwhile, exulted in the "kind reception . . . from my old and many new friends." Despite the ugly rumors spread by his political enemy, William Smith, over his failed mission against the Penns, he received "a more hearty welcome and . . . great cordiality" than he expected.[7]

Added to Ben's joy was his reacquaintance with Sally, by then an "amiable" nineteen-year-old who played the harpsichord he had sent her from England. He too was fond of music, and soon they played duets on the "armonica," an instrument he had invented in London. Ben's inspiration came from a 1761 concert he had attended in Cambridge, when a musician made music by rubbing his fingers over glass bottles. Ben's creation elaborated upon it. To do so, he crafted a series of graduated glass bowls with open necks through which he ran an iron rod connected to a foot pedal. As the rod spun the glasses, he ran a moistened finger over the glasses to produce the "sweet tones" similar to those made on a drinking glass.[8] Deborah was so enchanted with Ben's armonica she praised it as "the music of angels."[9]

In contrast to her delight was the imminent arrival of her stepson, Billy. Before he left for England he had been engaged to Elizabeth Graeme, the svelte, brunette daughter of Dr. Thomas and Ann Graeme. Ben had never approved of the match, because the Graemes were politically tied to the

Penns, but Billy remained betrothed. During his years in London, however, he wrote to Elizabeth only occasionally. After Ben clashed with the Penns there, the couple's correspondence faltered. Nevertheless, the Graemes' daughter assumed she was still betrothed to Billy.

Unfortunately, he had never informed his Philadelphia fiancée of his recent marriage. One day soon after Ben's return, Elizabeth appeared at the Franklins' door, stormed into the house, and demanded an explanation. Stunned, Deborah and Ben tried to calm her. Years later Elizabeth, by then married and the mother of two children, recalled that Ben sent her "fond" letters insisting he had "wished me to have been a member of his family."[10]

A few days after that visit, the Franklins were again interrupted, this time by the arrival of Ann Graeme, the jilted young woman's mother. After apologizing for her daughter's outburst, she explained that Elizabeth had become so hysterical that she was taken to the country to calm her nerves. Deborah and Ben listened politely but said little. To soothe her, Ben played music on his armonica.[11]

Still more trouble would come from Billy, for during his stay in London he had sired a son out of wedlock. Like his father, the young attorney never identified the mother. After naming the child William Temple Franklin and providing for him in his will, Billy hid the baby's identity. Through Strahan and Margaret Stevenson, Ben's former landlady in London, Billy sent money to an English woman to raise the boy. Knowing Deborah's dislike for Billy, Ben never told her about his grandson.

Out-of-wedlock births are often dismissed today but were considered disgraceful in the eighteenth century. All too often the child was teased or bullied because of his irregular birth. One wonders how then could Billy, who was often taunted for his origins, repeat his own history? Given his ambitions to be perceived as a highly respected gentleman it seems a remarkable coincidence, but birth control was then notoriously unreliable. Even legally married colonial women, as Ben observed in an earlier treatise on population increase, produced eight children on average. Left unsaid was the frequency of a mother's early death from childbirth.

Meanwhile in February 1763, Deborah braced herself for Billy's arrival. So, too, did Ben. Though Strahan told a mutual friend that Billy's bride was "very agreeable, sensible and good-natured," Ben merely shrugged.[12] Even when Jane congratulated him on Billy's governorship and marriage, Ben coolly replied, "As to the promotion and marriage . . . I shall now only say that the lady is of so amiable character that the latter gives more pleasure than the former."[13] Still, on that blustery February 26, when the newlyweds were expected to arrive, Ben, Sally, and several friends waited for them on the road, cheered their arrival, and escorted them to the Franklin home.

After receiving an "affectionate welcome" from Ben, warmed by heat from the Franklin stove, and comforted by Deborah's hearty meal served on English china, Billy described his and his bride's harrowing journey. In late December, after sailing from Portsmouth, their ship encountered such a violent storm that their captain returned to port. Days later the bad weather finally cleared and the ship embarked again. During the approach to the notoriously turbulent Bay of Biscay bordering France and Spain's west coast, another storm "broke through our windows and did considerable damage to our stores and baggage."[14]

Bad weather followed Billy and "Betsy" (as he called his bride), even when the ship crossed the Atlantic and approached the mouth of the Delaware. There, storms forced the newlyweds to remain offshore, bobbing in the ocean for another ten days. After landing, Billy learned the Delaware was so choked with ice that smaller boats could not sail upriver to Philadelphia. Nor could he obtain a covered carriage to take them overland. In desperation, Billy hired an open carriage and drove his shivering bride a hundred miles in blowing wind over the snowbound countryside. It was all he could do, Billy later wrote to Strahan, "to keep up poor Mrs. Franklin's [Betsy's] spirits."[15] To Deborah, his tale was still one more confirmation of the dangers of sea travel. Fortunately, such journeys were no longer a concern. From everything she knew, Ben was home to stay.

Four days later, her husband, Billy, and several "gentlemen in sleighs" left for Perth Amboy, the East Jersey capital where Billy was sworn in as governor.[16] By then Ben's anger had cooled and been replaced with "pleasure. . . . Seeing him . . . received with the utmost respect and even affection by all ranks of people."[17] After traveling to Princeton for other honors, father and son rode to Burlington, New Jersey's western capital, for bonfires and more celebrations. Since the town was only twenty miles from Philadelphia, Billy decided to make that his home.

Meanwhile his traumatized bride spent those two weeks huddled by the Franklin stove, brooding over the voyage and Pennsylvania's bleak winter. Deborah probably sympathized with her new daughter-in-law over the Atlantic crossing and tried to cheer Betsy by describing the joys of colonial life. Still Betsy remained doubtful. It was not until June that Billy wrote to Strahan that his wife was "pretty well reconciled to America."[18]

Ben, too, was ambivalent about living in the colonies. Despite Deborah's love, his friends' warmth, and his pride in Billy's promotion, he longed to return to England. A month after arriving in Philadelphia, he wrote Strahan: "In two years at farthest I hope to settle all my affairs in such a manner, as that I may then conveniently remove to England, provided we can persuade the good woman to cross the seas. That will be the greatest difficulty."[19] To him colonial life seemed dull compared to the intellectual, literary, and scientific stimulation he found in England.

Added to his restlessness were messages from Margaret, to whom Ben sent presents and letters. Suspiciously, he did not preserve them in his copy books. To ease Margaret's loneliness, he even invited her to join him and his family in Philadelphia. Her daughter, Polly, quickly discouraged the idea, leading Ben to apologize for failing to consider the "inconvenience of such a voyage to a person (Margaret) of her years and sex."[20]

Margaret's next letter invited Ben to return to England and bring his "better half and dear girlie" with him to London. Whether sincere or merely polite, her comment captures the cordial nature of Ben's landlady. For years she had written respectfully to Deborah and Sally, adding to the mystery of her relationship with Ben. Now Margaret's letter chattered on with news about her friends and her ailments. After apologizing for neglecting to correspond "with my best friends," she added, "All I ask is to be able to write for you to read that I am, dear sir, Your sincere friend and most obliged humble servant."[21]

Did Margaret mean to write "best friend" rather than "best friends"? Was that a hedge on her part or merely a slip of her pen? Whatever the intention, Ben's "landlady" longed to be with him. She missed him so much, in fact, that Polly's letter of March 11 admitted her mother was a "little jealous" of Ben's correspondence with others.[22] Two weeks later Ben also confessed to Polly that he regretted leaving London. "Of all the enviable things England has, I envy most its people. Why should that petty Island, when compared to America . . . enjoy in almost every neighborhood, more sensible, virtuous and elegant minds, than we can collect in ranging 100 leagues of our vast forests?"[23]

Within the first few weeks of Ben's return home, Deborah realized he had an overwhelming admiration for England and wanted to return. That shocked and saddened her. What, after all, could be better after their five-year separation than being reunited with his family and friends in Philadelphia? Filled with anger, disappointment, and hurt, she probably expressed that in no uncertain terms. Ben finally backed down and, to placate his "scolding" wife, promised to build a new house for them. Set on a deep lot on Market Street between Third and Fourth, the new three-story brick home seemed to symbolize the solidity of the Franklin marriage and Ben's commitment to remain in Philadelphia. By today's standards the new home was small, its footprint 34 feet by 34 feet with three rooms per floor and a kitchen in the basement. But compared to the Franklins' previously crowded quarters it seemed spacious, their version of a contemporary "dream house."

From Billy's perspective the new home seemed to settle his parents' argument. "My mother is so entirely averse to going to sea, that I believe my father will never be induced to see England again. He is now building a house," he reported to Strahan.[24] Even so, Ben still hoped to visit England again. "I do not forget your reason for my return to England . . . it is however impossible for me to execute the resolution this ensuing summer, having many affairs to arrange, but I trust I shall see you before you look much older," he assured Strahan.[25]

One of those "many affairs" concerned Ben's duties as the co-deputy postmaster general of the North American colonies. In April, after five months at home, he traveled to Virginia to meet his postmaster partner, John Foxcroft (who had replaced the deceased William Hunter), and planned to initiate more postal reforms.

Once again Deborah was alone and obliged to oversee Ben's affairs. Then he invited her to accompany him on his postal tour north, perhaps with the idea of "training" her to the idea of a future travel to England. Again Deborah refused. For all her spunk, she shied away from new situations and new acquaintances. A homebody at heart, Deborah was reluctant to leave Philadelphia. There she felt most comfortable, the place where she was surrounded by family and friends and where she was considered one of the city's most important women. As a businesswoman, assistant postmistress, and Ben's deputy representative, she often socialized with prominent citizens. Among them was her best friend, Deborah Norris, daughter of the speaker of the Assembly, and others: Dr. Benjamin Rush and his parents; Reverend Jacob Duche; Sarah Robert Bond; and poet-businesswoman Susanna Wright. Only twice in her life did Deborah leave Pennsylvania, once on an unrecorded trip to New England and a second time to New Jersey just before Ben sailed to England.

Deborah's refusal to travel infuriated Ben. If she would not accompany him, their daughter must. (She was then visiting Billy and Betsy in Burlington.) "I propose to take Sally at all events," Ben wrote his wife during a postal inspection in New York. "Write for her today to be ready to go in the packet that sails next Friday." Included in Ben's letter was a snipe suggesting that Deborah's decision to remain home was selfish. "You spent your Sunday very well, but I think you should go oftener to church."[26]

By mid-June he and Sally arrived in Rhode Island, where he had arranged to visit Katy Ray Greene. "I certainly could not have forgiven myself if I passed through New England without calling to see you and . . . finding you in the happy situation I used to wish for you," Ben had informed Katy ahead of their arrival.[27] By then his formerly flirtatious friend was the thirty-three-year-old wife of William Greene Jr.—son of the Rhode Island governor—and the mother of two daughters. Just before arriving at the Greenes' clapboard mansion in Warwick, Ben fell from the light carriage he was driving and dislocated his shoulder. Consequently, he and Sally spent several days at the Greenes' while he recovered. Then, despite Katy and Sally's plea for him to remain until he was healed, Ben insisted they proceed to Boston. Several days later while on an inspection in New Hampshire, he fell again and reinjured his shoulder.

On November 5 Ben and Sally returned to Philadelphia. Undoubtedly, Deborah was distressed that she had not accompanied him. To compensate she fussed over Ben's injuries, fully expecting that after his recovery he would complete plans for their still-unfinished house. But politics rather than plaster and porches preoccupied Ben, especially after thirty-nine-year-old John Penn, the initially friendly nephew of Robert Penn, became governor of Pennsylvania.

Less than a month after that appointment, the colony's civil peace was shattered. On December 14 Scotch-Irish backwoodsmen from Paxton, in western Pennsylvania, rode to Lancaster and killed six friendly Native Americans. The motive was revenge; for years the backwoodsmen had seethed over tribal massacres of their newly settled property that the Native Americans asserted were their ancestral lands. The murders in Lancaster were only the beginning of their rampage, as they and hundreds of other settlers resented Pennsylvania's Quaker-dominated Assembly's refusal to use force against the tribes. By December 27, 1763, they raised a mob of three hundred frontiersmen supported by Philadelphia's working-class German Lutherans and Scotch-Irish Presbyterians and swept into Philadelphia's workhouse, where they slaughtered the fourteen Native American men, women, and children who had been sheltered there to protect them from harm. The citizens were shocked.

So too was Ben, as expressed in his pamphlet, "A Narrative of the Late Massacres in Lancaster County." Within it he dubbed the attackers the "Paxton Boys," a gang that "committed the atrocious fact, in defiance of government, of all laws human and divine . . . to the eternal disgrace of their country and color, then mounted their horses . . . huzza'd in triumph as if they had gained a victory and rode off—unmolested." The natives, Ben solemnly observed, were the "remains of a tribe of the Six Nations" who had welcomed the arriving English nearly a century earlier with venison, corn, and skins. While "not making apologies for all Indians," he reminded citizens that Pennsylvania's tolerant founder, William Penn, had promised their lands would be respected 'As long as the sun should shine or the waters run in the rivers.'"[28]

Ben also insisted it was the colony's responsibility to stand up against those "barbarous men" who were acting "to the eternal disgrace of their country and color."[29] Quarreling factions soon churned out their own handbills and pamphlets reflecting Pennsylvania's social, ethnic, and religious groups and smearing each other with insults. Still, the peace-loving Quakers of the Assembly did nothing. Despite Ben's pleas for Governor Penn to stop new attacks, the official stalled. Once again Ben urged the citizens to form a new militia. By Saturday, February 4, as the mob advanced toward Philadelphia, the governor summoned British troops, ordered the arrest of the leaders, and urged residents to join the militia.

At midnight on February 5 a furious pounding on the front door woke Ben and Deborah. There in the shadows of a streetlight stood Governor Penn and his nervous advisers, begging for Ben's advice after the Paxton Boys charged into nearby Germantown with rifles and tomahawks. Within moments the Franklin home became the governor's headquarters for plans to stop the rebellion. For the second time in less than a year, the house was overrun with strangers whom the bleary-eyed Deborah must have provided with food and drink. Through the wee hours of that morning Ben begged Penn to use military force, but he refused. Instead the governor ordered Ben and his friends to arrange a peace accord with the Paxton Boys.

Days after a truce was finally declared, Ben complained to his English physician, Dr. Fothergill, that despite the governor's promise to punish the gang, he had suddenly dismissed "all inquiry after the murderers." Alarming, too, was Penn's disregard for the legislators who wanted to pursue the perpetrators. That, Ben added, brought the official "and his government into sudden contempt. All regard for him in the Assembly is lost. All hopes for happiness under a proprietary government are at an end."[30]

The governor was equally disgusted with Ben. On May 5 he wrote his uncle, Thomas Penn: "There will never be any prospect of ease and happiness while that villain [Franklin] has the liberty of spreading . . . the poison of that inveterate malice and ill nature . . . deeply implanted in his own black heart."[31] Inevitably, the Paxton riots signaled the start of Ben's second power struggle against the Penns. What that meant to Deborah—fright and fear that he would soon travel to England again—were all entirely possible.

In late May Ben, then serving as acting speaker of the Assembly, renewed the idea of removing the proprietors and converting Pennsylvania into a Crown colony. Despite the enemies he made over the Paxton Boys attack, he ran for reelection. But Ben's critics were many. Among them were the Germans who not only supported Governor Penn but remembered that Ben had called them "Palatine boors" in his 1751 pamphlet, "Observations Concerning Population Increase."[32] The Scotch-Irish settlers also deeply resented Ben, whose "A Narrative of the Late Massacres" denounced them as "Christian white savages" because of their racist hatred for Native Americans.[33] Other factions allied with the Penns despised Ben for his determination to free Pennsylvania from their authority. Cruel political cartoons, newspaper notices, and handbills soon appeared that portrayed Ben as a lecherous, corrupt political figure who had duped an innocent public through diplomatic chicanery while living luxuriously as their colonial agent in England.

That summer the Franklin home become campaign headquarters for Ben's reelection. One can only imagine how the stream of news and the political scheming of his followers disrupted the well-ordered Franklin home. Nor did it end there. Before long Ben's enemies dragged Deborah into the fray. One of the most blistering insults against her appeared in the pamphlet "What Is Sauce for the Goose Is Sauce for the Gander." In it, Ben was accused of having exploited Billy's mother as a "most valuable slave" for the "foster mother of his latest offspring who did his dirty work."[34] That "foster mother," of course, was Deborah, and her "dirty work" her duties to Ben as his devoted wife.

The pamphlet also accused Ben of having "piously withheld" from His Excellency's [Governor William Franklin's] mother the means to survive and had even starved her to death. Then Ben "stole her to her grave" without even a shroud to "cover her dignity, without a groan, a sign or a tear."[35]

To those and other insults, neither Deborah nor Ben publicly responded. Restraint in response to rage was a favorite Franklin tactic. Still, it cut deep. As Ben complained to Richard Jackson, Britain's colonial agent for Pennsylvania and a parliamentarian, "I bore the personal abuse of five scurrilous pamphlets, and three copperplate prints, from the proprietary party before I made the smallest return."[36] He did not mention how Deborah's reputation too was damaged. Like other women married to prominent men, her emotions were ignored.

In October Ben narrowly lost his election. With civil peace still threatened on Pennsylvania's frontier and the Penns' refusal to help, Ben's allies in the Assembly elected him again as their agent. "As it appeared to the General Assembly, that matters of the highest concern to the colonies in general and to this province in particular were depending in England, the House . . . resolve that you should embark with all convenient dispatch to Great Britain there to join with an assistant . . . Richard Jackson, Esq. In the agency of presenting, soliciting and transacting the affairs of their province for the ensuing year," read Ben's November 1 appointment.[37]

The task was heavy but no less heartbreaking than the question Ben now asked: Would Deborah accompany him to England? Again she refused. Nor would she allow Sally to join him. After arguing over their second separation, Ben demanded that Deborah write him only cheerful letters. If she would not travel to England with him, Deborah had no right to complain.

On November 5, Ben rode to Chester with an escort of three hundred allies to board the *King of Prussia* bound for England. From an island at the mouth of the Atlantic, he lectured Sally that "the more attentively dutiful and tender you are toward your good Mamma, the more you will recommend yourself to me. . . . You know I have many enemies (all indeed on the public account) . . . and you must expect that their enmity will extend in some degree to you, so your slightest indiscretions will be magnified into crimes . . . to wound and afflict me. It is therefore . . . necessary for you to be extremely circumspect in all your behavior that no advantage may be given to their malevolence."[38]

Ben had already warned Deborah to be similarly careful, promising all would be well: In a year he would return and complete their new house. As Deborah must have understood by then, the house was like her marriage: a project in transition that required seemingly endless patience.

From England on December 9, Ben admitted to Deborah that though his ship sailed swiftly across the Atlantic, they ran into "terrible weather; and I have often been thankful that our dear Sally was not with me. . . . I have no time to name names: you know whom I love and honor. Say all the proper things for me to everybody . . . I am, dear Debby, Your ever loving husband."[39]

Deborah was undoubtedly relieved to have received Ben's letter, but despite his admission of that rough transatlantic crossing, she remained defensive about her refusal to accompany him. Worrying that her letter might miss the next packet departure, Deborah dashed off a note explaining she wanted to avoid being found "wanting in my duty and you be displeased." In that letter—the first of Deborah's preserved correspondence—she wrote: "I long to know how your arm is . . . and hope you did not meet with any hurt in the passing."[40]

Her own hurt was not mentioned. While pragmatism rather than passion still dictated their union, Deborah was determined to keep Ben's affection afloat across the turbulent waters of the Atlantic.

"One Continued State of Suspense"

THE SILENT SUSPICIONS OF Ben's "good women" of Philadelphia and London are buried beneath their cordial exchange of messages, recipes, and goods. In February 1765, after Ben had resumed living with Margaret, he sent Deborah a trunk "with the blankets, bed ticks &etc. you wrote for." Among the contents was blue mohair "for the curtains of the blue chamber," intended for the new house. "The fashion" he added (probably with Margaret's advice), "is to make one curtain only for each window" with hooks "sent to fix the rails . . . at top."[1]

In the last paragraph he warned Deborah, "Let no one make you uneasy with their idle or malicious stories or scribblings, but enjoy yourself and friends and the comforts of life that God has bestowed on you, with a cheerful heart."[2] Was Ben referring to rumors about his efforts to petition the king—or to talk stirred by his renewed relationship with Margaret?

If Deborah worried about his landlady, Ben's closing comment dispelled her anxieties. "A few months, I hope, will finish affairs here . . . and bring me to retirement and repose with my little family, so suitable to my years, and which I have so long set my heart upon."[3]

Their letters crossed in the mail, but Deborah had just written Ben, assuring him she avoided behavior that might provoke more enemy attacks. "I have never said or done anything or any of our family, you may depend on it nor shall we. All our good friends call on us as usual and we have been asked out but I have not gone." That very day, for instance, some of their neighbors had attended an ox roast on the river, but Deborah had declined. "I partake of none of the diversions. I stay at home and flatter myself that the next packet will bring me a letter from you."[4]

Instead of socializing with others, she had turned her attention to completing details of their new house. "This day the man is putting up the fireplaces that came from London, the dark one in the parlor. The plasterer is finishing the lathing of the staircases and I am getting the lower part of the house cleaned out ready for the laying of the kitchen floor," she reported.[5] During that first year in England, Ben remained interested in the house and often questioned her about its progress. In June, after Deborah moved in, he asked about the kitchen, worrying that since it is "a mere machine and being new to you, I think you will scarce know how to work it." Ben also inquired about the furnace. "If that iron has not been set, let it alone until my return, when I shall bring a more convenient copper one."[6]

When Deborah reported that she had invited friends for a meal in the new dining room, Ben complained that he wanted more details. "You tell me only of a fault they found with the house, that it was too little, and not a word of anything they liked in it; nor how the kitchen chimneys perform, so I suppose you spare me some mortification, which is kind."[7]

He also worried that Deborah was unable to complete other important aspects of the house. "You should never be without tubs sufficient in the area to catch the rainwater, for if it overflows there often it may occasion the foundation to settle, and hurt the wall." Had Deborah "moved everything, and put all the papers and books in my room and do you keep it locked? Is the passage out to the top of house fixed with iron rails from chimney to chimney?" he asked in August.[8]

Comments like those, coupled with Deborah's insecurities about details usually left to husbands, intensified her anxieties. "O my child [as she often addressed Ben], there is a great odds between a man's being at home and abroad as everybody is afraid they shall do wrong so everything is left undone."[9] Despite her lament, Deborah sensed that if the house was ever to be completed, she would be the one to do it. Shrewdly, in spring 1765—with the independence that now characterized her life—she bought the empty lot next to the house, to create what became known as Franklin Court. Despite the steep price of 900 pounds, Deborah was relieved when Ben agreed it was a sensible decision. "I am very glad you do approve of my purchase and when it will please God to restore you to your [own] house I think you will be very much pleased . . . as it does make a fine square and an equal space on each side."[10]

Far less pleasant was Ben's dilemma in England. There his petition to the king was again postponed as Parliament debated how best to recoup losses from the French and Indian War. Added to those costs was Great Britain's plan to maintain a ten-thousand-man army in the colonies to defend the vast northern territories won from the French. By February 6, 1765, England's first minister, the flinty George Grenville, had a solution: a Stamp Act placed upon the American colonies, whose defense necessitated the expenses.

The act would become effective November 1. By its terms colonial newspapers, legal documents, and other papers were required to be produced on paper from England with an embossed revenue stamp. Alarmed, Ben suggested an alternate solution: a Parliament-regulated system of paper currency in the colonies. Grenville promptly dismissed it. "Our affairs are at a total stop here by the present unsettled state of the ministry," Ben complained to a Philadelphia friend. Even so, he intended to "go forward again as soon as that is fixed. Nothing yet appears that is discouraging."[11]

His optimism was far from reality, for the Stamp Act reignited simmering resentments in the colonies. On May 30 angry delegates in Virginia's House of Burgesses issued a set of "Resolves" protesting Britain's right to collect revenue through the Stamp Act without colonial permission. "Taxation of the people by themselves . . . is the only security against a burdensome taxation, and the distinguishing characteristic of British freedom, without which the ancient constitution cannot exist," the document proclaimed.[12] To Ben, a reasoned negotiation with the British government rather than colonial outbursts was the best way to end the proposed tax. To his Philadelphia friend John Hughes he predicted that the "rashness of the Assembly in Virginia" would be forgotten" and Pennsylvania would continue to "keep within the bounds of prudence and moderation."[13]

It was too late for that. By spring 1765, resistance to the Stamp Act had reached a fever pitch among the colonies, inciting riots, civil protests, boycotts of British goods, and the formation of rebellious groups like the Sons of Liberty of Massachusetts. Unfortunately, Ben had already obeyed Grenville's orders to appoint certain men as colonial stamp collectors. John Hughes, whom Ben had appointed, had received so many death threats that he obtained a gun to defend his home. Other colonies reported similar threats to stamp collector appointees. Even Cadwallader Colden, New York's acting governor, had to rush his son into a fort for protection. In Boston, a mob hung an effigy of the Massachusetts stamp collector, Andrew Oliver, and tore down his house.

Ben's enemies interpreted his compliance to Grenville as proof that he supported the Stamp Act, and they revived rumors of his disloyalty. On Wednesday, September 16, a gang of angry men gathered near Market Street intending to burn down Franklin Court. Deborah refused to let that happen. Having survived the Paxton Boys crisis and insults as Billy's "foster mother" during the Assembly election, the "hedgehog" in Ben's wife readied her quills.

"Something has been said relating to raising a mob in this place. I was for 9 days kept in one continued hurry by people to remove [leave]," Deborah wrote Ben a week later. After hustling Sally off to Billy's home in Burlington for safety, Deborah's cousin Josiah Davenport had arrived to protect her. "He stayed with me sometime towards night. I said he should fetch a gun or two as we had none. I sent to ask my brother to come and bring his gun . . . so we made one room into a magazine. I ordered some sort of defense upstairs such as I could manage myself."[14]

Throughout that night Deborah stood watch with a gun, determined to defend Ben's innocence. "I said . . . that I was very sure you had done nothing to hurt anybody nor would I stir or show the least uneasiness, but if anyone came to disturb me I would show a proper resentment and I should be very much affronted."[15] By morning a group of eight hundred Franklin supporters had gathered to threaten the mob, after which the gang finally disbanded.

Mindful of her promise to Ben to write only cheerful letters, Deborah's letter that September then switched to the subject of the new house. A mason had begun building a wall around the Franklin property despite a neighbor's claim that the new lot trespassed on his lot. The wall was finished but consequently "lays open on that side. Indeed I was afraid to have it done because of the objection. . . . I am afraid of giving any offense and content myself with thinking whatever is, is best." Stoic acceptance of life's events had tempered the once easily ruffled Deborah. Now, whatever Ben's relation was or had been with Margaret, Deborah seemed to accept her importance to Ben. If nothing else, she continued to remain polite and dignified as Ben's wife, in accordance with his "Rules and Maxims for Matrimonial Happiness." "My compliments to good Mrs. Stevenson, I will write to her . . . I like the curtains very well and everything that is sent," she praised Ben's landlady.[16]

Three weeks later, Deborah received several of Ben's "dear letters." A visitor also told her he recently saw her husband in England. "He tells me you look well which is next to seeing . . . you. I am pleased to read over and over again [your letter]. I call it a husband's love letter!" Though she wanted to share news about the political climate in Philadelphia, Deborah apologized for not relaying more information. "I . . . wrote several letters to you, one almost every day but then I could not forbear saying something to you about public affairs. . . . I would destroy it [the letter] and then begin again and burn it again and so on." Ultimately she decided to avoid writing "one word about them, as I believe you have better [information] than I could tell you."[17]

By November 9 Ben had read about the gang of ruffians who had threatened to burn his home and Deborah's steely defense. "I honor much the spirit and courage you showed, and the prudent preparations you made in that [time] of danger," he wrote her. Unfortunately, the original of that letter has been poorly preserved, leading scholars of the Franklin papers at Yale University to believe the next sentence read, "The [woman?] deserves a good [house] that [is?] determined . . . to defend it."[18]

Even before she received the letter, Deborah repeated her promise to avoid anything that might cast Ben in a negative light. "If I stay at home I may be as happy as possible while you are not here to make me quite so. I hope you are not to stay longer than the spring," she wistfully scrawled.[19]

But Ben's return was again postponed. The threat to the Franklin home, the alarmed messages, and newspapers and letters Ben received about colonial resistance to the Stamp Act prompted him to remain in England to campaign for its repeal. Week after week he met with sympathetic British officials, among them Lord Dartmouth and Lord Rockingham, who now replaced Grenville. To Deborah on February 22 he excused his delay thus: "I am excessively hurried, being, every hour that I am awake, either abroad to speak with members of Parliament or taken up with people coming to me at home concerning our American affairs."[20]

Rockingham and the Irish-born Edmund Burke called for a hearing in the House of Commons. One of the main speakers was Ben. The Stamp Act, he argued, was a violation of the English constitution by mandating a direct tax upon ordinary life events. If passed, "we shall have no commerce, make no exchange of property with each other, neither purchase nor grant, nor recover debts; we shall neither marry, nor make our wills, unless we pay such and such sums, and thus it is intended to extort our money from us; or ruin us by the consequences of refusing to pay it."[21] On March 16, 1766, at least partly because of Ben's testimony and tireless meetings with members of Parliament, the Stamp Act was repealed.

Still the ministry, a loose term referring to Crown advisers and Parliament, was fixed on the idea of making the colonists pay. The same day the Stamp Act was repealed, Parliament approved the Declaratory Act, reasserting Great Britain's authority to tax, "make laws and statutes of sufficient force and validity to bind the colonies and people of America, subjects of the crown of Great Britain."[22] So it was that British tyranny set the stage for Ben's decade-long battle for fair treatment of the American colonies.

In Philadelphia, Deborah would soon engage in a personal struggle for her own and Sally's independence. As the daughter of the famous Doctor Franklin, the young woman often attended teas, card games, and assembly balls with others from Philadelphia's best families. She also traveled to Burlington to visit her half-brother, Billy, and his wife, Betsy. There Sally's stylish sister-in-law groomed her before introducing her to prominent young men. In England, meanwhile, Ben worried that his twenty-three-year-old daughter was still single. In celebration of the repeal of the Stamp

Act and the end of the colonial boycott of British goods, he sent Deborah a new gown. For Sally there was "a fine piece of pompadour satin" for when she attended the elite dances, or "assemblies," of Philadelphia.[23]

Ironically, a death rather than a dance led to Sally's engagement. In August her friend Peggy Ross became gravely ill and on her deathbed asked her fiancé, Richard Bache, a handsome English merchant, "to marry her intimate friend, Sally Franklin."[24] In her grief, Sally asked Ben to send her a mourning ring. He complied but kept urging Sally to acquire more "friends" (beaus), little suspecting that she and Richard were romantically involved. In spring 1767, in a letter now lost, Sally explained she was in love with the Englishman.

In May, Richard sent Ben his own letter. That, too, has not been preserved, but judging from Ben's response, Sally's beau had declared his desire to marry her. The merchant also explained the circumstances that led to his current financial difficulties. In the early 1760s, Richard emigrated from England to work in his brother's successful marine insurance business in New York. Then, for reasons that remain unexplained, he moved to Philadelphia to open a dry goods store on Chestnut Street. At the peak of the colonial boycott of English goods, Richard bought and refurbished the *Charlestown*, a 110-ton ship that traded in Jamaica and in European ports. Allegedly he had an agreement with a partner in London, who somehow discounted it and left Richard in heavy debt.

Ben was horrified. It was bad enough that Sally planned to wed the mere owner of a dry goods store rather than an upper-class beau, but to marry a debtor? It was unthinkable that he, who famously offered others advice about money and authored the 1758 *The Way to Wealth* (an abridged version of the proverbs from his *Almanack*), would have a debtor for a son-in-law. That summer he wrote to Deborah that his "surrogate daughter" Polly had escaped a similar fate by ending an engagement with a "mean-spirted mercenary fellow" who was far less "valuable" than "she is as a girl."[25]

If only Sally would make a similar break, Ben thought, especially after reading a private letter from Billy. After asking around, the governor discovered Richard's debts were so great that the creditors had "agreed to give up their claim to damages, on account of its being a particular hard case."[26]

Even Richard's brother could not bail him out, because the debts exceeded his personal worth.

Still more damning was Billy's conversation with the father of Sally's deceased friend, Peggy Ross. Even before the *Charlestown* bankruptcy, Mr. Ross thought Richard a poor man even "if all his debts were paid." In sum, Richard seems to be "a mere fortune hunter, who wants to better his circumstances [by] marrying into a family that will support him," Billy advised his father. Still, he remained uncertain. "I don't know what to make of all the different accounts I hear of him; but I think it evident that these bills have involved him in a load of debt greatly more than he is worth, and that if Sally married him they must both be entirely dependent on you for subsistence." Worried about the confidentiality of the letter, Billy ended by instructing his father, "Burn this."[27]

Sally remained madly in love with Richard. In response to her beau's confession that he was ashamed of his debts, she encouraged him to avoid dwelling on them. "Nothing is worse for the health and spirits than reflecting for a long time on one subject. You ask me how I keep up my spirits; let me tell you that while I think you love me, it is out of the power of misfortune to make me truly unhappy." If others carped that Richard's financial "misfortunes" made him less than a desirable suitor, that mattered not. Sally simply adored him.[28]

Knowing the intensity of Sally's passion, Deborah did not dare to cross her daughter. Sally was so determined to marry Richard, she explained to Ben in May, that she did not criticize him. Besides, Deborah resentfully observed, with Ben absent, "I am obliged to be both father and mother." Aside from his debts, Richard was an affable and charming man. She therefore decided to "treat him well . . . for I think he deserves it." Deborah also thought it unwise to forbid Sally to see Richard. If she did, "it would only drive her to see him somewhere else which would give me great uneasiness." She also reminded Ben that Sally was a fine young woman who was so protective of her half-brother Billy that when he was once challenged in a duel, she had insisted upon accompanying him. "You see, this daughter of ours is a . . . champion and thinks she is to take care of us."[29]

In late May, Ben reluctantly conceded to the match. Unsure if he could return that summer, he wrote to Deborah, "I would not occasion a delay of her happiness if you thought the match a proper one."[30] Toward the end of that letter Ben briefly mentioned he had just sent Sally two summer hats. A month later Ben wrote Deborah that because he would probably remain in Britain another winter, she would have to decide about Sally's beau. "I suppose the sooner it is completed the better. In that case I would only advise that you do not make an expensive feasting wedding, but conduct everything with frugality and economy which our circumstances really now require."[31] Weddings of well-to-do Philadelphians, as the Franklins knew, were then expensive affairs involving a week of festivities.

Despite Ben's usual warnings about thrift, he had genuine financial concerns. In 1766 his eighteen-year publishing agreement with David Hall in Philadelphia ended, reducing his income by five hundred pounds per year. Moreover, given his resistance to the Stamp Act, his royal appointment as deputy postmaster general of the colonies was tenuous. If he lost that position, Ben wrote Deborah in June, "we should be reduced to our rent and interest on money for a subsistence which will by no means afford . . . [our usual] housekeeping and entertainments." While he lived as frugally as possible, London was costly. Deborah's expenses, too, were high because of the relatives who often stayed for weeks at the Franklin home. "In short, with frugality and prudent care we may subsist decently on what we have but without such care . . . it will melt away like butter in the sunshine; and we may live long enough to feel the miserable consequences of our indiscretion."[32]

It was true, Ben admitted, that he knew "very little of the gentleman or his character," but he hoped Richard had no expectations of "any fortune to be had with our daughter before our death. I can only say that if he proves a good husband to her, and a good son to me, he shall find me as good a father as I can be." So, if there had to be a wedding, he advised Deborah to provide Sally with clothes and furniture but to keep expenses under five hundred pounds. "For the rest, they must depend, as you and I did, on their own industry and care."[33]

Ben's long absence, her dashed hopes for his return, and Sally's romance led Deborah to decide on her own. That July, weary of inquiries from friends and business associates about Ben's return, she complained, "Some say you will come home this summer, others not. I can't say anything as I am in the dark and my life of old age is one continued state of suspense."[34] Coincidentally, that same day Ben wrote that he was sending Deborah a petticoat and one for Sally, along with a negligee, but he avoided mentioning more about the proposed wedding.

In a last-ditch effort to discourage the match, Ben wrote Richard on August 5. He politely expressed his sorrow "to hear of your misfortune" and hoped that "good management may in a few years replace what you have lost." Then his letter turned into a lecture. "Your own discretion will suggest to you how far it will be right to charge yourself with the expense of a family which if undertaken before you recover yourself, may forever prevent your emerging." To dispel any notion that he could support Richard and Sally, Ben added, "I love my daughter perhaps as well as ever parent did a child, but I have told you before my estate is small, scarce a sufficiency for the support of me and my wife, who are growing old and cannot now bustle for a living as we have done."[35]

That same day Ben wrote Deborah that he noticed her most recent letter did not mention "Mr. Bache." Again he repeated his hope that the young man's "misfortune" would prevent him from "entering hastily into a state that must require a great addition to his expense." To help Sally forget him, he even suggested that Deborah send her to London. It would, Ben declared, "be some amusement to Sally to visit her friends here and return with me, I should have no objection to her coming over with Capt. Faulkner, provided Mrs. Faulkner" agreed to accompany her. The trip, Ben insisted, "might be some improvement to her."[36]

If Deborah received that letter, she would again have refused. But somehow the letter miscarried. Meanwhile, Ben dashed off a second note in August announcing a trip to France. Over the next two months no letters followed, during which time neither Deborah nor Ben's friends heard from him. That, she wrote Ben, seemed "very surprising."[37] Undoubtedly, she must have wondered if he was angry about her support for Sally.

Or was he so upset about Richard's financial troubles that he was sulking in silence?

In reality, both were true. That summer Ben's mood was so sour that even the usually tolerant Margaret was taken aback. She was so distressed, in fact, that on September 18 she sent Deborah an unusually confidential letter. Within it Margaret explained that after hearing about Sally's match, she thrilled at the thought of outfitting the bride with fashionable English clothes. In response, Ben snapped at her and declared the marriage would not happen. Scolded for her giddy feminine enthusiasm, Margaret backed down. Since "your good man forbid it," Margaret wrote Deborah, she was simply sending Sally a silk negligee. Even if the young woman did not wed, the nightgown would not be "out of character for your daughter as Miss Franklin."[38]

Soon after that argument, Ben sailed to France. There, while celebrated by scientists, philosophers, and Louis XVI, he wrote Margaret an angry note. She was surprised, she admitted to Deborah, but conceded, as had his "good woman" in Philadelphia, that Ben "is the best judge." Sympathetically, Margaret added, "I truly think your expectations of seeing Mr. F from time to time has been too much for the tender affectionate wife to bear."[39] As an eighteenth-century woman-to-woman letter, Margaret's message was striking, a candid admission of the faults and foibles of the man she and Deborah knew and loved.

Deborah's response to Margaret has been lost, but for the first time in her life she withdrew from Ben. Finally. For years she had served Ben with devotion, keeping him informed about the current political climate, completing the new house, overseeing his affairs, sending him news about their friends, and wearily serving as his representative when others asked about him. In Ben's absence Deborah was the only one close to Sally, and worried about her daughter's emotional stability. All summer, after learning about Ben's disapproval of Richard, Sally looked pale and wan and seemed upset.

In October Deborah tried a different approach with Ben. Instead of pleading for understanding, she wrote a letter filled with news about their friends and relatives. Her one reference to Sally was that she "writes tomorrow. I shall say no more that she is better than she has been all summer, but

much disappointed as was Mr. Bache." She deliberately omitted the fact
that the couple remained passionately devoted to each other.[40] Two weeks
later, after Ben returned from France, he wrote Deborah about his "greatly
improved health. I hope this will find you and Sally and all we love . . . and
even those that don't, as well as I am."[41]

As it happened, Sally was not only "well," but ecstatic. "Last Thursday Evening [October 29] Mr. Richard Bache of this city, merchant, was
married to Miss Sally Franklin, the only daughter of the celebrated Doctor
Franklin, a young Lady of distinguished merit." The next day "all the ship-
ping in the harbor displayed their colors on the happy occasion," reported
the *Pennsylvania Chronicle*.[42]

For once, the women in Ben's life had their way by insisting that passion
must sometimes prevail over prudence.

"How I Long to See You"

BEN MUST HAVE NOTICED Deborah's unusually brief comment about Sally in her October letter. After that, her letters stopped. "I have this minute received letters by the packet of October from Billy and some other friends but not a line from you," Ben wrote her on November 17. "I suppose you have written by some other vessel; I long to hear of your and Sally's welfare from your own hands."[1]

Perhaps Deborah did announce Sally's marriage to Ben at last, but if she did, her letter was not preserved. Since he constantly corresponded with his Philadelphia friends, he must have known about the wedding. After learning about it, Ben fumed, his anger as white hot as the coals in the fireplaces at the Stevenson townhouse. Stoking his rage was his sister Jane's December 1 letter, probably inspired by Deborah, to persuade Ben to accept the wedding. "You are called to rejoice at the settling in marriage of your beloved daughter to a worthy gentleman whom she loves and the only one who can make her happy. I congratulate you . . . and wish it may give you lasting pleasure."[2]

It was not until late February 1768 that Ben frostily replied to Jane, "She [Sally] has pleased herself and her mother, and I hope she will do well; but I think they should have seen some better prospect . . . before they married how the family was to be maintained."[3]

To Deborah he expressed his anger by refusing to write. On Christmas Eve 1767 Ben communicated again in a letter now lost. That same day he hastily sent another note, asking Deborah to send German newspapers and a local stone used in Philadelphia for steps. "Your care in these particulars will greatly oblige your ever loving husband," he penned.[4]

By then Deborah had shipped crates of apples, cranberries, buckwheat meal, and nuts to Ben. On February 13 he received them, thanked her, and sent his love to Sally. Then, however, he added, "I forget to tell you that a certain very great lady, the best woman in England, was graciously pleased to accept some of your nuts and to say they were excellent. This to yourself only."[5]

A "very great lady"? The "best woman in England"? Any wife reading that would wonder at the words, let alone the intimidated Deborah. Was Margaret's approval the final judge of good food? Was not Deborah too "a very great lady" and the "best wife in North America"? Had she not served for years as Ben's "deputy husband" in Philadelphia, sending him news, informing others he was well, overseeing his business affairs? What was Ben getting at by praising Margaret so extravagantly? Did Deborah's decision to allow Sally's marriage put her in second place? Such thoughts may have at least fleetingly occurred to her.

For nearly a year, Ben's letters to his wife continued to convey his love to Sally but never mentioned Richard. In August 1768, ten months after the wedding, he finally wrote his new son-in-law. At the time the Baches were visiting relatives in Boston, but when Deborah received Ben's letter, she sent it on to Richard with an ecstatic note. "Well, the post brought letters from the packet and now Mr. Bache (or my son Bache) I give you joy; although there are no fine speeches, as some people would make, our father (or so I will call him) and you, I hope, will have many happy days together."[6]

Despite Deborah's expectations, Ben's letter to his son-in-law began with a rebuke. Though addressed to "Loving Son," he considered Richard's marriage "a very rash and precipitate one" that might bring "future unhappiness on my child, by involving her in the difficulty . . . that seemed connected with your circumstances." Then, softening, Ben added, "Time has made me easier. I hope too, that the accounts you give me of your better prospects are well-founded, and that by an industrious application to business you may retrieve your losses. I can only add at present, that my best wishes attend you, and that if you prove a good husband and son, you will find in me an affectionate father."[7]

Once that became a reality, Deborah told the newlyweds that "my heart will be more at rest than it has been for some time."[8] Her statement reflected the months of anxiety she felt during Richard's courtship of Sally, a stress already taking a toll on her increasingly heavy body. In response to Ben's announcement that he intended to arrive in Philadelphia that fall, Deborah urged the couple to return home to welcome him. But no sooner had they arrived than they learned Ben had canceled his trip.

The threat of violence in the colonies had thwarted his plans. For nearly a year Ben had brooded over reports of American protests of Great Britain's Townshend Acts. The acts, which demanded duties on essential goods such as glass, china, lead, paint, and tea, were the latest in a series of oppressive British measures meant to obtain revenue from the colonies. Just after Ben planned to return to America, he learned that Parliament was sending a thousand soldiers on a British man-of-war to Boston to demand payment of those duties. The situation boded ill. Soldiers, guns, and forceful payments almost certainly portended violence. This was not the time to return to Philadelphia for a family reunion. It was critically important that he remain in London. As a seasoned spokesman for Pennsylvania, indeed by then for all the American colonies, no one was as intimately acquainted with British politics as he. As Ben explained to his Assembly ally Galloway, he remained in England in the hopes of swaying members of the newly elected Parliament "to disapprove of the violent measures."[9]

Rushed, fearing interception of his letters by spies, or because politics was a man's realm, Ben did not explain to Deborah the reasons for his canceled return to Philadelphia. Devastated, she once again stopped writing.

"It feels very strange to me to have ships and packets come in and no letters from you. But I do not complain of it, because I know the reason is, my having written to you that I was coming home," Ben admitted on October 5. Instead of explaining why, he wrote about a brief escape from London "to breathe a little fresh air" at the country home of friends. "At my time of life," he added, he still enjoyed very good health, but "we are not to expect it will always be sunshine."[10]

In early 1769 some of that "sunshine" beamed on Deborah when Sally announced her first pregnancy. At sixty-one, the future grandmother was thrilled to see her daughter's body swelling with child. Mindful of Ben's warning to avoid any behavior that might incite his enemies, Deborah continued to entertain visitors and nurse sick friends, but she seldom visited others for social pleasure. Instead she wrote Ben, "I keep myself to myself."[11] The reality was a bit different. Deborah was rarely alone, for as Billy once predicted, the Baches lived with her at Franklin Court because of Richard's ongoing financial struggles.

Later that winter Deborah collapsed from a stroke. For weeks she had trouble speaking, seemed confused, and temporarily lost use of a hand. While the letters Sally and Billy sent Ben were not preserved, by late spring they had apparently reported on Deborah's gradual recovery. Ben, too, must have written Deborah, although those letters were also lost. Only one of his letters to Deborah from that period remains, written on June 3: "I rejoice to hear you so soon got over your late indisposition but am impatient for the next packet, which I hope will bring me that good news under your own hand."[12]

In Philadelphia that same day, Dr. Thomas Bond, the city's most prominent physician, advised Ben that his wife was unlikely to make a full recovery. "Your good Mrs. Franklin was affected . . . with a partial palsy in the tongue and a sudden loss of memory, but she soon recovered from them, though her constitution in general appears impaired. These are bad symptoms in advanced life and auger further injury on the nervous system."[13] Newly alarmed, Ben relayed that information to his friend Dr. John Pringle, physician to the queen, then sent Deborah his advice.

By August 31 Deborah was strong enough to write Ben about the birth and christening of Sally's son, Benjamin Franklin Bache, nicknamed Benny. "Our dear little boy was carried to Christ Church and was baptized by the name of Benj[amin]. Franklin. His uncle and aunt stood for him . . . and I was well enough to stand for myself."[14] In October Deborah wrote again, this time ecstatic over little Benny. "The baby was talking about you and is grown finely . . . and is one of the best-tempered child I ever saw . . . every-one says he is much like you, I wish you [could] . . . see him."[15]

Despite Deborah's delight in her grandson, Ben's absence wore on her. Nearly six years had passed since he had left. Before Ben's departure for England she had promised "never to make any complaints to you" but now could no longer remain silent. In late November Deborah wrote Ben that she believed her stroke was a result of their long years of separation. Just before it happened, she admitted she was tired from nursing a sick relative. Those long hours at the bedside merely "added to my dissatisfied distress at your staying so much longer . . . I tell my friends I was not sick but I was not [able] to bear any more so I fell down and could not get up again. Indeed it was not any sickness but too much disquiet of mind."[16] Although she assured Ben her memory was better, he noticed her handwriting was worse and her thoughts veered from one subject to another even more than in her earlier letters.

A month later Deborah wrote again, insisting she was "much better than I was when I wrote to you the last letter." She looked like her old self. Her sister (or sister-in-law, since the terms were often interchanged) had helped her recover. Now we "are as happy as we could expect to be in your absence, but we hope you will be [here] as soon as in the spring." In Ben's absence, the lonely grandmother poured her affections on "Kingbird," her pet name for Benny. "Our dear king bird is very well. He is sitting by me and is as fine a dear lad and sends his duty to you and . . . to good Mrs. Stevenson and Miss Polly."[17]

In an effort to cheer Deborah, Ben praised her in June 1770 as "the most punctual of all my correspondents . . . it is a particular satisfaction to me to hear from you when I have no letter from anyone else."[18] From a distance he also offered grandfatherly advice. Since smallpox still threatened Pennsylvania, Benny's parents had him inoculated. When the child failed to show post-inoculation symptoms, Ben became so worried he insisted the procedure be repeated. Despite his concern, his letters became increasingly detached. "I rejoice much in the pleasure you appear to take in him. It must be of use to your health," he replied in an impersonal tone.[19] Did

Deborah notice that? If so, she must have hoped her comment about the stroke would impel Ben to hurry home.

To the future founding father, there was no contest: The British noose of oppression was tightening around Boston. On March 16, 1770, when five Americans were shot by the British after a rowdy street skirmish, Ben's premonition proved true. Appalled by Great Britain's harsh treatment of the colonists, he nevertheless adopted a calm, reasoned manner in an effort to win support for the colonies from sympathetic members of Parliament. In politics as in love, prudence triumphed over Ben's passion. Shortly after the massacre, he revealed his real thoughts about the British to a Boston relative: "I was happy to find that neither you, nor any of your family, were in the way of those murderers. I hope that before this time the town is quite freed from such dangerous and mischievous inmates."[20]

From his previous encounters at Pennsylvania's frontier, Ben knew that once the sparks of rebellion were ignited, they would eventually burst into flame. To Galloway that June he predicted, "Party heats are at present a little abated: But many think the fire is only smothered, and will break out again before the meeting of Parliament."[21]

While civil protests, angry handbills, and newspaper accounts condemning British oppression in Pennsylvania and other colonies preoccupied most citizens, Deborah's one wish was to have Ben by her side. "I am very sorry to think I should not have it in my power to attend on you," she wrote her husband, referring to her declining health. "When will it be in your power to come home? How I long to see you." Then, reminded of the gravity of Ben's political responsibilities, Deborah backed off, assuring him, "I would not say one word that would give you one moment's trouble."[22]

But apparently she did. After reading a letter from Deborah describing one of Benny's illnesses, Ben dryly commented, "I am glad your little grandson recovered so soon." Was the phrase "your grandson" merely a "slip of the pen" from America's overworked spokesman? Or did it reveal an unconscious thought? "I see you are quite in love with him and your happiness wrapped up in his, since your long letter is made up of the history of his pretty actions," Ben practically yawned in print.[23] If nothing else, the comment revealed his conflicted allegiances: admiration for "the best woman in England" versus his dutiful and now-disabled wife, Deborah. Over time, sexual passion may have faded with both women, but the preservation of colonial rights now set him aflame.

Undeterred, Deborah persisted in her enthusiastic letters about Benny. When he became a toddler, she taught him to worship his important "Grandpa." "I showed him . . . grandfather's [picture], it pleased him and would kiss it. I told him who it was," she reported in early 1771.[24] By spring, "Grandpa" was so annoyed with the narrow subjects of Deborah's letters that he wrote, "You were not very attentive to money matters in your best days, and I apprehend that your memory is too impaired for the management of sums without damaging the future fortune of your daughter and grandson."[25] Perhaps fearing that as he, too, aged his memory might fail, Ben spent a portion of the summer of 1771 writing the first part of his *Autobiography* at the Twyford estate of his friend Joseph Shipley, the Bishop of Asaph, who lived there with his wife and five young daughters.

In late autumn Deborah sent Ben an account of recent expenditures. "I take notice of the considerable sums you have paid. I would not have you send me any receipts. I am satisfied with the accounts you give," he replied on January 28.[26] By then or soon afterward, Ben assigned his son-in-law Richard the power of attorney.

Still, Deborah insisted on proving her health had improved. As she did each autumn, she sent Ben produce from the Pennsylvania harvest. By late 1771 barrels of buckwheat, cornmeal, apples, and dried peaches had arrived at Craven Street. Somehow, too, Deborah had managed to have two squirrels caught, crated, and sent to Ben at the request of Bishop Shipley's curious daughters. "The squirrels came safe and well. You will see by the enclosed how welcome they are. A 1,000 thanks are sent you for them, and I thank you for the readiness with which you executed the commission," Ben replied. In that same letter he added that "Mrs. Steven [Stevenson] too loves to hear about your little Boy. Her own grandson (my godson) is a fine child, now nine months old. He has an attentive, observing sagacious look, as if he had a great deal of sense."[27]

Despite his annoyance with Deborah's enthusiasm for Benny, Ben had strong paternal instincts. Years earlier in Philadelphia he had mentored several young men and established his sister Jane's lackluster sons in various enterprises. During his second stay in England, he and the ever-obliging Margaret helped raise the motherless eleven-year-old daughter of a Franklin cousin. Most telling was Ben's unofficial adoption of young Temple, who had been raised from infancy by a hired woman in London. After befriending the boy, Ben enrolled him in a Kensington boarding school when he turned eight. During vacations Temple lived at Craven Street, where he and Margaret doted upon him.

Ben never mentioned Temple's existence to Deborah. Nor did he reveal to Margaret, Polly, or his English friends that the youngster was Billy's out-of-wedlock son. To them, Temple was an orphan whom Ben had taken under his wing. When one of the Stevensons' relatives asked about the boy, Polly merely replied, "Mr. Temple is a young gentleman, who is at school here . . . who is under the care of Dr. Franklin."[28]

During Ben's second stay in London, he grew even closer to Polly, whom he now considered his adopted "English daughter." On July 10, 1770, when she wed the brilliant physician and anatomist William Hewson, Ben stood in for her late father and gave Polly away. The following spring, when Polly delivered her first son, also named Billy, Ben became his godfather. To her the baby was almost Ben's own flesh and blood. Polly's letter of November 1771 even claimed the baby "resembles you in many particulars. He is generally serious, no great talker, but sometimes laughs very heartily." Then in a teasing reference to Ben's habit of sitting naked by an open window for health, Polly added her son "is very fond of being in his *Birthday Suit* and has not the least apprehension of catching cold in it . . . always seems delighted with fresh air."[29]

Ben was immensely flattered. "I thank you for your intelligence about my godson. I believe you are sincere when you say you think him as fine a child as you wish to see. . . . His being like me in some many particulars pleases me prodigiously."[30] No similar expressions of pride appear in Ben's letters to Deborah, in which she insisted Benny looked like him. That same November, Richard traveled to London and was greeted by Ben "with open arms" and then met Margaret and Polly. After seeing the newborn, Richard agreed with Polly that the "lower part of his [the baby's] face . . . [looked] something like Ben's."[31]

Jowls? The full cheeks of a well-fed baby? Perhaps Richard was being diplomatic, but whatever he meant, the resemblance of both babies to Ben seems a remarkable coincidence, one both families used to compete for his allegiance. Temporarily, at least, the London "family" won, as Ben soon matched Deborah's praise for Benny with his about Polly's son.

"Mrs. Stevenson sends her love to you all. Her grandson grows a very fine boy indeed," he wrote in early winter 1772.[32] In reply to Deborah's letters about Benny's superior qualities, Ben wrote in May, "I suppose he is master of the house. Tell him that Billy Hewson is as much thought of here as he can be there."[33]

Not to be outdone, Deborah kept coaching Benny about his absent grandfather. Her letter to Ben that same month described how she told the child she was writing to someone important. "I tell him to Grandpapa." In that same letter, Deborah confessed her health was failing: "I am very incapable of doing any business as I am not able to walk about and my memory so poorly and sometimes worse than others."[34]

Her next letter apologized for its ink blotches. "You may see what blunders by the scratching out that I am not capable of writing, so I shall only say that I find myself growing very feeble very fast." Even so, Deborah added another story about Benny. "This morning would [have] afforded you much pleasure with my kingbird. He went into the water [a bath] and as soon as he ate his breakfast he said he would go to school."[35]

Ben's letters to Deborah that summer and early autumn have disappeared, but one in December dwelled upon his own advancing years. While he still enjoyed "very good health and spirits I must not flatter myself it will continue much longer, as the course of nature brings on with age many infirmities."[36] In another letter he advised Deborah to "eat light foods, such as fowls, mutton &c. and but little beef or bacon, avoid strong tea and use what exercise you can. By these means, you will preserve your health better and be less subject to lowness of spirits."[37]

Either unable or unwilling to consider that the cause for Deborah's "low spirits" was his absence, Ben insisted they must both remain cheerful. "So swiftly does time fly," he wrote on January 6, 1773, his sixty-seventh birthday. "We have however great reason to be thankful that so much of our lives has passed so happily and that so great a share of health and strength remains as to render life yet comfortable."[38]

More discreetly reproachful was Ben's comment a month later. "In return for our history of your grandson, I must give you a little of the history of my godson. He is now 21 months old, very strong and healthy, begins to speak a little and even to sing. He was with us a few days last week, grew fond of me, and would not be contented to sit down to breakfast without coming to call, *Pa*, rejoicing when he had got me into my place." Then, fearing he sounded too fond, he added, "It makes me long to be at home to play with Benny."[39]

Still Ben did not return to Philadelphia. Sally, by then pregnant with a second child, was so worried about the ailing Deborah that she assumed the housekeeping and the family budget. As he had done earlier in her life, Ben lectured Sally on thrift. She must "get a habit of keeping exact accounts . . . remember, for [y]our encouragement in good economy that whatever a child saves of its parents money, will be its own another day. Study *Poor Richard* a little, and you may find some benefit from his instruction." More tenderly he then assured her, "I long to be with you all, and to see your son."[40]

On May 31, 1773, Sally delivered a second child, William, nicknamed Willy. In Ben's congratulatory letter to Deborah that July, he expressed the hope that the baby "will prove another pleasure to you." Delicately, he added, "I believe I told you that Mrs. Hewson has another son. Mrs. Stevenson was all along wishing for a granddaughter for herself and another for you. When I told her your new grandchild was a boy as well as hers, she says, *How provoking!*"[41]

Ben later praised Deborah's report about Benny's fondness for books, referred to him as a "precious little fellow," and added, "How much I long to see him!"—but made no commitment about returning to Philadelphia. Then in a September letter that must have deeply hurt Deborah, he wrote, "I begin to fear that when I return, I shall find myself a stranger in my own country . . . leaving so many friends there, it will seem leaving home."[42]

Possibly Deborah never received this correspondence, for two months later she wrote she was "very much distressed" at the absence of Ben's letters. Consequently, "I must endeavor to submit to what I am to bear," she lamented, in what had become her daily prayer.[43]

In London Ben waged an anonymously written newspaper campaign warning Great Britain it was destroying its own empire. To Billy he confided that he was "of the opinion that the Parliament has not the right to make any law whatever binding on the colonies." Unhappily, Ben realized that his son was still a "government man" loyal to Great Britain, despite the intercolonial cries for revolution.[44] Among the most prominent protesters were Sam and John Adams, who headed Boston's Sons of Liberty, the secret organization that first demanded independence. In a December 16, 1773, response to Britain's Tea Act, fifty "sons" disguised as Mohawk natives dumped 342 chests of tea from the English-owned East India Tea Company into Boston Harbor.

Ben condemned it as an "act of violent injustice on our part" but was soon dragged into an even more inflammatory position. The previous March he had sent copies of six letters to Thomas Cushing, speaker of the Massachusetts House, insisting they remain confidential. Written by Governor Thomas Hutchinson and his colonial secretary, Andrew Oliver, to Thomas Whately, commissioner of the royal Board of Trade, the letters were meant to disguise the governor's role in stoking the British oppression of Massachusetts. Simultaneously, the two-faced Hutchinson feigned sympathy for his constituents, thereby escaping blame for the protests in Boston that followed.

The so-called Whately letters, Ben had warned Speaker Cushing, must be shared with only a few political leaders and "great care . . . taken to keep our people quiet."[45] Nevertheless, Cushing and the Adamses leaked those letters to the newspapers, inciting riots, the burning of Hutchinson and Oliver effigies on Boston Common, and protests in other colonies. Once reports of the upheavals reached London, Ben was blamed as an "incendiary," and "the papers . . . filled with invectives against me," as he angrily informed Cushing.[46]

In early January 1774 Ben was summoned to the "Cockpit" to consider a colonial petition to remove Hutchinson as the Massachusetts governor. That octagonal inner room in the Privy Council, named for Henry VIII's favorite place for cockfights, soon became the setting for an equally brutal conflict. Sensing the hearing was only the first step to incrimination, Ben hired an attorney and delayed the meeting until the end of the month. On the 29th he stood calmly on the stand before a hostile audience of "all the courtiers," MPs, dignitaries, and "an immense crowd of other auditors . . . [came] as to an entertainment," as the caustic Solicitor General Alexander Wedderburn accused him of inciting colonial hostility.[47]

Later, Ben bitterly wrote to Cushing that "your agent [Ben] . . . stood there the butt of his invective and ribaldry for near an hour." After excoriating him for sending "private correspondence . . . hither held sacred" to the rebellious colonists, Wedderburn accused Ben of violating the "respect of societies and of men." In addition, the solicitor condemned Ben for keeping his part in the "Whately" affair secret for nearly a year. The Privy Council ultimately dismissed the Massachusetts petition against Hutchinson as "groundless, vexatious and scandalous."[48] The next day, the "disgraced" Ben was dismissed as postmaster general of the North American colonies.

After that, Ben's admiration for England ceased, and he became a fervent advocate for American independence. Although humiliated, rarely seen in public, and knowing he could best serve the colonies by returning home, Ben lingered in England. Historians still debate why. Was leaving Margaret and friends too difficult to bear? During the next ten months Ben wrote treatises in newspapers in defense of the colonies. Meanwhile Deborah, whose health was worsening, longed for his return. But once again Ben hedged. "I hoped to have been on the sea in my return by this time, but find I must stay a few weeks longer, perhaps for the summer ships. Thanks to God I continue well and hearty and hope to find you so when I have the happiness once more of seeing you," he wrote her in late April.[49]

A week after this correspondence, tragedy struck at Craven Street. "Our family here is in great distress. Poor Mrs. Hewson [Polly] has lost her husband and Mrs. Stevenson, her son-in-law. He died last Sunday morning of a fever which baffled the skills of our best physicians. He was an excellent young man, ingenious, industrious, useful and beloved by all. . . . She is left with two young children and a third soon expected. . . . All their schemes of life are now overthrown!" Ben wrote Deborah on May 5.[50] For days Dr. Hewson had been ill, but no one had expected his death, which left the pregnant Polly to face a lonely and financially uncertain future.

Two days later, in the midst of grieving, Ben suddenly realized he had had no recent letters from Deborah. "It is now a very long time indeed since I have had the pleasure of a line from you. I hope, however, that you are well as I am."[51] Ten weeks later Ben nervously penned, "I have had no line from you. I flatter myself it is owning not to indisposition but to the opinion of my having left England, which indeed I hope soon to do."[52] Yet still he remained in London.

By September Deborah's long silence alarmed Ben. "It is now nine long months since I received a letter from my dear Debby. I have supposed it owing to your continual expectation of my return. I have feared that some indisposition had rendered you unable to write. I have imagined anything rather than admit a supposition that your kind attention towards me was abated. . . . And yet when so many other old friends have dropped a line to me now and then, at a venture, taking the chance of finding me here or not, . . . why might I not have expected the same comfort from you who used to be so diligent and faithful a correspondent as to omit scarce an opportunity?"[53]

Historians do not know if Deborah received that letter or if she did, whether she was well enough to understand it. It had been ten years since she had seen Ben. On December 14, 1774, Deborah, age sixty-six, suffered another stroke.

On Christmas Eve Billy wrote Ben, "I came here on Thursday last to attend the funeral of my poor old mother who died the Monday noon . . . Mr. Bache and I followed as chief mourners. . . . She told me . . . that she never expected to see you unless you returned this winter, for she was sure she would not live till next summer. I heartily wish you had happened to come over in the fall, as I think the disappointment in that respect, preyed a good deal on her spirits."[54]

10

"I Desire That You May Love Me Forever"

DEBORAH WAS GONE AND so was the world Ben once knew. No sooner had he stepped onto the Philadelphia wharf on May 5, 1775, than he heard about the April 19 battle of Lexington and Concord. Then Ben learned the heartening news that the Redcoats had been forced into a humiliating retreat to Boston. Encouraged, Ben wrote the sympathetic parliamentarian David Hartley on May 6, "I arrived here last night and have the pleasure to learn . . . there is the most perfect unanimity throughout the colonies." Even New York had become "as hearty and zealous as the rest."[1]

By then Ben was happily settled at Franklin Court, where he and Temple (who accompanied him from England) were greeted by the newly pregnant Sally and her husband, Richard. Nearby played the two grandchildren born in Ben's absence: Deborah's "kingbird," five-year-old Benny, and two-year-old Willy.

As Ben walked through Franklin Court, he realized how carefully Deborah had followed his instructions. Every detail, from the sidewalk to the railings leading to the roof, was complete. The parlor contained a sideboard, two tables, a set of chairs, and a handsome English mirror. A large carpet covered the floor of the Blue Room, which housed the armonica and harpsichord. The dining room displayed the fine china and crystal Ben once sent from London; his own room was furnished with his desk, a sideboard with his papers, music, electrical equipment, and paintings. Indeed,

Deborah had "proved a good and a faithful helpmate," as Ben observed in his *Autobiography*.[2]

Still, there was little time for grief. That same morning, friends and neighbors rushed into his house with more news about the revolution. Philadelphia was in an uproar. Express riders appeared daily on lathered horses from Massachusetts with bulletins about the latest skirmishes with the British. Church bells announced their arrival; newspapers churned out reports, kiosks displayed handbills with the latest news as Patriots gathered in groups and readied arms. Added to the commotion were fifty-six delegates and their assistants arriving for the May 10 start of the Second Continental Congress. Some came in carriages; others arrived on vessels docked at the wharves and were then seen gathering for meals at the City Tavern and other fashionable eateries.

Regardless of the delegates' show of colonial "unanimity," the two men closest to Ben remained faithful to the Crown. One was his former political ally in the Assembly, Galloway. From England Ben vainly tried to explain the wisdom of the patriotic rebellion. Why, he had argued, should any colony "grant a revenue to a government that holds a sword over their head?"[3] Galloway dismissed the comment, although he and Ben remained friends. Soon after Ben's return Galloway invited him to his country house in Bucks County. For weeks, Galloway had hidden there after receiving death threats from the Patriots. Ben initially hesitated, claiming he was "so taken up with people coming in continually, that I cannot stir, and can scarce think what is proper or practicable."[4]

Even more disturbing was Billy's loyalty to the British. That May, Ben tried to convince his son that "independence is more honorable than any service" and warned him that if he insisted upon remaining in office as royal governor of New Jersey, the Patriots would seek revenge. Earlier he had warned that Billy would find himself "in no comfortable situation."[5] Now in 1775 Ben agreed to appear at Galloway's country house to meet with him and Billy. Temple had accompanied him and met his father for the first time, but after the three adults quarreled over the revolution, Ben left.

Once back in Philadelphia he threw himself into work at the Second Continental Congress. Ben held many positions: as a member of several committees, leader of Pennsylvania's defense committee, and postmaster for the newly united colonies. He also edited congressional documents, among them Thomas Jefferson's draft of the Declaration of Independence. Less than two weeks after it was circulated to the colonies, Billy was arrested as a "virulent enemy of this country."[6]

In contrast to Ben's bitterness toward Loyalists like Billy and Galloway, he exchanged friendly letters with his English friends. Especially poignant were letters from Margaret Stevenson, who desperately missed Ben. After a decade of companionship, his absence left her life feeling empty and hollow. Of course, it was not the first time they had been separated. In 1762 Ben left London abruptly when Billy was about to wed, but less than two years later the Colony of Pennsylvania sent him back to London. Remembering that, Margaret clung to the slender hope that he would return again. And now that Ben was widowed, she hoped he would marry her.

The same thought had occurred to Polly's friend, Dorothea Blunt, who had already written Ben while he was still at sea, "Mrs. Stevenson . . . gives frequent p[roof?] of weak spirits, which I am sure will be still [weak]er if your letter whenever it comes does not contain the strongest assurances of your return . . . for without the animating hope of spending the remainder of life with you, she would be very wretched indeed."[7]

Five days later, Margaret expressed her fervent desire to be reunited with Ben. "All your friends are well, except myself, and I am out of spirits, but I hope my dearest and dear friend . . . [your] writing will raise them by saying he shall soon return. Oh my dear Sir, I shall rejoice at that happy day." In his absence Margaret attended to Ben's papers and his personal property just as Deborah once did. Conscientiously, she wrote "I must make up your packet" and bring it "to the coffee house . . . myself that I see this Captain Price and beg his special care. I have enclosed all your letters. . . . My prayers and best wishes attend you in all place[s]."[8]

Even her daughter, Polly, who often wrote in her place, described Margaret's woeful state: "I asked my mother if she had anything to say. Only her love, and that her patience is almost exhausted, it will not hold out above ten days longer if she does not hear from you."[9]

One of Ben's surviving letters to Polly admitted he deeply missed his

"English family." Four days after signing the Declaration of Independence he even invited her to "come hither with your family," despite the discouraging "present situation of public affairs."[10] Ben may also have written other letters to Margaret, but the only one that has been preserved was dated July 17. In his letter he assured her he was "well and as happy as I can be" but was working "under the fatigue of more business than is suitable to my age and inclination."[11] His tone was oddly detached, just as it had been in his later letters to Deborah. The fight for colonial independence had become Ben's first priority. Love and its memories were left to languish in the hearts of his women.

Ben had not forgotten about his now-widowed sister, Jane. Frightened by the brutalities of British soldiers in Boston, the sixty-two-year-old had packed up her household goods and fled to the home of her Franklin relative, Katy Ray Greene in Warwick, Rhode Island. There Ben's former sweetheart and her husband, William, by then a justice of the Rhode Island Supreme Court, hosted Jane for weeks. On June 17, as the Battle of Bunker Hill raged in Boston, Ben wrote Jane that he intended to bring her to Philadelphia. The same day he wrote his old flame, insisting that while he welcomed seeing old friends, there was "none more than my dear Katy and her family." Her husband, he hoped, "will allow an old man of 70 to say he loves his wife [Katy]," since "it is an innocent affection." His letter also discouraged Katy, by then in her middle forties, from escorting Jane to Philadelphia herself. "It is much too long a journey for her who is no good horsewoman, and perhaps for you, though you used to ride admirably."[12]

Katy assured Ben that she considered Jane a friend and mother figure and that "we divert each other charmingly." Then she extended an invitation to Ben. "Do come and see us certain! Don't think of going home again. Do set down and enjoy the remainder of your days [here] in peace."[13]

Finally, after meeting with George Washington in Boston about instilling more discipline in the raw, undisciplined recruits of the new Continental Army, Ben traveled to the Greenes' home. Long resigned to loving Katy as an avuncular figure, he brought her son Ray along with Jane to Philadelphia. Their reunion was a unique moment for the brother and sister. As Jill

Lepore noted in her biography of Jane Franklin Mecom, the siblings "lived under the same roof for the first time since they were children."[14]

That reunion was short-lived, for on September 26 the financially strapped Congress appointed Ben a commissioner and directed him to seek funding in France. A month and a day later, Ben sailed to France on the American warship *Reprisal*. Temple, who was to serve as his private secretary, accompanied him, and so did eight-year-old Benny. What prompted Sally and Richard to let their bright first son leave with his grandfather is not known. Perhaps they welcomed Ben's offer to have Benny educated abroad. Or they tearfully conceded to Ben's plea that as a widower he was lonely and needed the comfort of his grandsons.

He needn't have worried. There would always be a woman willing to be at Ben's side. Inevitably in France, there would be more than one.

On December 3, 1776, the *Reprisal* arrived in the fishing village of Auray, Brittany. Despite the gravity of Ben's mission, the French turned out to greet him with festivities. Two decades had passed since that nation had celebrated Ben's electrical experiments, but he was still remembered as a genius. To them, as Anne-Robert Jacques Turgot, comptroller general of France, would later observe, Ben was a brilliant scientist-statesman, the man who "stole lightning from the heavens and the scepter from tyrants."[15] More bald, greyer, and heavier than in his 1767 visit to France, Ben appeared in a plain brown and white linen suit and a marten cap instead of a wig, but he was nevertheless hailed as a celebrity. As his carriage rumbled toward Paris, people gawked at him, waved, threw flowers, and cheered at "Bonhomme Richard," in remembrance of his *Almanack*.

Ironically, Ben's modest clothes added to his popularity—for the French, knowing he hailed from Pennsylvania, assumed he was a member of the Quakers, whose democratic attitudes they admired. Ben did nothing to dissuade them. In fact, as biographer Walter Isaacson observed, Ben deliberately exploited that image, which coincided with the popular French writer Rousseau's praise for the "purity" of man in his natural state. To the French, the American minister's plain appearance symbolized America's innocent values. Struck by the discrepancy between himself and the

bewigged and stylishly clothed French, Ben wrote Polly, "Figure to yourself an old man, with grey hair appearing under a marten fur cap, among
the powdered heads of Paris."[16]

Even before his 1776 arrival, Ben's name and face were well known.
Everyone from "kings courtiers, nobility . . . philosophers, . . . a valet
de chamber, coachman . . . to a lady's chambermaid" knew him, as John
Adams, who joined Ben as a commissioner in 1779, jealously observed.[17]
Indeed, Adams wrote his friend James Lowell that Franklin not only had "a
monopoly of reputation here" but "an indecency in displaying it."[18] One of
the most popular portraits of Ben depicted him bent over a book and peer-
ing through spectacles, a painting replicated in prints and on rings, snuff
boxes, and other decorative items. Equally famous was Ben's popularity
with the women who frequented the glittering salons held in the drawing
rooms and gilded halls around Paris.

A product of Enlightenment thought, the salons were often hosted by
aristocratic women to promote learning, cultivate manners, and encourage
social exchanges. By the time Ben arrived in France, widening divisions between the rich and poor had attracted the attention of the *philosophes*—the
intellectuals, scientists, and writers of France—who gathered in salons to
debate those social discrepancies. Imbued with Voltaire's plea for personal
freedom and Rousseau's belief in the natural "innocence" of man, the *philosophes* inadvertently fostered public discontent with the monarchy, which
would later inspire the French Revolution.

Ben frequented those salons, smiling, listening, rarely replying in his
faltering French, but understanding their drift. To Adams, Ben's attendance had less to do with intellectual stimulation than his interest in the
women who frequented the salons. While Ben accepted dinner invitations,
attended plays with highly placed members of French society, "and sometimes [met with] the philosophers, but most commonly to visit those ladies
who were complaisant enough to . . . procure sets of tea gear and make tea
for him. . . . After tea, the evenings were spent in hearing the ladies sing,
and play upon their piano fortes and other instruments . . . and in various
games."[19]

Adams's observations were probably accurate, but he never grasped something Ben intuitively knew: Winning the approval of elite French women was bound to influence their prominent husbands. One of the most famous images reflecting Ben's popularity with the ladies was Baron Jolly of Bruxelles's painting *Benjamin Franklin at the Court of France*, 1778. Painted to commemorate the French-American treaties of that year, Jolly depicted a drapery-festooned hall at the Court of Versailles, where gowned and coiffured women crowned Ben with a laurel wreath.

Despite Ben's diplomatic triumphs, his enemies spread rumors that he was lecherous, and shamelessly so. On October 11, 1779, after receiving a letter from Mrs. Elizabeth Partridge of Boston excoriating him for his behavior, Ben defended himself. "You mention the kindness of the French ladies to me. I must explain that matter. This is the civilest nation upon earth. . . . Somebody it seems, gave it out that I loved the ladies, and that everybody presented me their ladies . . . to be embraced, that is to have their necks kissed. For as to kissing of lips or cheeks, it is not the mode here. The first is reckoned rude & the other may rub off the paint. The French ladies have however, 1000 other ways of rending themselves agreeable; by their various attentions and civilities & their sensible conversation. 'Tis a delightful people to live with."[20]

Ben's defense came long after his arrival in Paris on December 21, 1776. At first he moved into the Hotel de Hambourg, where fellow commissioner Silas Deane, a thirty-nine-year-old merchant lawyer from Connecticut, was already assessing French reaction to the revolution. The public was wildly supportive, but that mattered far less than a commitment from the French Court for financial support. Ben's counterpart in those negotiations was the politically adept Charles Gravier de Vergennes, France's foreign minister and King Louis XVI's most trusted cabinet member.

Ben's first letter to Vergennes explained he had arrived to "propose and negotiate a treaty of amity and commerce between France and the United States." Diplomatically, he expressed his appearance as if it was a compliment to France: Congress, he said, had sent him to Paris in appreciation for "the just and generous treatment their [America's] trading ships have received, by . . . a free admission into the ports of this kingdom."[21] France had already secretly promised to send weapons and ammunition to the West

Indies, then to be shipped to America. However, that was minimal compared to the large funds Ben sought.

Ben consequently warned Congress to avoid expecting too much too soon. In the homey prose of *Poor Richard's Almanack,* he compared the United States to a young woman of marriageable age whose "virgin state should preserve the virgin character, and not go about suitoring for alliances." Ben's strategic approach was to wait "with decent dignity for the application of others."[22] While history suggested that France would aid America because of its long-standing enmity with England, he knew it would require time, diplomacy, and political duplicity to achieve that end.

Vergennes was equally coy. Ben's February 2 report to Congress reported that Vergennes met with him and his fellow commissioners Silas Deane and Arthur Lee but remained noncommittal. At that time the French minister merely "assured us of the protection of his court . . . due consideration . . . would be given to what we offered."[23] Vergennes had other reasons to hedge, for France's longtime ally, Spain, would also have to agree. Another obstacle was even more formidable: Official French support for the colonies would almost certainly spark another war with Great Britain.

To overcome those difficulties would require adept steps forward and graceful retreats much like the *contredanse allemande,* a dance made popular by Marie-Antoinette's 1774 marriage to Louis XVI. But after two months of formal bows and scrapes, Ben was so weary he moved to the nearby village of Passy, taking Temple and Benny with him. Claiming he did so for fresher air, Ben had accepted the invitation of the pro-American aristocratic industrialist Jacques-Donatien Le Ray de Chaumont.

At his host's insistence, Ben was to live there rent-free with his grandsons. Temple continued as his grandfather's secretary, and Benny was enrolled in the village school. Passy had other advantages over Paris, Ben realized, as he plotted his moves on the chessboard of French-English rivalries. Because the village was a half hour's ride from Paris, French officials could no longer observe his visitors. Inevitably that raised suspicions that Passy provided cover for Ben's negotiations with the British. That, too, would keep French officials on edge and serve as another goad to pry open the coffers of the royal treasury.

Dotted with villas, several chateaux, shops, and vineyards, Passy was located slightly west of Paris on a hill between the Seine and the Bois de Boulogne. Ben's home was a spacious pavilion on the grounds of Chaumont's baroque Hotel de Valentinois, a stately mansion surrounded by ten acres of formal gardens, an octagonal pool, and paths lined with linden trees. Years later Ben described his residence to the still-pining Margaret as a "fine house, situated in a neat village, on high ground, half a mile from Paris, with a large garden to walk in."[24] By the mid-nineteenth century, Passy and the neighboring villages of Auteuil and Chaillot had become part of the *seizième arrondissement* of Paris. Today it is still considered the city's most elite district.

In March 1777, soon after Ben began enjoying Passy's fresh country breezes, his introduction to Anne-Louise Boyvin d'Hardancourt Brillon de Jouy nearly took his breath away. Known as Madame Brillon, the petite, light-haired thirty-three-year-old had wide eyes and a stunning figure and was considered one of France's most beautiful women. She was also an accomplished musician and composer who favored the new piano over the harpsichord, a woman so gifted that Luigi Boccherini had dedicated his sixth sonata to her. In 1770 traveling music critic Charles Burney praised her as "one of the greatest lady players on the harpsichord in Europe and . . . the best performer on the pianoforte . . . just brought to Paris. . . . The lady . . . plays the most difficult pieces with great precision, taste and feeling."[25]

As French aristocratic custom demanded, her parents had married her at eighteen or nineteen to Jacques Brillon de Jouy, a wealthy treasury official twenty-four years her senior. It was a loveless marriage, although she bore him two daughters to whom she was devoted. Marriage, motherhood, and her status as a member of the elite consequently limited Madame Brillon's performances to entertaining friends in her high-toned (and high-haired) salons.

During that first meeting, Ben had so completely charmed the musician that she later worried that she had made a poor impression. When they spoke, he mentioned his fondness for Scottish tunes, leading her to beg their mutual friend Louis-Guillaume Le Veillard to obtain copies of that music. "I would try to play them and compose some in the same vein! I want my talent for music to please Mr. Franklin. This is not an affair of vanity. I have never taken pride in playing the harpsichord better than some others." Once she had copies of the Scottish music in hand, she hoped "to divert for a moment a great man from his affairs, and to procure myself the pleasure of seeing him."[26]

That spring Madame Brillon sent Ben several invitations to her estate, a lofty mansion surrounded by terraced gardens, lawns, and walking paths. Ben promptly accepted; as a lover of music and beautiful women, he saw no reason to decline. If nothing else, the musician's invitations provided welcome respite from monotonous carriage rides to Paris, where he met, smiled at, and tried to wheedle financial support from the French ministers.

Madame Brillon immediately schemed to capture Ben's heart. A seasoned flirt whose witty repartee, flashing eyes, and coy smile captivated men, she besieged him with invitations to luncheons, teas, and dinners. Franklin biographer Claude-Anne Lopez noted that her letters soon "glided from the formal 'Monsieur Franklin' to 'papa'," her pet name for her distinguished friend as they met to drink tea, play chess, and hear the Brillons' young daughters sing.[27] As the musician hoped, Ben was soon overwhelmed. While balding, overweight, and suffering from gout and boils, the seventy-two-year-old was flattered—and smitten.

Shamelessly, Madame Brillon flaunted her attachment to Ben before others at dinners, salons, and balls, despite the criticism she received as a result of "my pleasant habit of sitting on your knee, and yours of always asking me for what I always refuse."[28] Before long their meetings became part of Ben's weekly schedule. On Wednesdays and Saturdays he and the musician shared meals, attended concerts, and indulged in twilight strolls down the hundred steps of the Brillon terrace to the lush lawns and gardens below. They also matched wits over chess. By July 1777, Madame Brillon was so comfortable with Ben that, writing in the third person, she teased she was "miffed" by the six games in a row he won "so inhumanely . . . she warns him she will spare nothing" to get her revenge.[29]

Her good-natured husband, Jacques, also played chess. On at least one occasion the musician luxuriated in the bath as the two men matched wits over the game until late in the night. American readers heard about it and were scandalized, but the incident was more innocent. It was then the French custom for women to bathe as they entertained, with a plank covering the tub. Nor did Jacques seem concerned about his wife's infatuation with the American statesman. "I am certain that you have just been kissing my wife," Jacques accused Ben, but in the next line jauntily added, "My dear Doctor, allow me to kiss you in return."[30] Secretly he was sleeping with the governess to the Brillons' daughters, which may explain his cavalier reaction.

Needy, almost desperately so, Madame Brillon invested her affection in Ben. "Love" soon became the central theme of her letters. "It is a real source of joy . . . to think that she [Madame Brillon] can sometimes amuse Mr. Franklin whom she loves and esteems," she cooed.[31] Who could resist such adoration? Certainly not Ben. By then the musician considered herself what would be called today a "soul mate," a friend as deeply affected by the triumphs and defeats of another as she was by her own.

In reaction to the 1777 Patriots' victory at Saratoga, Madame Brillon seemed as overjoyed as Ben. "My heart is too full, too moved to control itself I yield to my overwhelming desire to write you . . . we [the sympathetic French] share your joy as fully as we love you. Farewell, I am about to compose a triumphal march to enliven the way of General Burgoyne."[32] Before long she had written the "Marche des Insurgents," a brisk piece most recently performed in a 2019 concert at Philadelphia's American Philosophical Society.

For Ben, 1777 was a year of frustrating flirtations, politically and personally. A week after his December 7 draft of a peace treaty, Ben and his fellow commissioners met again with Vergennes in Paris. Negotiations continued through the chill Parisian winter of early 1778 and finally resulted in a political thaw. On February 6 Ben and his fellow commissioners met in Silas Deane's second-floor Paris apartment in the Hotel de Coislin. There they signed the Treaty of Amity and Commerce and its sister agreement, the Treaty of Alliance. The first established a commercial agreement between the two nations. The second united them as allies for mutual defense, especially against Great Britain.

In contrast to that triumph was Ben's failure to consummate his relationship with Madame Brillon. If verbal pleas would not succeed, perhaps those described on paper would. The day after the French treaties, Ben composed an imaginative romp with the musician in the afterlife in which he asked her to save his soul. Gamely, Madame Brillon accepted, "as long as he loves God, America and me above all things, I absolve him of all his sins . . . and I promise him paradise where I shall lead him along a path strewn with roses."[33]

The next sentence shattered Ben's hopes. "The seventh—I shall not name it. All great men are tainted with it: it is called their weakness . . . you have loved, my dear brother, you have been kind and lovable, you have been loved in return! . . . Go on, doing great things and loving pretty women, provided that, pretty and lovable, though they may be, you never lose sight of my principle; always love God, America, and me above all."[34]

To the last part Ben agreed, "A commandment which, I confess, I have consistently violated . . . every time I have seen or thought of kind confessor. . . . I mean that which forbids coveting my neighbor's wife, and which *I confess* often as I see or think of my lovely confessor."[35]

Still, the "path of strewn roses" was not to be misconstrued. "Let us start from where we are," the musician reasoned. "You are a man. I am a woman, and while we may think along the same lines, we must speak and act differently. Perhaps there is no real harm in a man having desires and yielding to them; a woman may have desires, but she must not yield." Admittedly she was "as great a sinner as yourself. I have desired to see you, desired to know you, desired our esteem, desired your friendship . . . and now I desire that you may love me forever . . . this desire grows day by day in my heart and it will last all my life." Even so, "I have not the slightest doubt that all our desires will eventually lead us to Paradise."[36] Thus, an earthly consummation between Ben and Madame Billon was out of the question.

Were the months of their flirtation merely a game? If so, Ben had only been a pawn on Madame Brillon's chessboard. No woman was allowed to do that. Years ago he had tamed his lust for Katy Ray, if only out of respect for her youthful purity. But this was different. This was France, where affairs were not only permissible, but expected. The musician's declarations of love followed by denials were cruel, leaving Ben baffled. There was only one remedy: He must attend other dinners and salons where he would meet other attractive young women.

After discovering Ben's new social engagements, Madame Brillon exploded. "The dangerous system you are forever trying to demonstrate, my dear papa, that the friendship a man has for women can be divided *ad infinitum*—this is something I shall never put up with. My heart, while capable of great love, has chosen few objects on which to bestow it . . . you are the head of the list. When you scatter your friendships . . . , I shall try to be somewhat sterner toward your faults."[37]

To Ben, the musician's possessiveness was stifling. "You renounce and totally exclude arbitrarily everything corporal from our amour, except such a merely civil embrace now and then as you would permit to a country cousin. . . . Indeed it is I that have the most reason to complain," he wrote. Then, comparing himself to the cherubic image of a lovesick Cupid, he added, "My poor little boy, whom you ought . . . to have cherished, instead of being fat and jolly like those in your elegant drawings, is meagre and starved almost to death for want of the substantial nourishment which you, his mother, inhumanely deny him and yet would now clip his little wings to prevent his seeking it elsewhere!"[38]

Exhausted by the struggle, Ben proposed the draft of a "peace treaty." Among the clauses was an agreement for "eternal love" between them. Meanwhile, "he shall love no other woman than her, as long as he finds her agreeable."[39] The musician was temporarily placated. But after Ben announced he was restricting his visits to Saturdays, she raged, "You give up so easily a Wednesday with me? Then . . . you will say, as usual, *I love you furiously. I love you too much?* I, my dear papa, love you not furiously, but very tenderly; not too much, but enough to feel sorry every time I could see you but do not." Now, she challenged, "which of us two loves more and better?"[40]

After another of Ben's conciliations, Madame Brillon observed their conflict reflected two schools of Greek philosophy. "The gentleman, great philosopher that he is, goes by the doctrines of Anacreon and Epicures, but his lady is a Platonist. He wants a fat, chubby love, a love of flesh and bones, spoiled and pampered . . . the lady tries to blunt his little arrows, while giving him full freedom to run by hills and dales and attack anyone in sight . . . Platonism . . . is a convenient defense for the fair sex. Hence, the lady . . . advises the gentleman to fatten up his favorites, at other tables than hers, which will always offer a meager a diet for his greedy appetites." In closing, she reminded him of their tea-date the next day, and assured him of her "tender and inviolable love."[41]

On another occasion, Ben left one of her parties early. "Do you know, my good papa, that you played a mean trick on me?" she wrote the next day. After arranging his carriage for eight in the evening, Ben departed at half-past seven, leaving her to endure "the boredom of walking around with the ladies while I could have had fun, staying with you."[42] Again he apologized, explaining he had awakened at four a.m. that day, made a round trip to Paris, and found himself nodding off at her party. "Half an hour spent with an old man . . . is a mighty small matter, and you should not get angry over small things," Ben scolded Madame Brillon. "Saturday evening I shall stay with you until you long for my departure. . . . In spite of the usual courtesy of your words I shall know that the time to leave has arrived when you will refuse me a little kiss."[43]

So it continued for weeks. After they spent a late summer day at Moulin Joli, a flower-filled island in the Seine, Ben wrote a story about Madame Brillon's rejection. The main character was a grey-headed "ephemere," or fly, who, though knowing his days were limited, was grateful for the "sensible conversation of a few good Lady-Ephemeres, and now and then a kind smile and a tune from the ever-amiable Brillante."[44]

Still the musician flooded Ben with expressions of infinite love. Among them was her comment, "I will think every day that the day which has just passed brings me closer to the day when we will see each other again, and every day I will love you, as long as I live."[45] By then, Ben was resigned to the hopelessness of his passion. To resolve their difficulties, she proposed a new relationship. Rather than engaging with Ben as a lover, *"mon cher papa"* should become her surrogate father, a benevolent parent who would serve as adviser to a needy young woman. Since her own father had died years earlier, Madame Brillon longed for a paternal substitute.

In an echo of his romance with Katy Ray, Ben reluctantly agreed he would be "very happy in the parentage of such a good daughter." As he reminded the musician, "as, by coming to this country, I have lost the sweet company and respectful care of my own affectionate daughter, this loss shall be amended . . . and if I spend here the little remains of my days, another affectionate daughter will take care of me. . . . Yes, my dear child, I love you as a father, with all my heart."[46]

So it was that prudence again triumphed over passion. For the second time in his life, Ben was forced to restrain himself through the refusal of a young woman.

11

"By the Way, What Did You Do to That Shoulder?"

MADAME BRILLON'S RELATIONSHIP with Ben would not end there. Both of them had invested too much. To the musician, Ben had become an addiction, a cherished confidant who soothed her far better than the prize wines in her husband's cellar. Ben was also deeply attached to his former sweetheart. Despite his disappointment, he still enjoyed her beauty, declarations of love, and clever, if capricious, repartee.

Since he had agreed to become Madame Brillon's surrogate "father," they no longer met on Wednesdays and Saturdays. Instead, he accepted invitations from neighbors to their soirees on those days, but he was left longing for the musician's company. There was nothing wrong with meeting other women, he wrote Madame Brillon, "for if at my age, it is not fitting to say that I am in love with a young woman, there is nothing to prevent me from confessing that I admire and love an assemblage of all female virtues and of all admirable talents."[1]

Before long, Ben had befriended another extraordinary woman. He met Madame Helvétius in late summer 1778 at her salon in nearby Auteil through an invitation from Anne-Robert Jacques Turgot, comptroller general of France. Madame Helvétius was the wealthy widow of the late philosopher Claude-Adrien Helvétius; her guest list was a Who's Who of the era's brilliant thinkers, writers, and scientists. Among them, Voltaire and the Scottish historian/philosopher David Hume had once attended her salon. More recently so had the writer-philosopher Denis Diderot and mathematician d'Alembert (coauthors of the liberal *Encyclopédie*), scientist Antoine Lavoisier, and paleontologist/naturalist Georges Cuvier.

Once a renowned beauty, the widowed Madame Helvétius was still an attractive woman in her late fifties, known to her friends as "Minette" or "pussycat" because of her appealing but independent nature. Intrigued, Ben watched her flitting among the guests, amazed at how blithely she moved from group to group as she interrupted their conversations. No one seemed perturbed, although one friend later complained that "because of her beauty, unusual wit, and stimulating temperament, Madame Helvétius disturbed philosophical discussions considerably."[2]

After speaking with Ben, the widow invited him to other social events. In contrast to the temperamental moodiness of Madame Brillon, she seemed a breath of fresh air. Brisk, cheerful, and direct, Madame Helvétius glossed over difficulties with laughter and had an earthy appreciation for life. But as Ben's admiration grew, an incident revealed her carefree style had certain disadvantages. One October afternoon, when Ben arrived for dinner, a flustered Madame Helvétius apologized: She had forgotten her invitation and was then on the way to Paris to meet Turgot. Deftly, Ben soon turned the widow's faux pas into a compliment.

"I have been trying to form some hypothesis to account for your having so many friends and of such various kinds. I see that statesmen, philosophers, historians, poets and men of learning attach themselves to you as straws to a fine piece of amber," Ben began. In his opinion, those learned men liked her because she avoided flattery and "had no pretention[s] to any of their sciences . . . artless simplicity is a striking part of your character. . . . We find in your sweet society, that charming benevolence, that amiable attention to oblige, that disposition to please and be pleased . . . it springs from you."[3] Ben became such a frequent and favored guest at the Helvétius estate that his place was regularly set at the table.

Madame Helvétius, née Anne-Catherine de Ligniville d'Autricourt, had been the wife of the wealthy Claude-Adrien Helvétius, who owned many properties and was a tax-farmer, or royal official who collected taxes. After making his fortune, Helvétius retired and became a philosopher; his book,

Of Spirit, espoused atheism and scandalized the clergy. After his 1771 death, his widow threw off the traditions of an aristocratic wife and adopted an offbeat lifestyle. A case can be made that she returned to her own unconventional roots. The tenth of twenty children from an aristocratic family of Lorraine, she lacked a dowry. Despite her beauty, her parents shunted her off to a convent when she was fifteen. By the time she was thirty the allowance for support ran out; fortunately, a bohemian aunt who wrote novels and hosted a salon adopted her. Several suitors proposed, among them the young economist, Turgot, eight years her junior. Since he was poor, she married wealthy Claude-Adrien Helvétius instead.

Years later, when Madame Helvétius became widowed, she allowed her daughters to marry men of their own choice, against the usual aristocratic convention. Then in a final sweep of her former life, she gave each daughter one of the family chateaux, sold the Paris home, and purchased a small but comfortable estate in Auteuil bordering the leafy Bois de Boulogne.

Her new home also symbolized the widow's rebellion against the norm. The three acres surrounding her mansion were filled with dizzying varieties of plants, shrubs, and flowers in the rambling English style rather than the manicured French fashion. As passionate about animals as plants, Madame Helvétius stocked her park with deer, chickens, ducks, pigeons, cats, and dogs. Aviaries hung in the trees, where birds fluttered and nested. Within her home roamed eighteen cats over whom she doted and decorated with satin ribbons.

Abigail Adams, who visited the Helvétius estate in 1784 when her husband, John, replaced Silas Deane as a commissioner, found the widow's love for pets not only excessive but distasteful. After dinner the guests had adjourned to a drawing room, where Madame Helvétius unceremoniously "threw herself on a settee." Nearby was her "little lap-dog, who was next to the Doctor [Franklin], her favorite. This, she kissed and when he wet the floor, she wiped it up with her chemise."[4]

Ben was by then accustomed to the widow's disdain for social convention. In spite of her foibles, he found her free-spirited approach to life refreshing, in tune with his own liberal ideas. In France, where most women married and remarried, Madame Helvétius cherished her new independence. Soon after her husband's death, her former beau Turgot again proposed, but she turned him down a second time. Still, the economist remained one of the widow's closest friends.

Despite Madame Helvétius's declaration of independence, three men lived with her: two abbots and a medical student. People questioned the propriety of it, but she did not care. The widow's first lodger was the testy, middle-aged Abbé André Morellet, a prominent political economist and contributor to Diderot's anti-monarchical *Encyclopédie*. The second was the tall, handsome Abbé Martin Lefebvre de la Roche, a former Benedictine priest and devoté of Helvétius. After the philosopher's death he had moved into the widow's estate to organize her late husband's papers; finding it pleasant, he became a permanent resident. The third was a twenty-two-year-old medical student, Pierre-Georges Cabanis, whom Turgot had introduced to Madame Helvétius. Taking pity upon the young man's financial difficulties, the widow not only offered him a home but also "adopted" Cabanis as her surrogate son in place of the one she had lost in infancy.

That trio, which served as Madame Helvétius's "family," lived together harmoniously, sharing meals, walks, and conversations. Abbé Morellet was teased for his inordinate love of cream and fanciful theories; Abbé de la Roche only cared about books; and Madame Helvétius was inevitably disorganized but so regal and beloved that Ben dubbed her "Notre Dame d'Auteuil." All three lodgers became as fond of the American commissioner as he was of them. Morellet was so delighted with the drinking songs Ben presented that he wrote one of his own in honor of the American statesman, a man "cheerful and frank while founding an empire."[5]

Years later Abbé de la Roche recalled the good humor, earnest conversations, and friendly debates the three lodgers enjoyed with Ben at the Helvétius estate: "We were so happy, were we not, when sitting all together around a good table; when we discussed ethics, politics, philosophy; when Notre Dame d'Auteuil led you on to flirt, and the Abbé Morellet, while fighting for the cream, set his arguments in magnificent sequence, so as to convince us what we did not believe."[6]

An example of the way Madame Helvétius encouraged Ben to "flirt" appears in one of her rarely preserved notes. "Do you want, my dear friend, to have a dinner with me on Wednesday? I have the greatest desire to see you and embrace you—and a little bit your son, too [grandson Temple]."[7] Messages like that raised Ben's hopes for more than casual flirtation. "Of course I shall not fail to come next Wednesday. I get too much pleasure from seeing you, hearing you, too much happiness from holding you in my arms, to forget such a precious invitation," he promptly replied.[8]

To Ben's—and this biographer's—frustration, direct communication from the widow was unusual. Most of the time she delegated that task to her lodgers, who, acting as secretaries, sent notes and invitations on her behalf. Ben's replies were in turn communicated through that trio, who then conveyed them to Madame Helvétius. Whether playfully or out of an effort to communicate in proper French, his notes were written in the third person from "Mr. Franklin." Since they were read by at least one of the widow's residents, there were no secrets in the Helvétius household.

Simultaneously, Ben also wrestled with several political challenges. Not only was he surrounded by spies who related details of the American treaties to the English, but also his fellow diplomats quarreled bitterly. Their feud centered upon Silas Deane, one of the three American ministers to France, who was accused by his colleagues Arthur and Richard Lee and Ralph Izard of stealing millions from the French. After receiving complaints, Congress recalled Deane despite Ben's defense of his character. "I have no doubt that he will be able clearly to justify himself. . . . I esteem him a faithful, active, and able minister who . . . to my knowledge has done . . . great and important service to his country."[9]

Even so, the Lees continued to fume. When Arthur Lee discovered Deane was to escort the new French ambassador, Conrad Alexander Gerard, to America, he blamed Ben. For months, the founding father had held his tongue, but finally on April 3, 1778, he retorted, "If I have often received and borne your . . . snubbings and rebukes without reply, ascribe it to our mission, which would be hurt by our quarrelling. My love of peace, my respect for your good qualities, and my pity of your sick mind, which is forever tormenting itself with its jealousies, suspicions and fancies that others mean you ill, wrong you, or fail to respect you—if you do not cure your self of this temper it will end in insanity."[10] The next day Ben redrafted his response, then decided against sending that letter, too, "for of all things, I hate altercations."[11]

That same month, Ben's English friend and parliamentarian, David Hartley, warned that British agents were planning to murder him. Wryly, the founding father replied, "I thank you for your kind caution, but having nearly finished a long life, I set but little value on what remains of it . . . perhaps the best use an old fellow be put to, is to make a martyr of him."[12]

Despite Ben's alleged lack of concern for his life, he desperately wanted to share it with Madame Helvétius. Writing through Abbé Morellet, he assured her that "Mr. Franklin never forgets any party at which Madame Helvétius is to appear. He even believes that if he were to go to Paradise that morning, he would beg to be allowed to remain on earth until half past one, to receive the embrace she was kind enough to promise him at their meeting in M. Turgot's house."[13]

Nothing, however, was ever certain with her. The widow was so busy and so impulsive about seeing friends that she sometimes overlooked her own invitations. One morning after arriving at the Helvétius mansion, Ben described his disappointment over a forgotten brunch. "As the invitation was for eleven o'clock . . . I expected to find breakfast in the manner of a dinner . . . that there would be many guests, that we should have not only tea, but also coffee, chocolate, perhaps a ham and several other good things. I resolved to go there on foot. My shoes were a little too tight [from chronic symptoms of gout] I arrived nearly crippled."[14]

As Ben and his grandson Temple entered the courtyard, they realized they were the first to arrive. "We climb the stairs. No noise. We enter the dining room. No one but M. L'Abbé and Mr. C. The breakfast ended, eaten! Nothing on the table but some morsels of bread and a little butter. They exclaim. They run to tell Madame H. that we had come for breakfast."[15]

"Finally a new breakfast is ordered. But a watched pot never boils as Poor Richard's says. Madame departs for Paris, leaving us." The makeshift meal was poor. To compensate, the embarrassed "Mr. L'Abbé proposes a walk. My feet will not allow it. Consequently, we leave breakfast there and go up to his room in order to find something with which to finish our repast—his good books."[16]

After still another forgotten invitation in August or September 1779, Ben expressed his disappointment but filled it with endearments. "Mr. Franklin, having arisen, bathed, shaved, combed and beautified himself to look his best, completely dressed & about to go out, with his head full of the 4 Mesdames Helvétius [the widow and her three boarders] & the sweet kisses he proposed to steal . . . is quite mortified to discover the possibility of their felicity being put off until next Sunday."[17]

By then Ben was tired of mere flirtation. It was time to put bon mots aside and express his intentions. "He will be as patient as he can, hoping to see [her] at M. de Chaumont's on Wednesday. He will be there to see her enter with that grace and dignity that so charmed him seven weeks ago in the same place," he wrote Madam Helvétius in late summer 1779. Boldly, he then announced, "He even plans to stop her there and keep her at his house forever."[18]

Ben's declaration of love surprised her. While Madame Helvétius enjoyed him as a courtly companion, she considered his remarks merely flattering. Apparently she had either heard rumors about his earlier relationships, or she considered his pleas for love simply part of his playful style. In any case, she did not take him seriously. As she confided to a friend, "Franklin loves people only as long as he saw them."[19] Before long the comment reached Ben, and while he may have attempted to defend himself, the widow ignored his pleas. Instead, she thanked him for his "sweet letter . . . [which] made me feel all the more keenly my loss in not dining with you Wednesday. I hope that after putting pretty things on paper, you would come and tell me some, and now I am vexed for having hoped too much. For I confess that I love pretty things, especially those that come from you."[20]

Then, slyly she added, "I trust that I will have nothing but good tidings about the pain in your shoulder. By the way, what did you do to that shoulder? Would it be, by any chance, a rheumatism caught under the window of one of my rivals? Surely, you are young enough to go out and spend all clear fair nights playing the guitar, while blowing on your fingers."[21]

If that wounded Ben's vanity, he dismissed it as part of their ongoing repartee. Compared to the emotional problems he was still trying to solve with Madame Brillon, the widow's carefree attitude toward human folly was refreshing.

Nevertheless, certain outsiders wondered at Madame Helvétius's free-wheeling behavior. Among them was Abigail Adams, who recalled that while visiting Ben in Passy, the widow "entered the room with a careless, jaunty air, upon seeing the ladies who were strangers to her, she bawled out 'Ah! Mon Dieu, where's Franklin? Why did you not tell me there were ladies here?'"[22]

Her [Madame Helvétius's] hair was frizzled, over which she had a small straw hat, with a dirty gauzy, half-handkerchief behind. . . . She ran out of the room; when she returned the Doctor entered at one door, she at the other, upon which she ran forward to him, caught him by the hand. "Helas Franklin!", then gave him a double kiss, one upon each cheek; and another upon his forehead.

When we went into the room to dine she was placed between the Doctor and Mr. Adams. She carried on the chief of the conversation at dinner, frequently locking her hand into the Doctor's . . . and sometimes spreading her arms upon the back of both the gentlemen's chairs, then throwing her arms carelessly upon the Doctor's neck.

I should have been greatly astonished at this conduct, if the good Doctor had not told me that in this lady should see a genuine French-woman, wholly free from affectation or stiffness of behavior, and one of the best women in the world.[23]

Abigail's description of Madame Helvétius's behavior may lead the reader to wonder how Ben remained captivated by her. Until then he had been the one to set the boundaries of relationships with women—with Deborah, Sally, Katy, Margaret, and probably the "older" mistress he once praised in his letter of advice to a young man.

Between 1778 and the early 1780s, Ben ricocheted between his passion for the widow and his attention to Madame Brillon. That led the musician, who admitted she was jealous of her "amiable rival," to tighten her grip on Ben.[24] Insisting she was special and should be cherished as such, she reminded him, "Your daughter is not content to please you by the kind of charms you can meet any day, and to a higher degree in many other women, but by a combination of all virtues, which will make her your friend."[25]

To support that new role, Madame Brillon vowed to behave more properly with Ben before others. Since some of her acquaintances criticized her for the "familiarity . . . between us," she would no longer behave so fondly in public. "Though I may not sit upon your knee so often, it certainly will not be because I love you less . . . but we shall have shut the mouths of evil speakers, and that is no small feat even for a sage."[26]

Simultaneously, the "sage" kept quiet about a secret in the Brillon marriage. On April 10, 1778, when John Adams attended a dinner with Ben at the Brillon estate, he was stunned to meet the hostess. Madame Brillon, he recalled, was "one of the most beautiful women in France—all softness, sweetness and politeness."[27] During that visit he consequently became appalled to learn that Mademoiselle Jupin, the "plain and clumsy woman," the Brillons' daughters' governess, was the "amie" or mistress of their host, Jacques.[28]

In his *Autobiography* Adams claimed that Ben, his grandson Temple, and others already aware of the affair told him about it. The prim New Englander was outraged. To him it seemed "astonishing . . . that these people could live together in such apparent friendship and indeed without cutting each other's throats."[29] In reality Adams was mistaken, because Madame Brillon remained ignorant of her husband's liaison. A year after discovering it, she fell ill and abruptly dismissed the governess. Still, she continued to fret that Jacques "will perhaps for a long time [be] under her spell."[30] Her anxiety about the governess even extended to Ben, whom she worried might hire the governess as his housekeeper.

On May 3, 1779, Madam Brillon had admitted to Ben that her health was better but "my soul is very sick. It is that soul, honest and too sensitive, that is killing me. Would you, could you receive me Wednesday, the day after tomorrow. At ten in the morning and close your door for an hour, so that my soul can open itself to you, and receive comfort and advice? . . . You are my father. It is the father's love that I need more than ever."[31]

At this time, Ben was not only consumed with duties as the newly appointed minister plenipotentiary to France but was also suffering from gout. Two months earlier, after attending court at Versailles for an audience with Louis XVI, he had returned home and spent a week in bed. Still crippled with pain, he and the French minster of maritime affairs were also planning an attack on the British coast with John Paul Jones and Lafayette. Somehow, though, he found time to meet with Madame Brillon.

On May 8 she thanked him. "My soul is calmer, my dear papa, since it has unburdened itself in yours."[32] More than likely, Ben listened more than spoke and said less than he thought, just as he once advised readers of his *Almanack*.

In one of her letters, Madame Brillon complained about how she had been wronged. As a young woman, she had been forced by her parents into wedding Jacques, since "marriages in this country are made by the weight of gold."[33] No one had considered the temperaments of the couple, and theirs did not match. Jacques was crass, in her opinion: she was refined, imbued with a deep appreciation of the arts. That mismatch, combined with her "extreme sensitivity, her frankness, her too easy affability, no distrustfulness to shield her from evil . . . not being capable of evil herself," had led her into a "terrible trap" by hiring that governess. Consequently, she wrote that she became so ill that "I almost paid with my life the ingratitude, the falsity with which she deceived me."[34]

Gently, Ben agreed her heart was "too sensitive." Only obliquely did he refer to the musician's egotism and moodiness. "A keen awareness of our own faults is good because it leads us to avoid them in the future. But to be very sensitive to, and afflicted by the faults of other people—that is not good. As for us, we should preserve that tranquility that is the just portion of innocence and virtue."[35] Rather than seeking revenge, he advised her to continue leading an exemplary life. "My very dear and always amiable daughter, the good resolution that you have so wisely taken, to continue to fulfill all your duties as good mother, good wife, good friend, good neighbor, good Christian etc. without forgetting to be a good daughter to your papa; and to neglect and forget, if you can, the wrongs you may be suffering at present."[36]

Ironically, Ben was then so emotionally involved with Madame Helvétius that he forgot his own advice about seeking "tranquility." Nor could he
forget the "wrongs" he was "suffering at present," because of the widow's
lighthearted replies to his passionate notes. Was he only a plaything to her?
That would not do. He wanted to be much more than that, especially because, at seventy-three, time was running out. Unable to contain himself
any longer, Ben's letter of September 19 announced, "If the lady likes to
spend her days with him, he would like to spend his nights with her and as
he has already given many of his days though he had so little left to give, it
seems ungrateful to have never given him one of her nights."[37]

The widow's response, if there was one, has not been preserved. Scholars believe that before the end of 1779 Ben had formally proposed marriage.
Caught between her admiration for Ben and her desire for independence,
Madame Helvétius turned to Turgot for advice. In reply, the economist
bluntly declared that she and Ben were too old for romance. His answer
insulted the widow. Even if his answer had been more "chivalrous," Turgot
felt "quite certain I would not have elicited more gratitude," he confided to
a friend.[38]

To Ben, that proposal was only the first move. As a master chess player,
he knew capture required a persistence strategy if he was to win the handsome widow. In contrast to the conventional rules of the game, he sought
conquest not of the king but of the queen, "Notre Dame d'Auteuil."

12

"Prudence Is Not Your Strongest Point"

ON NEW YEAR'S EVE 1779 Ben arrived at Madame Helvétius's estate, where he had been invited to dinner. The moment seemed right: The night marked the start of a new year and a new decade. Filled with hope, Ben proposed marriage. The widow vehemently refused. Unhappily, Ben returned to his home in Passy and spent the rest of the night brooding.

"Vexed by your barbarous resolution, announced so positively last night to remain single all your life in respect to your dear husband, I went home, fell on my bed, and believing myself dead, found myself in the Elysian Fields," Ben wrote her the next day.[1] He was not about to give up. If passionate expressions of love would not move Madame Helvétius, perhaps an appeal to reason could. With that in mind, Ben sent her a tale about meeting her late husband in heaven.

His ideas about love in the afterlife were not new. Months earlier he had proposed similar thoughts to Madame Brillon, with disappointing results. Now, though, he reconfigured his story into a dramatic fantasy. It opened with comments from the spirit of the widow's late husband, Claude-Adrien Helvétius. "Ah! You remind me of my former felicity—but it is necessary to forget it in order to be happy here," he told Ben. The philosopher had taken another wife, one who most closely resembled his earthly spouse. While she was not "so completely beautiful [as Madame Helvétius] . . . she has as much good sense, a good deal of spirit, and she loves me infinitely," Helvétius claimed.[2] If Ben waited a few moments, he would meet her.

If his heavenly wife was still alive, she would have "absolutely rejected me for love of you." Just at that moment, the new Madame Helvétius appeared. Ben was stunned. "I recognized her to be Madame Franklin, my old American friend. I called out to her, but she answered coldly, 'I have been your good wife for forty-four years and four months, nearly half a century, be content with that.'" Offended, Ben returned to earth "to see again the sunshine and you. Here I am. Let us take revenge!"[3]

Ben's cautionary tale about the folly of living in the past did not change Madame Helvétius's decision. Though she enjoyed his wit, intelligence, and conviviality, she vowed to remain single. Her insistent claim of loyalty to her late husband was not the only reason. As a widow, she was free to do as she pleased. No one told her what to do or how to act. Having a second husband would change that. Unlike other women, as her friend Denis Diderot once observed, "She refused to be a slave."[4]

Her denial stung Ben to the quick. Perhaps not coincidentally, he was soon writing long-delayed letters to other women who adored him. On January 10 he wrote his "English daughter," Polly Stevenson Hewson, knowing she would share the missive with her mother, Margaret, who rarely wrote. Occasionally she sent Ben a letter and reiterated her love, but worries about spelling errors and a new palsy in her hands discouraged her from doing so. Most of her messages to Ben were relayed through her daughter.

"I hear your affairs are settled to your satisfaction," Ben wrote Polly. "You end your letter with this endearing expression of friendship, 'I wish we could meet'—and now, why may we not meet? I live here in a pleasant village within two miles of Paris, a lofty situation with good air, have a fine large garden & neighboring woods to walk in, in which village you might find lodgings of a small course to accommodate yourself, [your] good mother & children."[5]

In January, Ben also sent a long-delayed reply to Georgiana Shipley, the fourth daughter of his friend Bishop Shipley. After Ben's summer visits in 1771 they had occasionally exchanged letters. The previous May, Georgiana had written that she wished he could visit Twyford again but did not "dare to allow myself to think that such a happiness is reserved for us." She also reported that one of the squirrels Deborah had sent years earlier was "still living and much caressed. Poor fellow! He is grown quite old & has lost his eyesight but preserves his spirts & wonted activity." After mentioning some of the family's mutual friends, she asked Ben to send his portrait and a lock of his "own dear grey hair."[6]

After delaying for months, Ben mailed Georgiana a snuff box with his portrait on it and a lock of his hair. On February 3 Georgiana replied. "How shall I sufficiently express my rapture on receiving your dear delightful letter & most valuable present . . . the beloved little lock of hair. I kissed both that & the picture a 1000 times. The miniature is . . . my very own dear Doctor Franklin himself. I can almost fancy you are present; nay I even think I see you smile at the excess of my happiness . . . it will ever be my constant & favorite companion . . . no time nor circumstance can lessen the affection with which I subscribe myself."[7]

While flattered, Ben continued to obsess over Madame Helvétius. Like anyone who feels rejected, he must have had moments of self-doubt. Had the widow rejected him because she disliked his fondness for other women? Or, as the jealous Turgot had suggested, was it because he was too old? It was true: He was bald, fat, and suffering from gout, boils, and kidney stones, but those ailments had not prevented other women from loving him.

If such questions ran through Ben's head, he kept them to himself. As he once warned readers of *Poor Richard's*: "Let thy discontents be secrets."[8] Politically, he was more involved in responsibilities than ever before, for by then Congress had elected him minister plenipotentiary. After Lafayette delivered news of that appointment in February 1779, Ben assumed sole responsibility for obtaining additional funds and supplies from France, sidestepping spies and confounding the English. At least there was one advantage to his new position. No longer did he have to consult with his contentious former fellow ministers, Richard and Arthur Lee and Ralph Izard. As he wryly observed in April 1780 after they left, "no soul regrets their departure."[9] But already 1780 seemed a year of frequently frustrating requests. "I have long been humiliated with the idea of our running about from court to court begging for money and friendships, which are the more withheld the more eagerly they are solicited," he wrote to John Adams, who would soon seek funds in the Dutch Republic.[10]

By then only Ben's grandson Temple and a clerk were his assistants. His home at Passy was quieter for other reasons, too, for he had recently moved Benny from the village school to a boarding school in Geneva. As the long grey winter broke into a spring filled with flowering magnolia and chestnut trees, Ben maintained a busy schedule. On Tuesdays he rode the rutted roads from Passy to court in Versailles; other days he heard diplomatic arguments over Spanish territories in America, monitored reports about American privateers, negotiated deals to free American prisoners of war, and supervised plans for a French-American attack upon the English coast. Still, his nights were beset with hopes of winning the hand of Madame Helvétius.

He continued to pursue her relentlessly. By early summer he realized she was annoyed, and he even admitted as much to her boarder, Cabanis. But she was so polite in her rebuffs that Ben remained hopeful. "I now and then offend our good lady, who cannot long retain her displeasure, but sitting in state on her sofa, extends graciously her long handsome arm and says, 'là: baisez ma main, je vous pardonne,' with all the dignity of a sultaness."[11] Superficially Madame Helvétius seemed to "forgive" him, but privately she was disquieted by Ben's insistence. To her it seemed an exploitation of her warmth toward Ben and an assault upon her usual good humor.

Several days before Ben's letter to Cabanis, Turgot described Madame Helvétius's private turmoil to a friend. When he visited the usually cheerful widow, he found her "in pretty poor shape. Her tranquility has been again troubled and always by the same vagaries."[12] Why did Ben refuse to accept her refusal to wed? Why did he fail to respect the line she had drawn? And how could she stop Ben's proposals but maintain him as a cherished friend?

Turgot consequently explained that Madame Helvétius "has decided to . . . spend the summer in Tours, at the home of a relative . . . she will settle in the country, and busy herself only with her health and that of her daughter, that she may forget, if possible, all the turmoil that has tormented her. . . . She has arranged her departure for Monday." Turgot had agreed with her decision, finding it "most appropriate, not only for her own tranquility but also to reestablish in that other head [Franklin] that has agitated so ill-advisedly."[13]

In the past, historians and biographers have ignored Madame Helvétius's reaction and the depth of despair it revealed. More often than not they maintained that Ben's flirtatious escapades were no more than exercises in wit, charm, and flattery, harmless parlor games meant to delight and flatter women. His flirtations, biographer Van Doren claimed, "had a general warmth which, while no doubt sexual in origin, made them strong, tender, imaginative and humorous beyond the reach of mere desire."[14] Pulitzer Prize–winning author Gordon S. Wood agreed that Ben's flirtations never cut deep into his heart but were "always with a certain playful detachment."[15] Biographer Walter Isaacson echoed that interpretation: "By September 1779, he was ardently proposing marriage in a way that was more than half-serious but retained enough ironic detachment to preserve their [his and Madame Helvétius's] dignities."[16]

Notwithstanding the brilliance of those biographers on scientific and political aspects of Ben's life, their comments gloss over the heated emotions leading to his insistent proposals and the panicked reaction they produced in the usually poised Madame Helvétius. The result has been a less than fully human portrait of the founding father. Viewed from a postfeminist perspective, a more realistic picture appears. Ben had harassed Madame Helvétius to the point that she became distraught and felt forced to flee. Once again, passion had overruled Ben's usual prudence.

Questions remain. Were Ben's hopes for marriage related to the need for physical intimacy, even though he was in his mid-seventies? Or was fear of a lonely old age his motive for marriage? Ben's *Autobiography* and letters leave few clues. His letter of June 1779 to his son-in-law, Richard, admitted that he worried about his future as he grew older. He noted the comfort of having two of his grandsons with him while he was "in a foreign country, where, if I am sick . . . I have a child to close my eyes and take care of my remains."[17] However, neither grandson (one still a child) was likely to care for him as tenderly as a woman—especially a certain French widow and her trio of devoted household companions.

Yet the thought of returning to the United States worried Ben. He still had many enemies in Pennsylvania—so many, in fact, that his colony was the only one that refused to support his election to the position of minister plenipotentiary. Now that the Lees and Izard had returned to America, they too would have blackened his reputation. More than likely, Ben would thus receive a cold reception if he returned to America. Besides, with the exception of the two years when he had returned to Philadelphia, Ben had lived overseas for nearly thirty years. As he once admitted to Deborah and to Billy, "I have been so long abroad that I shall now be almost a stranger in my country."[18]

At the same time, Ben remained immensely popular in France, revered not only as the scientist-statesman who was cheered in the streets as "Bonhomme Richard" but also as a rustic symbol of Enlightenment liberty. Nor did it matter that he was elderly, for as John Adams archly observed, French women had "an unaccountable passion for old age."[19] As Ben would later write Billy, "I am here among a people that love and respect me, a most amiable nation to live with . . . perhaps I may conclude to die here."[20]

The same week that Madame Helvétius fled to Tours, Madame Brillon wrote Ben that she was very ill. "Did the bloodletting relieve you?" Ben anxiously inquired on July 10. Sternly he then observed, "It seems to me that when you are in good health, you do not take enough exercise . . . I advise you to take a walk every day for an hour in your beautiful garden if the weather is good, otherwise in your home . . . go up and down the steps in your garden or in your house every day for a quarter of an hour."[21]

Ben's former sweetheart was too ill for that. "My good papa, I have had a violent attack and am now exceedingly weak. . . . Fate has destined me to suffer. . . . I take some exercise, I live moderately, I love my friends and especially my papa," she faintly replied.[22]

Then came more troubling news from America. In May the British had defeated the Patriots at Charlestown. By summer the value of the "Continentals," the paper bills issued by Congress, had collapsed. In September George Washington's favorite general, Benedict Arnold, turned traitor and sided with the British. The list of unfortunate events boded ill for the success of the revolution, further delaying France's willingness to provide more funds.

Taking a lesson from his own guidebook *The Morals of Chess,* Ben refused to be discouraged. "Life is a kind of chess game filled with uncertain-
ties," it had reminded players, but advised them to avoid being "discouraged
by present bad appearances." It was better to hope for a "favorable change"
and find the means to achieve it.[23] Ben consequently met cheerfully with
French dignitaries, patiently listened to their doubts about the American
Revolution, and smiled. But the stress took its toll.

In October Ben had a severe attack of gout, probably resulting from
long hours at work, a lack of exercise, and his fondness for fine wines and
rich foods. Paradoxically, the man who once preached "Eat to live, and
not live to eat" and had warned "many dishes, many diseases" forgot his
own advice.[24] Housekeeping records from Passy reveal that his dinners,
while often including friends, were large. A typical menu included hors
d'oeuvres, joints of beef, veal or mutton, poultry or game, sweets, vegetables, pastries, cheese, pickles, fruits, and desserts. Ben's cellar at Passy
included over a thousand bottles of wine, some for himself and guests,
lesser ones for servants.

That autumn it became Madame Brillon's turn to reprimand Ben. His
diet had contributed to his ailment. To prove it she sent him her poem
"The Sage and the Gout." "Prudence," she wrote, "is not your strongest
point. . . . You eat too much, you covet women, you no longer walk, &
you spend your time in chess, & sometimes in checkers." In addition, "you
drink a little . . . in those sweet pastimes mood collects." Ben's personal
habits, in other words, were destroying his health, and, she wrote, "it's a
crime."[25]

With his aching feet propped up in bed, Ben scrawled his agreement
that her criticism was partly valid, with one important correction. While
Madame Brillon blamed his attacks of gout on his fondness for "a pretty
mistress, sometimes two-three—four & etcetera," he wrote, "I believe . . .
the exact opposite." As a young man, "I enjoyed more of the favors of the
sex than I do at present, I had no gout. Hence, if the ladies of Passy had
shown more of that Christian charity that I have so often recommended to
you in vain, I should not be suffering from the gout now."[26]

Probably smiling to herself, Madame Brillon blandly replied that "nothing remains but the faculty of loving my friends." Then in an echo of their old argument she added, "I will do my best for you, in a spirit of Christian charity—but to the exclusion of *your* brand of Christian charity."[27]

Inspired by Madame Brillon's writings, Ben embellished upon it in "The Dialogue Between the Gout and Mr. Franklin." In this piece, a stern character named Gout accused Ben of spending too much time at that "abominable game of chess" and "taking a carriage instead of walking." In self-mockery, Ben's Gout also scoffed that "you philosophers are sages in your maxims and fools in your conduct." Thus reprimanded, "Mr. Franklin" promised "never more to play chess but to take exercise daily and live temperately." Gout remained skeptical: "After a few months of good health, you will return to your old habits. . . . I leave you with an assurance of visiting you again at a proper time and place, for my object is your good, and you are sensible now that I am your *real friend.*"[28]

By November 18, after showing the "Dialogue" to Madame Brillon, Ben sent a copy to a friend to improve his poor French, then sent her the corrected version. She objected to that, insisting the original mistakes were delightfully expressive; paradoxically, they even strengthened his arguments. "A few purists must argue with us, but those birds [grammarians] weigh words on the scale of cold erudition." In contrast, Madam Brillon claimed that she neither weighed nor judged his prose but simply enjoyed it for its content. After all, she asserted, "I am a female guided by instinct and since you seem to express yourself more forcefully than a grammarian, my judgment goes in your favor."[29]

She (and perhaps other women who attended salons) resented the dominance of the male *philosophes*. In reaction to their incessant intellectualization Madame Brillon added, "I might build long dissertations on the basis of my instinct, yet my reasoning might not be more unreasonable than those of your abominable Encyclopedists—economists—naturalists—journalists—theologians—atheists—moralists—and all imaginable sorts of 'ists!"[30]

Diplomatically, Ben backed off. Instead he blandly observed that "human reason, my dear daughter, must be a very uncertain thing, since two sensible persons, like you and me, can draw diametrically opposed conclusions from the same premises." While agreeing that "reason is a blind guide" and "true and sure instincts" were more reliable, Ben made a stunning confession. While married to Deborah he claimed he had acquired the "habit of letting myself be guided by her in difficult matters, for women, I believe, have a certain feel, which is more reliable than mere reasoning."[31]

Was Ben being honest? Or had he written that merely to placate Madame Brillon? The reader (and this biographer) is left to wonder just which "difficult matters" Deborah influenced. Certainly not his favoritism for his son William; his narrow attitude toward his daughter, Sarah; his 1764 decision to travel overseas without Deborah; and his refusal to return home in the months before her death. Studies of Ben's life confirm that he was fiercely independent, making decisions in business, politics, and diplomacy on the basis of "reason" and "logic."

Years earlier when Ben was living at Craven Street, Margaret was on a brief trip, and he reminded her, "I find such a satisfaction in being a little more my own master . . . I value my own liberty above all the advantage of others' services."[32]

Having ignored Madame Brillon's suggestions to retain the original French in his first version, Ben sent the "Dialogue" on to Cabanis for additional correction. Since nothing remained private in the Helvétius household, the young physician shared it with Madame Helvétius, who had just returned from Tours. News about Ben's illness, his "Dialogue," and Madame Brillon's inspiration for it caught her immediate attention. The widow promptly called for her carriage and rode to Ben's home in Passy. There she found him in bed or perhaps hobbling around on swollen feet. Appalled by his unkempt quarters, the disarray of his papers, and the clutter of dirty glasses, Madame Helvétius took charge. First she had Ben's quarters cleaned, then had his room and possessions put in order. Clearly the widow still cared. After that, she and Ben reconciled and became close friends.

Madame Helvétius's purge of his messy household led Ben to compose still another short story, or "bagatelle" as he called it, and he later printed it on his private press at Passy. The tale was titled "The Flies," and its main characters were a Greek-like chorus of insects. For weeks they had lived happily on the dregs of punch left in glasses "under the hospitable roof of the said good man." The one threat to their tranquility was spiders, which constantly tried to trap them in nets. Now, in their "best language and their recognition for the protection" of "Mrs. H.," they thanked her for removing the "assassins" from their master's rooms. But even as Ben concluded his story, he could not resist a final pitch for the widow's hand. "We have only one thing left to wish for the perpetuation of our happiness, let us say it. Bizz izzz," the flies announced. "It's only that you live together in one household."[33]

Another visitor to Ben's sickroom was Madame Brillon's husband, Jacques, who arrived not only as a substitute for his ailing wife but also because he enjoyed the statesman's company. During those meetings the two men played chess, exchanged ideas, and regaled each other with stories. Paradoxically, that displeased the possessive Madame Brillon. "My fat husband often goes to visit you and tell you stories. I am worried to death that he has stolen some [stories] I have been keeping for the day of our reunion," she fretted.[34] She had no reason to worry, Ben assured her. She could tell the stories again, because "coming from your lips, they will always please me."[35]

By December 10 Ben had recovered. So, too, had Madame Brillon, who invited Ben and his grandson Temple to visit. "I shall come to see you, dear daughter, tomorrow morning with great pleasure. And if it is too much trouble for you to come down, I shall be strong enough, perhaps, to climb your steps," Ben replied.[36]

Later that month Ben returned again and on New Year's Day was welcomed to the Brillons' estate as a beloved family friend. Similarly warm invitations also came from the Helvétius estate at Auteuil. "Love hath made thee a tamed snake," William Shakespeare had observed two centuries earlier.[37] So it was that Ben's passion for his two French sweethearts had been forced to curl back upon itself, from its once vibrant posture into that of a friendly pet.

Meanwhile, the success of the revolution continued to show little promise. By late 1780 Congress was in such dire financial straits that Washington warned, "Our present situation makes one of two things essential to us; a peace, or the most vigorous aid of our allies, particularly . . . money."[38]

From his sick bed, Ben sent papers to Vergennes describing the Continental Army's desperate need for funds. "I lately received from America the enclosed letters, and resolutions of Congress. Such unexpected drafts on me give me much pain; as they oblige me either to give your Excellency the trouble of fresh applications, or to protest their bills, which would be absolute ruin [for America]. Hopefully, your Excellency will see the pressing necessity that has driven the Congress into this measure."[39] Boldly Ben requested sixty-five million livres, but the Court thought that excessive. Ultimately, Vergennes was able to obtain six million livres from the royal treasury, which enabled Congress to barely continue the revolution.

Disappointed and still weak from his long illness, Ben wrote Samuel Huntington, president of Congress, that he wished to resign. "I find that the long and severe fit of the gout which I have had since last winter, has shaken me exceedingly and I am yet far from having recovered the bodily strength I before enjoyed. I do not know that my mental facilities are impaired . . . but I am sensible of great diminution in my activity. . . . I propose to remain here at last till the peace; perhaps maybe for the remainder of my life."[40]

Left unsaid was the lonely prospect of dying without a caring woman by his side.

*"As Long as We Will Exist
You Will Not Be Abandoned"*

THE CORRESPONDENCE BETWEEN BEN and his English friends was unreliable. Polly's January 11, 1779, letter to Ben explained that she had received his letter but that her mother had received none. "You hurt her, not only by not writing to her immediately but by not answering some particulars that she wrote to you," scolded Ben's "English daughter."[1]

Two weeks later Ben apologized to Margaret. In that letter he explained he seldom wrote in order to protect his friends from British authorities who might suspect them of being spies. "If I do not write to you as often as I used to . . . it is owning to the present difficulty of sure communication, and partly to an apprehension of . . . possible inconvenience that my correspondence might occasion you."[2]

He, in turn, complained that he seldom heard directly from her and usually only through Polly. "Why do you never write to me? I used to love to read your letters and I regret your long silence. They were seasoned with good sense and friendship. . . . Even your spelling pleased me," Ben penned. Then, in a sudden burst of nostalgia, Ben added, "It is always with great pleasure when I think of our long continued friendship which had not the least interruption of twenty years (some of the happiest in my life) that I spent under your roof in your company."[3]

Margaret's April letter thanked Ben for "writing to gratify a poor old woman." At seventy-three she felt old but assured him that "my feelings of friendship and gratitude will always remain." In the absence of Ben's letters, she admitted she had become increasingly insecure about their relationship. "I was afraid of your esteem lessening and although I never expect to see you more, if I hear you are well it gives me pleasure, more if you were happy." Her silence did not reflect any anger over an absence of Ben's letters. She had not deliberately stopped writing. Nor was she sulking "in a pie crust as you used to tell me." Then she admitted sheepishly, "maybe a little." Aside from the tremor in her hands she felt well and continued to bake and perform household chores. Before closing Margaret cheekily warned that since a friend was planning a trip to France, "don't be surprised if I pack myself up with her."[4]

The idea of living together had been a recurrent theme between them for years. Soon after Ben had returned to Philadelphia in 1775, he had invited Margaret to join him. The idea had overwhelmed her. "If I could get to America I should be happy but that is such a distant prospect that I fear never will be, so I shall never see you my dearest friend," she had wistfully replied.[5]

Now in April 1779, with only the English Channel separating them, a meeting seemed more probable. Polly, while never sentimental, also wrote Ben a month later: "I wish we could meet."[6] The mail between Ben and his British friends was often delayed or lost, and it was not until January 1780 that Ben received Polly's note. "You end your letter with this endearing expression of friendship, 'I wish we could meet'—And now why may we not?" he wrote. "I live here in a pleasant village within two miles of Paris, a lofty situation with good air, have a fine large garden and neighboring woods. . . . You formerly had thoughts of coming hither. Think again and tell me the result."[7]

Polly apparently never received Ben's invitation. On April 2 she complained, "Though you do not write, I trust you do not forget us, nor wish us to forget you." After explaining that Margaret had "an alarming attack several months earlier . . . but is now quite recovered," Polly described her children's progress in school and conveyed their regards to "Papa Franklin."[8]

A week later Margaret received one of Ben's letters dated the previous

December. Mysteriously, it had been forwarded in an unknown hand and arrived through London's mail delivery system. After that Polly suggested that Ben should not "fear putting it in the post . . . and if it should be opened I am sure no state matters will be revealed."[9]

Once again Polly received no reply. "A whole year has elapsed since we received one line from you," she unhappily reminded him on December 23, 1781. "Perhaps you meant to drop all correspondence with us, but we will not let you off quite so easy . . . for whenever an opportunity offers, I shall send you a letter." Margaret's health remained fragile. "She has been much indisposed of late, and her spirits are extremely low. She has taken up the idea that she has dropsy [edema in the arms or legs from congestive heart failure], though no one can discern the least appearance of it . . . I wish she were with you, for you could raise her spirits and reason her out of this notion, but I fear you are not destined ever to meet again."[10]

Another factor that probably delayed their correspondence was Polly's move to Kensington, then a suburb of London. Ben consequently assumed the letter was lost but assured her it was not important. After all, "it only expresses what you always knew, that I love you both very much and very sincerely. . . . I am very well, as happy as the situation of public affairs will permit, only capable made more so if you were here with me."[11]

The "situation" Ben mentioned was Washington's October 19 triumph over General Lord Charles Cornwallis's army at Yorktown, Virginia, which signaled the end of the revolution. News of the victory reached Prime Minister Vergennes in France a month later. He immediately shared it with Ben, who published the news on his printing press and distributed it to friends and colleagues. As he anticipated, the peace treaty would change his life, for once the terms were signed he would be released from his duties as America's minister plenipotentiary. Inevitably that raised the question of where he should live and with whom. Since Madame Helvétius would not marry him, Ben considered other options.

During his long friendship with Madame Brillon he often praised her two pretty daughters, whom he dubbed the *étoiles*, or stars, of the family. By 1781 the oldest, Cunegonde, was of marriageable age. So too was Ben's twenty-one-year-old grandson, Temple. From the time he arrived with his grandfather in France, Temple faithfully served as Ben's secretary, but at heart he was self-indulgent, favoring parties and luxury over hard work. But like many grandparents, Ben seemed oblivious to Temple's faults and suggested the marriage to Cunegonde's father, Jacques Brillon.

While waiting for a reply, Ben wrote Madame Brillon to promote the benefits of the match. "I love the whole family without exception . . . and [a marriage will] tighten . . . the tender liaisons of our friendship. Having almost lost my daughter by the vast distance between us I was hoping to find one in you, and another in your daughter to look after my old age if I stayed in France."[12] During the six years Ben lived in Passy, he watched Cunegonde grow up. Consequently, he told Madame Brillon, he had "a very good opinion of this amiable young lady." Temple, "who has no vices," would surely "make a good husband." The pair were already good friends, and Temple approved the idea of a marriage. He had only one concern: If his grandfather returned to America, he would be alone in France. That would never happen, Ben assured Madame Brillon. If there was a wedding, "I would stay until the end of my days in France." Only at the end of Ben's letter to Madame Brillon did he concede that Temple was still young. Perhaps, he admitted, "the partiality of a [grand]father had made me think too advantageous of him."[13]

Privately, the Brillons thought so too. In what must have been a difficult letter to write, Madame Brillon explained that while she and Jacques thought Temple had "everything it takes to become a distinguished man and make a woman happy," he would eventually want to return to America. Still another objection had to do with Jacques's plans to retire soon. Thus he needed a son-in-law to take his place, someone "educated in the laws and forms [customs] of our country."[14] Another worrisome factor was the couple's different religions, for Cunegonde was Catholic and Temple, Protestant.

For those reasons, Madame Brillon and her husband had to decline Ben's "flattering proposition," even though it "costs our hearts not to be able to accept it." Still she assured Ben "of our tenderness forever . . . as long as we will exist you will not be abandoned . . . we are your friends, and we will give you at all times the care that will be in our power."[15] Stoically, Ben accepted the Brillons' decision. "Hence, the affair is finished," he replied, observing "there may be other objections he [Jacques] has not communicated to me."[16]

While Temple's proposed marriage to Cunegonde was thus dismissed, Madame Brillon was deeply disappointed. Still weak from her long illness and embittered by Jacques's affair, the emotionally fragile musician retreated to her mother's estate, La Thuillerie. "I am in a beautiful country . . . with a good mother who loves me dearly, whom [I] love myself . . . they treat me . . . cherish me. . . . well." Even so, while "far from you, I think of your pleasures," she wrote Ben on June 5.[17]

A week passed without a new letter from him. That worried her, especially since Ben had attended the opera on June 8, the night of a great fire in Paris. "What, not a word, my sweet papa? Have you forgotten your daughter? Have you found pretty ladies on your way who will have distracted you?" Could he already have forgotten her? That was something she could not allow. "Remember then this friendship, this feeling so sweet and so sure that your daughter has for you," she insisted. "I know you had been at the opera on the day of the appalling fire, my heart was deeply moved by the danger you ran. . . . Life is limited . . . friendship makes me cherish my existence . . . there are so many sorrows and so few pleasures for the sensitive being; there are so many . . . deprivations for our sex but friendship consoles me and takes the place of what [I] may have missed elsewhere."[18]

By then Madame Brillon was so depressed that her doctor recommended a bland diet and a trip south. In late September the Brillons packed their household and took their daughters on a long journey to Nice on the Mediterranean coast.

As their carriage passed through bumpy country roads, Ben worried about his former sweetheart's health. "I continually think of the fatigues that you must suffer in such a long journey, bad hotels, bad beds, bad kitchens. . . . I fear for your tender & delicate fabric. These ideas make me sad. I am angry that I am not the Angel Gabriel with large wings, for if I were, I could spare you all these inconveniences."[19]

Surprisingly, Ben missed her more than he had expected. In the flowery style so favored by Madame Brillon, and perhaps even in imitation, he admitted he tended to distance himself from his sweethearts. "In my youth I loved strongly at a distance of a thousand. . . . Now though I find that I have been deceived, for although you are more and more distant from me . . . you are always present to my imagination."[20]

Madame Brillon's mood gradually improved as the family rode through the craggy hills and valleys of Provence, passing tiny villages, vineyards, and caves to arrive at the seaside city of Nice. To lift her spirits, Ben had already sent several letters ahead. Within them he apologized for his French, whose nuances he struggled to master. In reply, the musician explained Ben's efforts to write in perfect French "denied me" of his deepest feelings. Besides, "some lines of your bad French I . . . find very good." In fact, if he did not write more frequently, "out of spite I will learn English."[21]

By early January Madame Brillon was pleased with Nice, delighting in its salty air and mild winter climate. The town had "a sky always serene, a sun always warm and bright, trees always green, flowers of all kinds." Her daughters attended balls three times a week, which pleased her enormously—but pleasant as that Mediterranean town was, "nothing will ever take the place of a letter from you."[22] Two weeks later she related an incident that had political implications neither she nor Ben could have predicted.

Once settled in Nice, the Brillons made new friends. Mostly they were wealthy English families who traveled to Nice for its climate and in an effort "to cure their consumptions." Some of them bitterly resented France's alliance with America, but others were quietly sympathetic. One of their neighbors was Milady Rivers the Baroness Chatham, the widow of the late statesman William Pitt the Elder. At sixty, the baroness was "still magnificent and . . . [has] spirit . . . like you and even has a little bit of the expression of your character," Madame Brillon gushed.[23]

The baroness, who was secretly sympathetic to American independence, invited Madame Brillon to give a concert in her home. Among the guests was the Duchess of Ancaster, a close friend of Queen Charlotte of England. The musician discreetly tried to avoid politics as she chatted with the guests. To her surprise and embarrassment, the roguish governor of Nice asked her to play "Marche des Insurgents," the piece she wrote for Ben in celebration of the 1777 victory at Saratoga. Reluctantly Madame

Brillon played it, hoping no one would ask about its history. The duchess applauded, but the governor then announced the title and history of the march. Fortunately, the duchess dismissed the implications and declared the "pleasure of music" was what counted.[24]

Afterward, Lord Cholmondeley, a handsome young man and flute player, complimented Madame Brillon on her performance. Learning that she was one of Ben's friends, he became excited. "He tells me that he had many friends who were also yours, that he had left England because he could no longer bear the unreason of the court," Madame Brillon wrote Ben, gleefully adding he even promised "to come and have tea with me at Passy."[25]

In February Madame Brillon met him again and promptly wrote Ben that Cholmondeley "would be overwhelmed to meet you." In fact he "would give everything in the world" to do so.[26] A month later, while the Brillons were still in Nice, Ben received a letter from the English aristocrat. After sending his compliments to Dr. Franklin, Cholmondeley explained he was leaving "for London tomorrow evening" but "should be glad to see him for five minutes before he went. Lord Cholmondeley will call upon him [Ben] at any time in the morning he shall please to appoint [name]."[27]

The next morning, Ben welcomed him to his home in Passy. After exchanging news about their mutual friends in Nice, Cholmondeley explained the real reason for his visit. The Whig statesman Lord Shelburne had "great regard for me [Ben], that he was sure his Lordship would be pleased to hear from me, and that if I would write a line, he would have a pleasure to carrying it."[28] Stunned, Ben dashed off a letter. There was no reason to hesitate: A personal invitation from Shelburne meant he and other high-ranking men were amenable to a peace treaty.

Still the British hesitated. It was not until March 1782 that Congress assigned Ben, John Adams, Thomas Jefferson, John Jay, and Henry Laurens to negotiate a treaty with Britain. Meanwhile, as Ben waited, he was the only peace commissioner in Paris to confront the challenge of conflicting political interests. America had initially promised to "treat" or negotiate a settlement first with France, but Britain kept pressing for its own series of talks. Complicating that was the Rockingham government's dispatch of two rival ministers to Paris, Foreign Secretary Charles Fox and Colonial Secretary Lord Shelburne. Decades earlier, Ben had warned readers of *Poor Richard's Almanack*, "Don't think to hunt two hares with one dog."[29] Before long the wisdom of that remark would prove painfully true. Despite Fox's arrival in France, Ben favored Shelburne.

That same spring Margaret renewed her plans to see Ben. "My mother talks of visiting you this summer and if she can get a companion I believe she will. I rejoice in the prospect of peace," Polly wrote Ben on May 1.[30] Deftly avoiding discussion of his political problems, Ben wrote, "The truth is I love you both very well, and wish to be with you anywhere—but I dread exposing my good old friends to the fatigues and inconvenience of such a journey . . . therefore say no more of that *at present*."[31]

Even before receiving his letter Polly decided the trip was impractical, for once again Margaret had been ill. But after her mother had recovered, Polly assured Ben that "she seems to have given up the thought of visiting you."[32]

Six weeks later, Britain's prime minister, Lord Rockingham, died from influenza and was succeeded by Lord Shelburne. From London, the new prime minister appointed Richard Oswald his representative and sent him to France. Ben, who had met Oswald years earlier in the colonies, welcomed the one-eyed London merchant and former slave trader, praising him for his "candor, probity, good understanding and good will to both continents."[33] Through Oswald Ben sent Shelburne his conditions for a peace treaty. Foremost among them were four "necessary" conditions: full recognition of the United States, removal of British troops, secure boundaries, and fishing rights off the Canadian coast.

Ben also sent a second list of "advisable" provisions: reparations for the destruction of American property, acknowledgment of British guilt, a free-trade agreement, and American ownership of Canada. Fully aware of France's disapproval of the last—American dominion over Canada—he nevertheless included it to secure his country's borders and reduce American dependence on France. Then in an effort to obtain reparations, Ben produced a newspaper from his Passy printing press portraying the horrors of British brutality upon Americans. After a series of frustrating delays and political intrigues, the British finally agreed to a peace conference with France.

By midsummer 1782 Ben's old nemesis, the gout, had reappeared. That August his toes, feet, and legs became so painful and badly swollen he could barely walk. Then he was seized with an attack of kidney stones. Today doctors attribute both ailments to an excess of uric acid, which can be treated with medications. Not so in 1782, however; that summer Ben had become so incapacitated that John Jay was summoned to Paris to continue treaty negotiations in his place.

From her nearby estate in Passy, Madame Brillon expressed her concern and tried to cheer the bedridden Ben. "I hope that by Monday you shall be strong on your legs, and that the Wednesday and Saturday teas and the Sunday morning teas will resume in all their glory. . . . My fat husband will make us laugh . . . Pere Pagin will play "Dieu d'Amour" on the violin, I will play the "March" on the piano, you will play "Petites Oiseaux" on the armonica . . . oh, my friend after evil days, one enjoys the happy ones all the more!"[34]

By winter, in pursuit of her own "happy days," the musician and her family had moved to Paris to introduce their daughters to society. Ten months later Cunegonde, the Brillons' elder daughter, married an aristocratic Frenchman, Colonel Marie-Antoine Paris d'Illinis.

Perhaps the Brillons' departure for Paris was the final goad. Or perhaps the severity of Ben's recent illness, while followed by recovery and his return to negotiations, was responsible. Regardless of the motive, Ben turned increasingly to those he loved from his past through letters. On July 17 Polly wrote she was "highly delighted with the importance I am grown into since the charge [change] of affairs . . . still more so with the frequent opportunities of hearing from you and writing to you. . . . A letter arrived two days ago by penny post which I know to be your hand but . . . addressed to my mother."[35]

Ben's illness, worries about old age, the Brillons' rejection of Temple as a son-in-law, and Madame Helvétius's refusal to wed had intensified his desire to be surrounded by loved ones. By July 1784, after having his fourteen-year-old grandson, Benny, returned to Passy from a Geneva boarding school, Ben hoped to send him to England with Polly's sons. Graciously she replied, "I enclose the rules of the school where my boys are. I should have great pleasure in placing Bache there."[36]

A month later, still suffering from gout, Ben repeated his hopes "to see peace and my friends, whose continued regard for me after so long and so thorough an acquaintance . . . I esteem among my honors and felicities. . . . In this observation I include your good mother, from whom I had lately the pleasure of receiving a few lines."[37] Five months later Ben wrote again, explaining he had been ill "until very lately." Yet "nothing would give me greatest pleasure than to see you both [Margaret and Polly] once more, well and happy." The final terms of the peace treaty were imminent, and once signed, he would be free to travel again. Would it, he asked Polly, be "prudent in me to visit England before I return to America? I have no other call there, but the pleasure of seeing my friends."[38]

Polly's next letter of January 13, 1783, probably crossed Ben's in the mail. After thanking him for a packet of books, she added, "My mother was much disappointed . . . there was no letter in the parcel." Her next sentence sliced through Ben's heart. "I know you will pay the tribute of a sigh for the loss of one who loved you with the most ardent affection. She lingered under a most painful disorder many weeks and departed the first day of this year."[39]

Margaret, with whom Ben had spent "some of the happiest [days] of my life," had slipped away.[40]

14

"We Are Apt to Forget That We Are Grown Old"

"THE DEPARTURE OF MY dearest friend . . . greatly affects me. To meet with her once more in this life, was one of the principal motives of my proposing to visit England again. We never had among us the smallest misunderstanding. Our friendship has been all clear sunshine," Ben replied to Polly on Margaret's death. Memories of the years they shared at Craven Street flooded over him, filling him with longing for the past: Margaret's tender care when he was ill, their conversations over dinner, the friends they shared, the concerts and plays they attended, and the private times too. Margaret's death, the fifth of Ben's friends in the past year, moved him so deeply that he pleaded, *"the fewer we become, the more let us love one another."* [1]

Of course, he had always loved Polly and had admired her from the start, not only as Margaret's daughter but also because she was curious and intelligent. If he had met Polly in a different era, Ben probably would have courted her. Nor was he the only one who admired her. As his literary friend Dr. John Hawkesworth once said, Polly had the most "logical head of any woman he ever knew." Ben's admiration transcended that. The spring before Margaret's death, he had admitted to Polly that his "head" was only one aspect of his affection and "rather a project of my heart." [2]

That comment, coupled with Ben's tender attachment to Polly, led historians to suspect their relationship was secretly sexual. Yet given Ben's devotion to Margaret, that seems unlikely.

In February Polly invited Ben to visit her in Cheam, a village eleven miles southwest of London where her two sons attended school. Ben, by then seventy-seven, thanked her for the invitation but explained he wanted to return to Philadelphia. "The little left of life at my age will perhaps hurry me home as soon as I can quit my employment here. I should indeed have great pleasure in seeing you, and in being some time with you and our little family: I cannot have all I wish."[3]

Ben's comment "I cannot have all I wish" had become his private mantra as he completed negotiations for a peace treaty with Great Britain. Now, with the official end of the war, life—literally and figuratively—was on the upswing. A week before the September 3, 1783, signing of the Peace of Paris, Ben watched a balloon filled with hydrogen ascend over the Champs-de-Mars in Paris, following the Montgolfier brothers' experiment with a hot-air balloon that rose over a field in Lyon in July. Despite public excitement, a skeptic asked what good was a balloon? Ben famously replied, "What good is a newborn baby?"[4] On a more serious note he wrote his friend Sir Joseph Bank of Britain's Royal Society, expressing the hope that man's first ascension into the sky might "possibly give a new turn to human affairs. Convincing sovereigns of the folly of wars may perhaps be one effect . . . since it will be impracticable for the most potent of them to guard his dominions."[5]

With peace at last a reality, Ben again asked Polly if his grandson Benny could join her sons at their school in Cheam. After years studying at Geneva's Pension Marignac, the teenager's English was rusty. Once again Polly agreed, but worried about the youth's adjustment to a new country. "How will my young friend like to lay aside his powder and curls, and return to the simplicity of a rustic school boy? I fear he will think us all so unpolished he will scarcely be able to endure us." Still, "if English cordiality will make amends for French refinement, we may have some chance for making him happy."[6]

In December Ben decided against the idea. After four and a half years in Switzerland away from his grandfather, Benny was thrilled to be with him again. The affection was mutual, for Ben found him a pleasant and engaging youth. In warm weather Benny accompanied Ben to other balloon launchings, flew kites, and swam in the Seine. In winter he skated on the river, chatted with Ben's visitors at Passy, and enjoyed the magic tricks his cousin Temple played to amuse him. As Benny noted in his journal, "Grand Papa was different from other old people, for they were fretting and complaining and dissatisfied, and my Grand Papa is laughing and cheerful, like a young person."[7]

When Ben mentioned sending him to England, the boy vehemently objected. Consequently Ben wrote, "I concluded to keep him til I should go over myself. He behaves very well."[8]

The same could not be said about Temple. Dejected by the Brillons' rejection, he became ill but after recovering threw himself into the temptations of Parisian night life. Among his romances was one with a countess "without backbone, who can't say no," and another with an Italian mistress. He was also "spicing the affair with some little adventures left and right."[9] Simultaneously, Temple began courting the Brillons' younger daughter, Aldegonde.

Hearing about this courtship infuriated their mutual family friend, Louis-Guillaume Le Veillard, the neighbor who had once introduced Ben to Madame Brillon. After reminding Temple that Jacques Brillon "care[d] nothing about the young man's sighs," Le Veillard sarcastically reprimanded Temple for neglecting "two most interesting liaisons," then rebuked him for hiding them from a certain "inexperienced fifteen-year-old demoiselle" [Aldegonde].[10]

Despite his escapades, Temple still might have married the Brillons' second daughter. A year after their older daughter wed, Jacques was so disgusted with his new son-in-law that he suddenly became amenable to the idea of Temple's marriage to Aldegonde. The union had obvious benefits. Not only would Temple receive a "fat dowry" and the inheritance of Jacques's post as tax collector, but Ben would also have a reason to remain in France.[11] Once more the statesman's hopes were dashed when one of Temple's mistresses, Blanchette Caillot, the wife of a famous actor, gave birth to his son.

As historians famously observed, Ben's great-grandson, born out of wedlock, was sired by the son, also born out of wedlock, of the son Ben had conceived before marrying Deborah. But before little Theodore was five, the triple Franklin fault line foundered when the child died of smallpox.

While Ben continued to overlook Temple's instability, the youth's flamboyant tendencies were probably fanned by the circumstances surrounding his birth. Soon after Temple's birth, Billy had arranged for a hired woman to raise him. After Ben's second return to London he found Temple and befriended him; when the boy turned eight he placed him in a boarding school. On school holidays the boy stayed at Craven Street; though treated warmly, he was known as Ben's charitable ward. In 1775, when his grandfather brought him to Pennsylvania, Temple finally met and lived briefly with Billy, and by 1783 he longed to see his Loyalist father again. Subsequent to his imprisonment in revolutionary-era America, Billy was freed and moved to England.

Billy, too, hoped for reconciliation with his own father. "Dear and honored father, ever since the termination of the unhappy contest between Great Britain and America, I have been anxious to write to you, and . . . endeavor to revive that affectionate intercourse and connections which, until the commencement of the late troubles, had been the pride and happiness of my life," he wrote Ben. Brashly he insisted upon adding, "If I have been mistaken, I cannot help it . . . were the same circumstances to occur again tomorrow, my conduct would be exactly similar to what it was." Still he hoped to visit Ben in France.[12]

Still seething about his son's disloyalty, he replied, "Indeed, nothing has ever hurt me so much and affected me with such keen sensations as to find myself in my old age deserted by my only son: and not only deserted, but to find him taking up arms against me, in a cause where my good fame fortune and life were all at stake."[13] After discouraging Billy from traveling to France, Ben announced he was sending Temple to London in his place.

In London the young man was celebrated as the grandson of the famous Benjamin Franklin. The Royal Society honored him, the Lord Mayor and prominent ladies invited him to teas, and Gilbert Stuart even painted his portrait. A friend provided Temple with a list of London's best tailors and bootmakers along with a private list of "the following safe girls who I think are quite handsome."[14]

Such introductions may have contributed to Temple's delay in meeting Polly in November. She had anticipated his visit for weeks; a decade had passed since she remembered him as a boarding school student who had occasionally lived at Craven Street. On November 18 Polly eagerly wrote, "I depend upon seeing you next Sunday. I have a bed ready for you and will get one for your servants."[15]

But Temple failed to appear and offered a flimsy explanation. Angrily Polly replied, "I expected a letter instead of yourself today, though I had not suggested so handsome an excuse as you have found."[16] Six days went by and still Temple had not arrived. By then Polly was alarmed. "This comes of not keeping your appointment. I received your letter on Sunday morning and wrote an answer which a gentleman took to town to put in the penny post . . . and informed you where I should be yesterday evening. We have looked for you all this morning and inquired for you at every town but in vain. Something I do suppose has prevented your setting out."[17]

Temple finally did visit Polly and her children, after which she wrote Ben how surprised she was by how much he had grown. "We are all pleased with our old friend Temple changed into young Franklin." Then, having no reason to hold back any longer she admitted, "We see a strong resemblance of you." Years earlier she and her mother "pretended to be ignorant" about Temple's origins, even though they sensed he was Billy's son born out of wedlock. Diplomatically Polly added, "I believe you may have been handsomer than your grandson, but then you were never so genteel; and if he has a little less philosophy he has more polish."[18]

Despite her reservations about Temple's character, he persuaded her to visit Ben. By early winter 1785 she and her children arrived in Passy, where they lived with Ben. It had been ten years since they had met, and while Polly noticed how much her "surrogate father" had aged, she wrote her sister-in-law, Barbara Hewson, that Ben's conversation was as "amusing and instructive" as ever.[19]

In good weather she walked to the village where her two sons attended school. On other occasions she met the visitors who came to see Ben. Among them were Madame Brillon, who entertained them with music, physicist Jean-Baptiste Le Roy, the chemist Lavoisier, Abbé Morellet, and

members of the Masonic Lodge of the Nine Sisters. Only once did Polly
visit Paris to attend the Comédie, because Temple monopolized Ben's carriage. "He has such a love of dress and is so absorbed in self-importance
and so engaged in the pursuit of pleasure that he is not an amiable nor a
respectable character," Polly complained to her sister-in-law. In contrast to
his hardworking, serious-minded grandfather, Temple was fit to be nothing
more than "the gallant of the French ladies."[20]

Benny, in contrast, was "sensible and manly in his manner without the
slightest tincture of the coxcomb," wrote Polly; his admirable "simplicity
of character" was like that of his grandfather.[21] Already Ben had prepared
him for a useful occupation. Since Ben's efforts to have Congress appoint
Temple to a diplomatic post failed, he decided to prepare Benny for a trade.
Not surprisingly, Ben turned to the one he knew best: printing. By the time
Polly arrived, Benny was an accomplished typesetter who had trained at
his grandfather's press in Passy. Deborah's praise for Benny as a promising
child—her "kingbird"—seemed prophetic.

Once back in England in April, Polly thanked Ben for his "kindness,"
adding "my thoughts have incessantly turned to Passy."[22] Ben insisted that
he was the one who owed her a debt. "My dear dear friend . . . you talk
of obligation to me, when in fact I am the person obliged. I passed a long
winter in a manner that made it appear the shortest of any I ever passed.
Such is the effect of pleasing society with friends one loves." Just before
writing that note, Ben had received permission from Congress to return
to America. "However happy that circumstance may make me, your joining me there will surely made me happier." If she agreed to come, Ben
promised to "prepare a house for you, as near me . . . convenient for you
as possible."[23]

Ben's next letter of July 4 was even more insistent. By then he had arranged a "fine ship" to bring him to America, with "a large convenient
cabin with good lodging places" and with "plenty of room for you and
yours." Polly must seriously consider sailing with him, he added, because
"you may never have so good an opportunity of passing to America . . .
think of it."[24] Initially Polly declined Ben's invitation. Three weeks later,
when his ship was underway, she confessed she was a "fool" to reject his

offer. While she could not have been ready "to embark in so short a time . . . I do not give up on the intention of taking the voyage."[25]

In addition to the comfort of living near her surrogate father, America offered Polly other advantages. As Ben had once explained, her sons could less expensively be established in America compared to the costly schools and traditions required to raise them as English gentlemen. Polly's friends objected to her departure, but she now agreed that America offered her sons "better prospects" than England.[26]

Ben's French friends were also upset with his departure. While relations with his two former sweethearts had evolved into friendships, both women were distraught. "I have a heavy heart. The thought that you will leave is like a nightmare," Madame Brillon admitted. To remember him, she had his portrait painted.[27] Ben, in turn, presented his "very dear daughter" with a collection of the bagatelles he had written at Passy.

On July 10, two days before Ben's departure, a tearful Madame Brillon met him for the last time. The next day she explained she could not attend his farewell. "My heart was so heavy yesterday, when I left you, that I feared, for you and for myself, another such moment would have only added to my misery, without further proving the tender, unchanging love I have devoted to you forever. . . . If it ever pleases you to remember the woman who loved you the most, think of me. Farewell. My heart was not meant to be separated from yours but it shall not be, you shall find it near yours, speak to it and it shall answer you."[28]

Ben's departure from the Helvétius estate at Auteuil was equally emotional. As Cabanis tersely wrote, "Many honorable tears were shed on both sides."[29] To ease the departure of the gout-ridden minister, Queen Marie-Antoinette sent her royal litter to bring Ben to the port of Le Havre. On July 12, after settling his accounts and dinner with his host, Chaumont, Ben climbed onto the royal sedan chair. Surrounding him was "a very great concourse of the people of Passy. A mournful silence reigned around him and was only interrupted by a few sobs," Benny recalled in his journal.[30]

Just after his departure Madame Helvétius scribbled a hurried note. "I cannot get accustomed to the idea that you have left us, my dear friend, that you are no longer in Passy, that I shall never see you again. I can picture you in your litter, further from us at every step, already lost to me and to your friends, who loved you so much and regret you so." Fearing the journey was too difficult for the seventy-nine-year-old, she begged, "Come back, my dear friend, come back to us. My little retreat will be the better for your presence, you will like it because of the friendship you will find here and the care we will take of you. . . . You will make our life happier, we shall contribute to your happiness . . . for sure that you have read in my heart and that of my friends."[31]

From the port of Le Havre Ben replied to the widow. While he regretted leaving France, "the country I love the most in the world" as well as "my dear Helvetia" and felt uncertain about his happiness in America, he could not return to Passy. "I must go back [to Philadelphia]. I feel sometimes that things are badly arranged in this world when I consider that people so well matched to be happy together are forced to separate." In closing he added, "I will not tell you of my love. For one would say that there is nothing re-markable or praiseworthy about it, since everybody loves you. I only hope you will love me some."[32]

Far less sentimental was Ben's meeting with Billy at the Star Tavern in Southampton, England. Tensions ran through their four days together, for Ben's goal was recompense rather than regrets. In businesslike tones he in-sisted Billy assign the deeds to his New Jersey property to Temple at a below-market price. Ben also claimed ownership of his son's New York property in repayment of a fifteen-hundred-pound debt. One of the few sentences in Ben's diary about Billy read, "Gave a power to my son to re-cover what may be due to me from the British government."[33]

Brightening Ben's mood was the arrival of old friends who wanted to bid him farewell. Among his favorites were Bishop Shipley, his wife, and their youngest daughter, Catherine. During the afternoon of July 27, the Shipleys joined Ben when he boarded the *London Pacquet*. "We go down in a shallop to the ship. The captain entertains us at supper. The company stays all night." By the time Ben awoke the next morning they were gone and the ship was under sail. On September 14, after seven weeks at sea, Ben reported in his journal, "A light breeze brought us above Gloucester Point, in view of dear Philadelphia. . . . My son-in-law came with a boat for us."[34]

Already an earlier vessel had arrived and alerted the city to Ben's arrival with Temple and Benny. No sooner had Richard's boat landed at the Market Street wharf with Ben than he was "received by a crowd of people with huzzas, and accompanied with acclamations quite to my door."[35] Cannons sounded in his honor and church bells pealed as the grey-haired statesman approached Franklin Court. Perhaps he deliberately took his time. Nearly ten years had passed since his departure in 1776. Despite the British occupation of Philadelphia in 1778–79, the city had grown and prospered and was now the largest and most refined urban center in America. Where empty lots once stood were new homes and buildings housing shops, importing firms, tailors, and bootmakers. The paved roads Ben had advocated for were crowded with carriages, wagons, and carts, and the city's wharves bustled with vessels and goods.

Ben gazed at Franklin Court. Compared to the elegant buildings of Paris and Passy, the "dream house" he once designed for himself and Deborah looked plain, its clapboard exterior dingy. That was no surprise, for Richard continued to struggle financially on his modest salary as postmaster of Philadelphia. Still, Ben was home. There Sally, heavier with the years, was surrounded by the four new grandchildren born since his departure. Smiles, tears, and laughter marked their reunion as the little ones danced around "Grand Papa." Emotions ran high. Even the usually understated Ben wrote in his diary that day, "Found my family well. God be praised and thanked for all his mercies!"[36]

The next morning legislators from the Pennsylvania Assembly appeared to pay their respects, followed the next day by professors from the College of Pennsylvania. On Saturday, September 17, members of the state's Constitutional Society celebrated him "as the father of our free and excellent constitution."[37] Later that day a group of "respectable citizens" at Byrne's Tavern nominated Ben to Pennsylvania's Supreme Executive Council. The honors continued. On Monday the 19th the general and officers of the Pennsylvania Militia expressed their gratitude for establishing the unit forty years earlier. The *Pennsylvania Packet* praised Ben on Tuesday for his "endeavors . . . to promote the prosperity of the human race."[38] Relieved that the ugly rumors spread by the Lees and Adamses had faded, Ben wrote

John Jay, "The affectionate welcome I met with from fellow-citizens was far beyond my expectations."[39]

A week later, other institutions that Ben had founded honored him, among them, the Union Fire Company and the American Philosophical Society. On October 11, Ben became a member of Pennsylvania's Supreme Executive Council, and on the 7th he was elected president of the Commonwealth of Pennsylvania. Thrilled to be involved again, he wrote Polly he was "plunged into public business as deep as ever."[40] Only Jane, his seventy-four-year-old sister, disapproved. Whatever possessed him, she angrily scrawled, to accept "all solicitations to burden yourself . . . with the outcomes for the public. . . . If I were with you I should enjoy a little familiar domestic chit chat like common folks."[41]

At Franklin Court Ben engaged in "familiar domestic chit chat" with Sally, his amiable son-in-law, Richard, and his adoring grandchildren, but he still missed the conversations he once had with Polly. Within a year the English daughter of his "heart" announced she was "finally inclined to come over."[42] By then the eighty-year-old Ben had busied himself with still other projects. In between meetings as president of Pennsylvania, he planned renovations to Franklin Court, which had become too small for the Baches' growing family.

To enlarge the house, Ben tore down three old buildings bordering Franklin Court and had space cleared for a two-building addition connected by an arched passage wide enough for a carriage to pass through. One building had a cellar for wood; above it was a dining room that could accommodate twenty-four. Above that was Ben's library, which housed his four thousand books in floor-to-ceiling shelves. To retrieve a volume from the top shelf Ben invented a mechanical arm, which is still in use in some libraries today. Above the library were bedrooms and an attic. Sheepishly, Ben admitted to Jane that taking on such a project in his eighties probably seemed overly ambitious. "I hardly know how to justify building a library at an age that will so soon oblige me to quit, but we are apt to forget that we are grown old and building is an amusement."[43]

As Philadelphia expanded, so had the produce stalls along Market Street, including one that stood near Franklin Court. Because produce was readily available there, Ben saw no reason to maintain the land inside the Court as a garden. There, during the last ten years of her life, Deborah used to grow vegetables and herbs, some of which she sent to him overseas. Recalling the beautiful terraces and grounds on the estates of Madame Brillon and Madame Helvétius, Ben converted the land into a French-style garden with gravel paths, shrubs, and a mulberry tree. During Philadelphia's scorching summers, it became a favorite place for Ben and his family to cool off. A visitor once described seeing Ben there, "sitting upon a grassplot, under a very large mulberry tree with several other gentleman and two or three ladies . . . the tea table was spread under the tree and Mrs. Bache . . . the only daughter of the Doctor . . . served it out to the company. She had three of her children about her. They seemed to be excessively fond of their grandpapa."[44]

By mid-October 1786 his "English daughter" Polly and her children arrived. Even before her ship landed in Philadelphia she wrote Ben, "we are arrived in sight of your land and hope to see you soon." Despite her excitement, the ever-practical Polly asked Ben to "procure a lodging for us . . . we shall want three beds for ourselves and one for my maid. That and one room to eat in is all we care for."[45]

Only a few details exist about their final years together. After years of exchanged letters between Philadelphia and Craven Street, Sally and Polly finally met. Emotions must have run high as the two women eyed each other and probably embraced. Later, as they became better acquainted, they may have even exchanged fond stories about Ben. However, as biographer Claude-Anne Lopez commented, they remained polite to each other but were never friends. It was understandable. From Sally's perspective, Polly was an intruder, her father's "surrogate daughter" upon whom he lavished his affection while sending his "real" daughter stern letters about economy and thrift. Polly must have sensed that too but was so devoted to Ben that she brushed aside her discomfort with Sally.

In May 1787, at eighty-one, Ben was elected a delegate to the Constitutional Convention at the State House. To celebrate the arrival of General Washington, he opened his new dining room and toasted him and other men with food and a cask of beer. But on May 28, the opening day of

Congress, Ben awoke with a new attack of kidney stones, which prevented his attendance. Still in pain two weeks later, he arrived in a sedan chair carried by four prisoners from the Walnut Street jail. Despite Ben's exalted status as the Convention's oldest and most seasoned political member, he spoke little. After a futile attempt to argue for the efficiency of a unicameral Congress, the "short, fat, trunched old man in a plain Quaker dress, bald pate and short white locks" listened to the delegates squabble over states' rights and the unequal voting power of large and small states.[46]

As William Pierce, a delegate from Georgia, later recalled, Ben was "well known to be the greatest philosopher of the present age . . . he does not shine much in public council: he is no speaker, nor does he seem to let politics engage his attention." Ben's reticence in the wake of the vitriolic arguments that echoed through the stifling temperatures of the State House rooms had less to do with Ben's age than his seasoned political style. Pierce noted, "He is, however, a most extraordinary man, and tells a story in a style more engaging than anything I ever heard. . . . He is eighty-two and possesses an activity of mind equal to a youth of twenty-five years of age."[47]

Ben never wholeheartedly approved of the Constitution. However, he famously agreed to it "with all its faults—if they are such—because I think a general government necessary for us. . . . I doubt too, whether any other convention we can obtain may be able to make a better Constitution for when you assemble a number of men to have the advantage of their joint wisdom, you inevitably assemble with those men all their prejudices, their passions . . . errors of opinion . . . local interest and . . . self views. From such an assembly can a perfect production be expected?"[48]

Over the next two years, as Ben's health failed, he contented himself with similar thoughts about his own imperfect life. On bad days he rested in his room or in bed. Often his grandchildren visited him there, delighting in his stories and interest in their education. One of the youngest, seven- or eight-year-old Deborah, named after Ben's wife, recalled sitting on "a little stool near a Windsor bottom chair" as she practiced her writing. If she took too long, Ben asked, "Debby is not that line of spelling ready yet?"[49] In September 1788 Sally delivered another little girl named Sarah, adding to

Ben's pride in his growing number of descendants. Occasionally his oldest grandsons visited: Benny, a recent graduate of the College of Pennsylvania, and Temple, by then the restless owner of his father's New Jersey farm.

During the last year of his life Ben was bedridden, his pain only partially relieved by laudanum. Sally assumed the burden of his daily care. Ben now described her as "the comfort of my declining years . . . a kind attentive nurse when I am at any time indisposed."[50]

Polly too attended him at the bedside, reading him poetry and discussing religion. Like earlier in his life, Ben was indifferent to her inquiries, believing the essence of religion was to help others. Rather than being threatened by the approach of death, he seemed to accept it peacefully. As he once wrote the charismatic preacher George Whitfield, "That Being who gave me existence . . . and has been continually showering his favors upon me . . . can I doubt that he loves me? And if he loves me, can I doubt that he will go on to take care of me, not only here, but hereafter?"[51]

Even as his health declined, Ben maintained a positive attitude. "No repining, no peevish expression ever escaped him during a confinement of two years," Polly recalled. "When the pain was not too violent to be amused, he employed himself with his books, his pen, or in conversation with friends."[52] Nor did Ben care that Polly, unlike Sally, was not his flesh and blood, for as he once observed in the *Almanack*, "Generous minds are all of kin."[53] What mattered was Sally's and Polly's presence, the devoted daughters of the two women he had once loved.

So it was that when the end came on April 17, 1790, the founding father's struggles with passion and prudence were finally at peace.

ACKNOWLEDGMENTS

When is the idea for a book born? Like many authors, I cannot name a specific time or date when the concept finally gelled, but even after that, it was many years before I began writing. Once I did, the work was enhanced by experts, readers, and friends to whom I remain indebted.

With appreciation to my agent, Joelle Delbourgo, for her advice, support, and encouragement from inception to publication. Her faith in my work has brightened the long months spent creating this manuscript.

Special thanks are due to Gayatri Patnaik, associate director and editorial director at Beacon Press, who believed in my work and urged me to expand the scope of this book to include Franklin's French sweethearts.

And to Beacon Press senior editor Joanna Green, whose discerning eye and penetrating questions helped me focus on Franklin's women and do so despite the looming vision of the scientist-statesman that threatened to dominate the story. Thank you too, Joanna, for seeing the ironies of Franklin's relation to women and sharing laughter as you completed the edit over Valentine's Day 2021.

To Alison Rodriguez, editorial assistant at Beacon Press, for her patience and assistance with technical issues of the notes in the manuscript.

To Laura Kenney, whose thoughtful suggestions as copyeditor greatly enhanced the final version of the manuscript. To Janet Vail, Travis Cohen, and the rest of the staff at Beacon Press for their enthusiastic and diligent efforts to introduce the book to readers everywhere.

To historian and author Dr. Larry Tise, former director of the Franklin Memorial at the Franklin Institute, whose advice about sources twenty-four years ago, ongoing interest in the project, and comments on a late draft of the book were invaluable. Along the way our conversations led me to new insights about Franklin as a man well beyond his worldly achievements.

To Ellen R. Cohn, editor of *The Papers of Benjamin Franklin* at Yale University, for her suggestions about sources for Franklin and his women.

To Amy Jacaruso, editorial assistant at Yale University's *The Papers of Benjamin Franklin*, for advice about permissions. Thank you for your assistance in locating page numbers for letters that appeared in the Library of Congress's digitized Benjamin Franklin papers but were listed as "unpublished."

To the Women's Writing Lives Seminar at the Graduate Center of the City University, whose meetings over the years helped illuminate the challenges and techniques of writing biographies about women.

To Dr. Patrick Spero, executive director of the American Philosophical Society, and Dr. Kyle Roberts for their support and excitement about the book's publication.

To my friends Alvina Baxter-Moran, for her encouraging comments about the manuscript, and Madeline Holt, for her interest and valuable thoughts about early chapters. Thanks are also due to Linda Selman, whose ongoing support for my work has always been a source of inspiration. I am also indebted to author Barbara Struna, who helped me with several computer issues in a late draft of the book.

With special thanks to my sister, Wendy, who carefully read each chapter of the evolving book, offered valuable comments, and shared her opinion about Franklin from a contemporary woman's perspective, often to our mutual delight.

Above all, with gratitude to my dear husband, Bill, who read an early proposal about Deborah Franklin, located and visited the Franklin townhouse with me in London, critiqued subsequent drafts of the manuscript, cheerfully endured my long hours at the computer, and remains my most loving and devoted fan.

NOTES

ABBREVIATIONS

Archives

FP Benjamin Franklin Papers Online, Library of Congress, https://www.loc.gov
  /collections/benjamin-franklin-papers/about-this-collection

YBFP Yale University published volumes, *The Papers of Benjamin Franklin*
  (excluded from the online version)

Individuals

BF Benjamin Franklin
DF Deborah Read Franklin
CRG Catharine (Katy) Ray Greene
JM Jane Franklin Mecom
MB Madame Brillon (Anne-Louise d'Hardancourt Brillon de Jouy)
MH Madame Helvétius (Anne-Catherine de Ligniville d'Autricourt Helvétius)
MS Margaret Stevenson
PSH Mary (Polly) Stevenson Hewson
WF William (Billy) Franklin
WS William Strahan
WTF William (Temple) Franklin

INTRODUCTION

1 BF to MB, October 12, 1781, FP 35: 584.
2 Franklin, *Almanacks*, 163.
3 "A Scolding Wife," July 5, 1733, Labaree, *Papers of Benjamin Franklin*, 1: 325–27.
4 DF to BF, October 13–18?, 1767, FP 14: 278.
5 BF to MS, January 25, 1779, FP 28: 42.
6 Franklin, *Almanacks*, 147.

CHAPTER 1

"A Most Awkward Ridiculous Appearance"

1 Labaree et al., *Autobiography of Benjamin Franklin*, 76.
2 Labaree et al., *Autobiography*, 79.
3 Labaree et al., *Autobiography*, 79.
4 Labaree et al., *Autobiography*, 78.

5 Labaree et al., *Autobiography*, 68.
6 "Letters of Silence Dogood, September 24, 1722, FP 1: 41.
7 Labaree et al., *Autobiography*, 79.
8 Labaree et al., *Autobiography*, 79.
9 Labaree et al., *Autobiography*, 79.
10 Labaree et al., *Autobiography*, 79.
11 Labaree et al., *Autobiography*, 89.
12 Labaree et al., *Autobiography*, 81.
13 Labaree et al., *Autobiography*, 83.
14 Labaree et al., *Autobiography*, 92.
15 Labaree et al., *Autobiography*, 92.
16 Labaree et al., *Autobiography*, 89.
17 Riley, "Deborah Franklin Correspondence," 239.
18 Benjamin Franklin, *Poor Richard: The Almanacks for the Years 1733–1758*, 36, 67.

19 Labaree et al., *Autobiography*, 89.
20 Labaree et al., *Autobiography*, 94.
21 Labaree et al., *Autobiography*, 95.
22 Franklin, *Almanacks*, 172.
23 Labaree et al., *Autobiography*, 96.
24 Labaree et al., *Autobiography*, 107.
25 Labaree et al., *Autobiography*, 98.
26 Labaree et al., *Autobiography*, 99.
27 Franklin, *Almanacks*, 28.
28 Labaree et al., *Autobiography*, 105.
29 Labaree et al., *Autobiography*, 106–7.
30 Labaree et al., *Autobiography*, 107.
31 Labaree et al., *Autobiography*, 128–29.

CHAPTER 2
"A Man and Not an Angel"

1 Labaree et al., *Autobiography*, 129.
2 Labaree et al., *Autobiography*, 29.
3 Labaree et al., *Autobiography*, 29.
4 Labaree et al., *Autobiography*, 29.
5 Labaree et al., *Autobiography*, 29.
6 Labaree et al., *Autobiography*, 125–26.
7 Labaree et al., *Autobiography*, 125–26.
8 Franklin, *Almanacks*, 242.
9 Labaree et al., *Autobiography*, 111.
10 Labaree et al., *Autobiography*, 112.
11 Labaree et al., *Autobiography*, 127.
12 "Old Mistress Apologue," June 25, 1745, FP, 3: 27.
13 Labaree et al., *Autobiography*, 128.
14 Labaree et al., *Autobiography*, 128.
15 Labaree et al., *Autobiography*, 128.
16 Labaree et al., *Autobiography*, 115.
17 Labaree et al., *Autobiography*, 116.
18 Labaree et al., *Autobiography*, 120.
19 Labaree et al., *Autobiography*, 122.
20 Labaree et al., *Autobiography*, 123–24.
21 "The Nature and Necessity of a Paper Currency," April 3, 1729, FP 1: 39.
22 Labaree et al., *Autobiography*, 123.
23 Labaree et al., *Autobiography*, 145.
24 "Extracts from the Gazette," August 19, 1731, FP 1: 219.
25 Federalist Papers Project, "Rules and Maxims."
26 Federalist Papers Project, "Rules and Maxims."
27 Federalist Papers Project, "Rules and Maxims."
28 Federalist Papers Project, "Rules and Maxims."
29 Gillespie, *A Book of Remembrance*, 17.
30 Skemp, *Benjamin and William Franklin*, 12.
31 Lopez and Herbert, *The Private Franklin*, 23.
32 BF to Abiah Franklin, Thursday, April 12, 1750, FP 3: 474.
33 BF to Sarah Davenport, June 1730, FP 1: 171.

CHAPTER 3
"Like a Faithful Pair of Doves"

1 "The Death of Infants," *Pennsylvania Gazette*, June 20, 1734.
2 Franklin, *Almanacks*, 66.
3 Labaree et al., *Autobiography*, 145.
4 Labaree, *Papers of Benjamin Franklin*, 1: 194–99.
5 Franklin, *Almanacks*, 3.
6 Franklin, *Almanacks*, 3.
7 Franklin, *Almanacks*, viii.
8 Lopez and Herbert, *The Private Franklin*, 30.
9 Franklin, *Almanacks*, 13.
10 Franklin, *Almanacks*, 13.
11 "A Scolding Wife," July 5, 1733, Labaree, *Papers of Benjamin Franklin*, 1: 325–27.
12 Franklin, *Almanacks*, 15.
13 Franklin, *Almanacks*, 20.
14 Franklin, *Almanacks*, 15.
15 Franklin, *Almanacks*, 28.
16 Franklin, *Almanacks*, 40.
17 "Extracts from the Gazette," March 4, 1731, FP 1: 214.
18 Labaree et al., *Autobiography*, 170.
19 BF to JM, January 13, 1772, FP 19: 28.
20 "On the Death of His Son," December 30, 1736, FP 2: 154.

21 Coss, "What Led Benjamin Franklin," 76.

22 "To Bethia Alexander," June 24, 1782, FP 36: 519.

23 Power of Attorney to Deborah Franklin, August 30, 1733, FP 1: 331, http://franklinpapers.org/framedVolumes.jsp?vol=1&page=325a.

24 Labaree et al., *Autobiography*, 169.

25 "Reply to a Piece of Advice," *Pennsylvania Gazette*, March 4, 1734/5, Labaree, *Papers*, 2: 21–26.

26 "Reply to a Piece of Advice," *Pennsylvania Gazette*, March 4, 1734/5, Labaree, *Papers*, 2: 21–26.

27 "Reply to a Piece of Advice," *Pennsylvania Gazette*, March 4, 1734/5, Labaree, *Papers*, 2: 21–26.

28 Skemp, "Family Partnerships," in Tise, *Benjamin Franklin and Women*, 24.

29 "I Sing My Plain Country Joan," FP 2: 352–54.

CHAPTER 4
"In the Dark, All Cats Are Grey"

1   Franklin, *Almanacks*, 29.

2   "A Scolding Wife," July 5, 1733, Labaree, *Papers of Benjamin Franklin*, 1: 325–27.

3   BF to Cadwallader Colden, November 4, 1743, FP 2: 387.

4   "An Account of the New Invented Pennsylvania Fire-Place," Labaree, *Papers*, 2: 419–46.

5   "An Account of the New Invented Pennsylvania Fire-Place," Labaree, *Papers*, 2: 419–46.

6   Labaree et al., *Autobiography*, 192.

7   BF to James Read Jr., August 17, 1745, FP 3: 39.

8   Fisher and Howard, "Extracts from the Diary of Daniel Fisher, 1755," 276.

9   Sarah Broughton to BF, July 3, 1766, FP 13: 329.

10 Franklin, *Almanacks*, 59.

11 Fisher and Howard, "Extracts," 272.

12 Seavey, *Becoming Benjamin Franklin*, 170.

13 Daniel T. Morgan, *The Devious Dr. Franklin*, 17.

14 Conner, *Poor Richard's Politicks*, 215.

15 Fry, "'Extraordinary Freedom and Great Humility,'" 167–68.

16 Coss, "What Led Benjamin Franklin," 76.

17 DF to BF, January 8, 1765, FP 12: 13.

18 BF to William Dunlap, April 4, 1757, FP 7: 168.

19 Fisher and Howard, "Extracts," 272.

20 Fisher and Howard, "Extracts," 272.

21 "Plain Truth," November 17, 1747, FP 3: 180.

22 Cummings, *Richard Peters*, 134–36.

23 Wood, *Americanization of Benjamin Franklin*, 69.

24 "A Proposal for Promoting Useful Knowledge," May 14, 1743, Labaree, *Papers*, 2: 378–83.

25 "Proposals Relating to the Education of Youth in Pennsylvania," Labaree, *Papers*, 3: 397–421.

26 "Old Mistress Apologue," June 25, 1745, FP 3: 27.

27 "Old Mistress Apologue," June 25, 1745, FP 3: 27.

28 "Old Mistress Apologue," June 25, 1745, FP 3: 27.

29 "Old Mistress Apologue," June 25, 1745, FP 3: 27.

30 "The Speech of Miss Polly Baker," April 15, 1747, FP 3: 120.

31 BF to Abiah Franklin, April 12, 1750, FP 3: 474.

32 Isaacson, *Benjamin Franklin*, 128.

33 BF to Cadwallader Colden, September 29, 1748, FP 3: 317.

34 BF to Peter Collinson, May 25, 1747, FP 3: 126.

35 BF to John Franklin, December 24, 1750, FP 4: 82.

36 Peter Collinson to BF, February 5, 1750, FP 4: 459.

37 Peter Collinson to BF, September 27, 1752, FP 4: 357.
38 "The Kite Experiment," October 19, 1752, Labaree, *Papers*, 4: 360–69.
39 Franklin, *Almanacks*, 223.
40 Lopez and Herbert, *The Private Franklin*, 49.
41 Lopez and Herbert, *The Private Franklin*, 49.
42 BF to DF, June 10, 1758, FP 8: 90.

CHAPTER 5
"Kisses in the Wind"

1 DF to Margaret Strahan, December 24, 1751, FP 4: 224.
2 BF to Abiah Franklin, October 1, 1747, FP 3: 179.
3 BF to Abiah Franklin, April 12, 1750, FP 3: 474.
4 BF to WS, June 2, 1750, FP 4: 478.
5 BF to WS, June 2, 1750, FP 4: 478.
6 Franklin, *Almanacks*, 245.
7 Fisher and Howard, "Extracts from the Diary," 276.
8 BF to Abiah Franklin, April 12, 1750, FP 3: 474.
9 Roelker, *Benjamin Franklin and Catharine Ray Greene*, 7.
10 BF to CRG, September 11, 1755, FP 6: 182.
11 BF to CRG, October 16, 1755, FP, 6: 225.
12 BF to CRG, March 4, 1755, FP 5: 502.
13 BF to CRG, March 4, 1755, FP 5: 502.
14 BF to CRG, March 4, 1755, FP 5: 502.
15 BF to CRG, March/April 1755, FP 5: 535.
16 CRG to BF, June 28, 1755, FP 6: 96.
17 BF to CRG, September 11, 1755, FP 6: 182.
18 BF to CRG, September 11, 1755, FP 6: 182.
19 BF to CRG, September 11, 1755, FP 6: 182.
20 BF to CRG, October 16, 1755, FP 6: 182.
21 BF to CRG, October 16, 1755, FP 6: 182.
22 Wood, *Americanization of Benjamin Franklin*, 69.

23 BF to Peter Collinson, November 5, 1756, FP 6: 9.
24 Fisher and Howard, "Extracts from the Diary," 276.
25 Lemay, *Life of Benjamin Franklin*, 3: 509.
26 BF to DF, January 25, 1756, FP 6: 364.
27 BF to DF, January 30, 1756, FP 6: 378.
28 Fry, "'Extraordinary Freedom,'" 181.
29 LeMay, *Life of Benjamin Franklin*, 3: 470–72.
30 BF to CRG, March 3, 1757, FP 7: 143.

CHAPTER 6
The Ghost Wife

1 Franklin, *Almanacks*, 170.
2 BF to DF, April 5, 1757, FP 7: 173.
3 BF to William Dunlap, April 4, 1757, FP 7: 168.
4 Power of Attorney to Deborah Franklin, April 4, 1757, FP 7: 169.
5 BF to DF, May 27, 1757, FP 7: 217.
6 Fry, "'Extraordinary Freedom and Great Humility,'" 192.
7 Fry, "'Extraordinary Freedom and Great Humility,'" 192.
8 Lopez and Herbert, *The Private Franklin*, 69.
9 BF to DF, November 22, 1757, FP 7: 272.
10 Labaree et al., *Autobiography*, 262–63.
11 Labaree et al., *Autobiography*, 263.
12 BF to DF, November 22, 1757, FP.
13 BF to DF, November 22, 1757, FP.
14 BF to DF, February 19, 1758, FP 7: 379.
15 BF to DF, November 22, 1757, FP 7: 272.
16 BF to Joseph Galloway, February 17, 1758, FP 7: 373.
17 WS to DF, December 13, 1757, FP 7: 29.
18 WS to DF, December 13, 1757, FP 7: 29.
19 BF to DF, November 22, 1757, FP 7: 272.
20 BF to DF, January 14, 1758, FP 7: 359.
21 Lopez and Herbert, *The Private Franklin*, 80.
22 BF to DF, February 19, 1758, FP 7: 379.
23 BF to DF, February 19, 1758, FP 7: 379.

24 BF to DF, February 19, 1758, FP 7: 379.

25 BF to DF, February 19, 1758, FP 7: 379.

26 BF to DF, September 6, 1758, FP 8: 133.

27 BF to DF, June 10, 1758, FP 8: 90.

28 Lopez and Herbert, *The Private Franklin*, 91.

29 BF extract to Isaac Norris, January 14, 1758, FP 7: 360.

30 BF to Isaac Norris, January 19, 1759, FP 8: 232.

31 BF to Isaac Norris, January 19, 1759, FP 8: 232.

32 "Order in Council," September 2, 1760, FP 9: 196.

33 BF to DF, August 29, 1759, FP 8: 430.

34 BF to DF, June 27, 1760, FP 9: 173.

35 BF to DF, June 10, 1758, FP 8: 90.

36 BF to DF, November? 1761, FP 9: 394.

37 BF to DF, January 21, 1758, FP 8: 363.

38 BF to DF, November 22, 1757, FP 8: 272.

39 BF to DF, February 19, 1758, FP 8: 379.

40 BF to PSH, 1759, FP 8: 455.

41 PSH to BF, September 16, 1760, FP 9: 217.

42 BF to PSH, March 8, 1762, FP 10: 64.

43 BF to DF, June 27, 1760, FP 9: 173.

44 BF to DF, March 28?, 1760, FP 9: 37.

45 BF to PSH, June 7, 1762, FP 10: 102.

46 BF to PSH, August 11, 1762, FP 10: 142.

47 BF to WS, August 23, 1762, FP 10: 142.

48 BF to DF, March 24, 1762, FP 10: 69.

CHAPTER 7

Home, but Not in His Heart

1 Deborah Franklin: Account of Expenses, May 1762, FP 10: 100.

2 BF to WS, December 2, 1762, FP 10: 161.

3 BF to JM, November 11, 1762, FP 10: 153.

4 BF to JM, November 11, 1762, FP 10: 153.

5 BF to WS, December 2, 1762, FP 10: 161.

6 BF to JM, November 25, 1762, FP 10: 154.

7 BF to WS, December 7, 1762, FP 10: 166.

8 BF to Giambatista Beccaria, July 13, 1762, FP 10: 116.

9 Franklin Institute, "Benjamin Franklin's Glass Armonica."

10 Lopez and Herbert, *The Private Franklin*, 98.

11 Lopez and Herbert, *The Private Franklin*, 99.

12 Lopez and Herbert, *The Private Franklin*, 99.

13 BF to JM, November 25, 1762, FP 10: 154.

14 Hart, *Letters from William Franklin to William Strahan*, 11.

15 Hart, *Letters from William Franklin to William Strahan*, 11.

16 Lopez and Herbert, *The Private Franklin*, 100.

17 BF to WS, March 28, 1763, FP 10: 235.

18 Hart, *Letters*, 14.

19 BF to WS, December 7, 1762, FP 10: 166.

20 PSH to BF, August 30, 1763, FP 10: 333.

21 MS to BF, March [1763?], FP 10: 427.

22 PSH to BF, March 11, 1763, FP 10: 216.

23 BF to PSH, March 25, 1763, FP 10: 23.

24 Hart, *Letters*, 12.

25 BF to WS, March 28, 1763, FP 10: 235.

26 BF to DF, June 16, 1763, FP 10: 290.

27 BF to CRG, June 6, 1763, FP 10: 272.

28 "A Narrative of the Late Massacres," January 30, 1754, FP 5: 42.

29 "A Narrative of the Late Massacres," January 30, 1754, FP 5: 42.

30 BF to Dr. John Fothergill, March 14, 1764, FP 11: 101.

31 Van Doren, *Benjamin Franklin*, 311.

32 "Observations Concerning the Increase of Mankind," 1751, FP 3: 225.

33 "A Narrative of the Late Massacres," January 30, 1754, FP 5: 42.

34 Lopez and Herbert, *The Private Franklin*, 120.

35 Lopez and Herbert, *The Private Franklin*, 120.

36 BF to Richard Jackson, September 1, 1764, FP 11: 326.

37 "From Pennsylvania Assembly Committee of Correspondence to Richard Jackson," November 1, 1764, FP 11: 423.

38 BF to SF, November 8, 1764, FP 11: 447.

39 BF to DF, December 9, 1764, FP 11: 534.

40 DF to BF, January 8, 1765, FP 12: 13.

CHAPTER 8
"One Continued State of Suspense"

1 BF to DF, February 14, 1765, FP 12: 62.

2 BF to DF, February 14, 1765, FP 12: 62.

3 BF to DF, February 14, 1765, FP 12: 62.

4 DF to BF, February 10, 1765, FP 12: 43.

5 DF to BF, February 10, 1765, FP 12: 43.

6 BF to DF, June 4, 1765, FP 12: 166.

7 BF to DF, July DF to BF, October 6–13?, 1765, FP 12: 292.

8 BF to DF, August 1765, FP 12: 224.

9 DF to BF, October 6–13?, 1765, FP 12: 292.

10 DF to BF, August 1765, FP 12: 250.

11 BF to Hugh Roberts, July 7, 1765, FP 12: 201.

12 Virginia Resolves on the Stamp Act, 1765.

13 BF to John Hughes, August 9, 1765, FP 12: 234.

14 DF to BF, September 22, 1765, FP 12: 270.

15 DF to BF, September 22, 1765, FP 12: 270.

16 DF to BF, September 22, 1765, FP 12: 270.

17 DF to BF, October 8 1765, FP 12: 299.

18 BF to DF, November 9, 1765, FP 12: 360.

19 DF to BF, November 3, 1765, FP 12: 350.

20 BF to DF, February 22, 1766, FP 13: 165.

21 "Examination before the Committee of the Whole of the House Commons," February 13, 1766, FP 13: 124.

22 Declaratory Act, March 16, 1766.

23 BF to DF, April 6, 1766, FP 13: 233.

24 Gillespie, *A Book of Remembrance*, 25.

25 BF to DF, June 22, 1767, FP 14: 192.

26 WF to BF, May? 1767, FP 14: 17.

27 WF to BF, May? 1767, FP 14: 17.

28 Lopez and Herbert, *The Private Franklin*, 139.

29 DF to BF, May 16, 1767 (I), FP 14: 156.

30 BF to DF, May 23, 1757, FP 14: 166.

31 BF to DF, June 22, 1767, FP 14: 192.

32 BF to DF, June 22, 1767, FP 14: 192.

33 BF to DF, June 22, 1767, FP 14: 192.

34 DF to BF, July 3, 1767, FP 14: 206.

35 BF to RB, August 5, 1767, FP 14: 220.

36 BF to DF, August 5, 1767, FP 14: 224.

37 DF to BF, October 13–18?, 1767, FP 14: 278.

38 Lopez and Herbert, *The Private Franklin*, 141.

39 Lopez and Herbert, *The Private Franklin*, 141.

40 DF to BF, October 13–18?, 1767, FP 14: 278.

41 BF to DF, November 2, 1767, FP 14: 299.

42 Lopez and Herbert, *The Private Franklin*, 142.

CHAPTER 9
"How I Long to See You"

1 BF to DF, November 17, 1767, FP 14: 305.

2 JM to BF, December 1, 1767, FP 14: 333.

3 BF to JM, February 21, 1768, FP 5: 57.

4 BF to DF, December 24, 1767, FP 14: 343.

5 BF to DF, February 13, 1768, FP 15: 45.

6 Lopez and Herbert, *The Private Franklin*, 143.

7 BF to RB, August 13, 1768, FP 15: 185.

8 Lopez and Herbert, *The Private Franklin*, 144.

9 BF to Joseph Galloway, August 20, 1768, FP 15: 189.

10 BF to DF, October 5, 1768, FP 15: 223.

11 Lopez and Herbert, *The Private Franklin*, 131.

12 BF to DF, June 3, 1769, FP 16: 14.

13 Dr. Thomas Bond to BF, June 7, 1769, FP 16: 152.

14 DF to BF, August 31, 1769, FP 16: 187.

15 DF to BF, October 4, 1769, FP 16: 212.

16 DF to BF, November 20–[27], 1769, FP 16: 230.

17 DF to BF, December 13, 1769, FP 16: 262.

18 BF to DF, June 10, 1770, FP 17: 166.

19 BF to DF, June 10, 1770, FP 17: 166.

20 BF to Samuel Franklin, June 8, 1770, FP 17: 165.

21 BF to Joseph Galloway, June 26, 1770, FP 17: 180.

22 DF to BF, August 16, 1770, FP 17: 205.

23 BF to DF, October 3, 1770, FP 17: 239.

24 DF to BF, March 30, 1771, FP 18: 63.

25 BF to DF, May 1, 1771, FP 18: 90.

26 BF to DF, January 28, 1772, FP 19: 42.

27 BF to DF, January 28, 1772, FP 19: 42.

28 Lopez and Herbert, *The Private Franklin*, 154.

29 PSH to BF, November 2, 1771, FP 18: 238.

30 BF to PSH, with a postscript to Dorothea Blunt, November 25, 1771, FP 18: 252.

31 RB to DF, December 3, 1771, FP 8: 257.

32 BF to DF, February 3, 1772, FP 19: 55.

33 BF to DF, May 5, 1772, FP 19: 130.

34 DF to BF, May 14, 1772, FP 19: 140.

35 DF to BF, June 30, 1772, FP 19: 192.

36 BF to DF, November 19, 1772, FP 19: 376.

37 BF to DF, December 1, 1772, FP 19: 395.

38 BF to DF, January 6, 1773, FP 20: 15.

39 BF to DF, February 2, 1773, FP 20: 34.

40 BF to SF, April 6, 1773, FP 20: 141.

41 BF to DF, July 15, 1773, FP 20: 317.

42 BF to DF, September 1, 1773, FP 20: 383.

43 DF to BF, October 29, 1773, FP 20: 449.

44 BF to WF, October 6, 1773, FP 20: 436.

45 BF to Thomas Cushing, December 2, 1772, FP 19: 399.

46 BF to Thomas Cushing, February 15–[19], 1774, FP 21: 86.

47 BF to Thomas Cushing, February 15–[19], 1774, FP 21: 86.

48 BF to Thomas Cushing, February 15–[19], 1774, FP 21: 86.

49 BF to DF, April 28, 1774, FP 21: 205.

50 BF to DF, May 5, 1774, FP 21: 208.

51 BF to DF, May 7, 1774, FP 21: 210.

52 BF to DF, July 22, 1774, FP 21: 246.

53 BF to DF, September 10, 1774, FP 21: 303.

54 WF to BF, December 24, 1774, FP 21: 402.

CHAPTER 10

"I Desire That You May Love Me Forever"

1 BF to David Hartley, May 8, 1775, FP 22: 34.

2 Labaree, *Autobiography*, 129.

3 BF to JG, February 25, 1775, FP 21: 508.

4 BF to JG, May 8, 1775, FP 22: 32.

5 BF to WF, May 7, 1775 [1774?], FP 21: 211.

6 Skemp, *Benjamin and William Franklin*, 144.

7 Dorothea Blunt to BF, April 19, 1775, FP 22: 25.

8 MS to BF, April 24, 1775, FP 22: 27.

9 PSH to BF, June 10, 1775, FP 22: 62.

10 BF to PSH, July 8, 1775, FP 22: 99.

11 BF to MS, July 17, 1775, FP 22: 108.

12 BF to CRG, June 17, 1775, FP.22: 66.

13 CRG to BF, July 18?, 1775, FP 22: 109.

14 Lepore, *Book of Ages*, 179.

15 Turgot, *The Monthly Anthology*, 167.

16 BF to PHS, January 12, 1777, FP 23: 155.

17 Charles Francis Adams, *Works of John Adams*, 1: 660.

18 Butterfield, *Adams Family Correspondence*, 4: 118–19.

19 Butterfield, *Adams Family Correspon-dence*, 4: 118.

20 Ziff, *The Portable Benjamin Franklin*, 496.

21 The American Commissioners to the Comte de Vergennes, December 23, 1776, FP 23: 82.

22 Smyth, *The Writings of Benjamin Franklin*, 7: 55.

23 The American Commissioners to the Committee of Secret Correspondence, January 17–22, 1777, FP 23: 194.

24 BF to MS, January 25, 1779, FP 28: 421.

25 Lopez, *Mon Cher Papa*, 30.

26 MB to Louis-Guillaume Le Veillard, Monday morning [March 1777?], FP 23: 542.

27 Lopez, *Mon Cher Papa*, 36.

28 MB to BF, Sunday 20 [December 1778?], FP 28: 316.

29 MB to BF, July 30, 1777, FP 24: 376.

30 Monsieur Brillon de Jouy to BF, May 15, 1778, FP 26: 464.

31 MB to BF, July 30, 1777, FP 24: 376.

32 MB to BF, December 4, 1777, FP 25: 241.

33 MB to BF, March 7, 1778, FP 26: 75.

34 MB to BF, March 7, 1778, FP 26: 75.

35 BF to MB, March 10, 1778, FP 26: 85.

36 MB to BF, March 16, 1778, FP 26: 116.

37 Exchanges with Anne-Louise Boyvin d'Hardancourt Brillon de Jouy, six let-ters circa July 27, 1778 (V), FP 27: 162.

38 Exchanges with Anne-Louise Boyvin d'Hardancourt Brillon de Jouy, six let-ters circa July 27, 1778 (VI), FP 27: 164.

39 Exchanges with Anne-Louise Boyvin d'Hardancourt Brillon de Jouy, six let-ters circa July 27, 1778 (III), FP 27: 162.

40 Exchanges with Anne-Louise Boyvin d'Hardancourt Brillon de Jouy, six let-ters circa July 27, 1778 (I), FP 27: 160.

41 Exchanges with Anne-Louise Boyvin d'Hardancourt Brillon de Jouy, six let-ters circa July 27, 1778 (III), FP 27: 162.

42 Exchanges with Anne-Louise Boyvin d'Hardancourt Brillon de Jouy, six

letters circa July 27, 1778 (III), FP 27: 162.

43 Exchanges with Anne-Louise Boyvin d'Hardancourt Brillon de Jouy, six let-ters circa July 27, 1778 (IV), FP 27: 162.

44 BF to MB, "The Ephemera," September 20, 1778, FP 27: 437.

45 MB to BF, September 17, 1778, FP 27: 416.

46 BF to MB, September 15, 1778, FP 27: 403.

CHAPTER 11
"By the Way, What Did You Do to That Shoulder?"

1   BF to MB, September 15, 1778, FP 27: 403.

2   Lopez, *Mon Cher Papa*, 246.

3   BF to MH, October 1778?, FP 27: 670.

4   Charles Francis Adams, *Letters of Mrs. Adams*, 2: 55–56.

5   The Abbé André Morellet's song in honor of Franklin, July 5, 1779, FP 30: 47.

6   Lopez, *Mon Cher Papa*, 255.

7   MH with Benjamin Franklin's reply (unpublished), 1782, FP 37.

8   BF to MH, 1782, FP 37.

9   BF to Henry Laurens, March 31, 1778, FP 26: 203.

10 BF to Arthur Lee, April 3, 1778, FP 26: 223.

11 BF to Arthur Lee, April 4, 1778, FP 26: 231.

12 BF to David Hartley, April 29, 1778, FP 26: 374.

13 Amacher, *Franklin's Wit and Folly*, 60–62.

14 Amacher, *Franklin's Wit and Folly*, 60–62.

15 Amacher, *Franklin's Wit and Folly*, 60–62.

16 Amacher, *Franklin's Wit and Folly*, 60–62.

17 Franklin and Madame Helvétius: An Exchange through Cabanis, August 1, 1779, FP 30: 278.

18 Franklin and Madame Helvétius: An Exchange through Cabanis, August 11, 1779, FP 30: 279.

19 Lopez, *Mon Cher Papa*, 260–62.

20 Lopez, *Mon Cher Papa*, 262.

21 Lopez, *Mon Cher Papa*, 262.

22 Charles Francis Adams, *Letters of Mrs. Adams*, 2: 55–56.

23 Charles Francis Adams, *Letters of Mrs. Adams*, 2: 55–56.

24 From Madame Brillon circa 1778 Saturday morning, FP 28: 315.

25 MB to BF, June 4, [1779], FP 29: 625.

26 MB to BF, January 22, 1779, FP 28: 411.

27 Butterfield, Faber, and Garrett, *The Adams Papers*, 4: 50.

28 Lopez, *Mon Cher Papa*, 60.

29 Butterfield, *Adams Family Correspondence*, 4: 50–51.

30 MB to BF, May 8, 1779, FP 29: 450.

31 MB to BF, May 3, 1779, FP 29: 417.

32 MB to BF, May 8, 1779, FP 29: 450.

33 MB to BF, June 4, 1779, FP 29: 625.

34 MB to BF, May 8, 1779, FP 29: 450.

35 BF to MB, May 10 [May 11 or after, 1779], FP 29: 465.

36 BF to MB, May 10 [May 11 or after, 1779], FP 29: 465.

37 BF to Cabanis for Madame Helvétius, September 19, 1779, FP 30: 373.

38 Lopez, *Mon Cher Papa*, 264.

CHAPTER 12
"Prudence Is Not Your Strongest Point"

1 BF to MH, Saturday, January 1, 1780, FP 31: 322.

2 BF to MH, Saturday, January 1, 1780, FP 31: 322.

3 BF to MH, Saturday, January 1, 1780, FP 31: 322.

4 Dennis Diderot as quoted in Guillois, *Le Salon de Madame Helvétius*, 16.

5 BF to PSH, January 10, 1780, FP 31: 360.

6 Georgiana Shipley to BF, May 1, 1779, FP 29: 407.

7 Georgiana Shipley to BF, February 3, 1780, FP 31: 444.

8 Franklin, *Almanacks*, 68.

9 Van Doren, *Benjamin Franklin*, 609.

10 BF to John Adams, October 2, 1780, FP 33: 353.

11 BF to Cabanis, June 30, 1780, FP 32: 624.

12 Lopez, *Mon Cher Papa*, 270.

13 Lopez, *Mon Cher Papa*, 270.

14 Van Doren, *Benjamin Franklin*, 653–54.

15 Wood, *Americanization of Benjamin Franklin*, 209.

16 Isaacson, *Benjamin Franklin*, 365.

17 BF to RB, June 2, 1779, FP 29: 597.

18 BF to WF, August 16, 1784, FP (unpublished).

19 Wood, *Americanization of Benjamin Franklin*, 209.

20 BF to WF, August 16, 1784, FP (unpublished).

21 BF to MB, July 10, 1780, FP 33: 45.

22 MB to BF, "after July 10, 1780," FP 33: 56.

23 "The Morals of Chess" [before 28 June 1779], Oberg, *Papers of Benjamin Franklin* 29, 750–57.

24 Franklin, *Almanacks* 7, 15.

25 "Dialogue Entre La Goute et M. F.," November 17, 1780, FP 34: 11.

26 BF to MB, November 17, 1780, FP 34: 20.

27 MB to BF, November 18, 780, FP 33: 25.

28 "Dialogue Entre La Goute et M. F.," November 17, 1780, FP 34: 11.

29 MB to BF, November 18, 1780, FP 34: 20.

30 MB to BF, November 26, 1780, FP 34: 61.

31 BF to MB, November 23, 1780, FP 34: 47.

32 BF to MS, November 3, 1767, FP 14: 299.

33 "Les Mouches à Mme Helvétius" [December? 1780], Oberg, Papers of Benjamin Franklin, 34: 226–27.

34 MB to BF December 7, 1780, FP 34: 135.
35 BF to MB, December 10, 1780, FP 34: 145.
36 BF to MB, December 10, 1780, FP 34: 145.
37 William Shakespeare, *As You Like It*, act IV, scene 3.
38 George Washington to BF, October 9, 1780, FP 33: 398.
39 BF to Vergennes, November 19, 1780, FP 34: 28.
40 BF to Samuel Huntington, March 12 [April 12], 1781, FP 34: 443.

CHAPTER 13
*"As Long as We Will Exist
You Will Not Be Abandoned"*

1 PSH to BF, January 11, 1779, FP 28: 365.
2 BF to MS, January 25, 1779, FP 28: 421.
3 BF to MS, January 25, 1779, FP 28: 421.
4 MS to BF, March 16 [April 11], 1779, FP 29: 136.
5 MS to BF, November 16, 1775, FP 22: 263.
6 PSH to BF, May 30, 1779, FP 29: 578.
7 BF to PSH, January 10, 1780, FP 31: 360.
8 PSH to BF, April 2, 1780, FP 32: 205.
9 PSH to BF, April 8, 1781, FP 34: 523.
10 PSH to BF, December 23, 1781, FP 35: 287.
11 BF to PSH, April 19, 1782, FP 37: 172.
12 BF to MB, before April 20, 1781, FP 34: 560.
13 BF to MB, before April 20, 1781, FP 34: 560.
14 MB to BF, before April 20, 1781, FP 34: 560.
15 MB to BF, before April 20, 1781, FP 34: 560.
16 BF to MB, June 5, 1781, FP 35: 124.
17 MB to BF, June 13, 1781, FP 35: 155.
18 MB to BF, October 12, 1781, FP 35: 543.
19 BF to MB, October 12, 1781, FP 35: 543.
20 BF to MB, November 26, 1781, FP 36: 120.
21 MB to BF, January 8, 1782, FP 36: 408.
22 MB to BF, January 20, 1782, FP 36: 456.
23 MB to BF, January 20, 1782, FP 36: 456.
24 MB to BF, January 20, 1782, FP 36: 456.
25 MB to BF, January 20, 1782, FP 36: 456.
26 MB to BF, February 1782, FP 36: 504.
27 Lopez, *Mon Cher Papa*, 115.
28 Lopez, *Mon Cher Papa*, 115.
29 Franklin, *Almanacks*, 17.
30 PSH to BF, May 1, 1782, FP 37: 259.
31 BF to PSH, May 13, 1782, FP 37: 363.
32 PSH to BF, May 23, 1782, FP 37: 403.
33 BF to Richard Oswald, June 27, 1782, FP 37: 558.
34 MB to BF, October 13, 1782, FP (unpublished); YBFP 38, 218–19.
35 PSH to BF, July 19, 1782, FP 37: 650.
36 PSH to BF, July 19, 1782, FP 37: 650.
37 BF to PSH, August 17, 1782, FP 37: 650 (unpublished).
38 BF to PSH, January 8, 1783, FP (unpublished); YBFP 38: 566–68.
39 PSH to BF, January 13, 1783, YPBF 38: 578 (unpublished).
40 BF to MS, January 25, 1779, FP 28: 421.

CHAPTER 14
*"We Are Apt to Forget
That We Are Grown Old"*

1 BF to PSH, January 27, 1783, FP 39: 67 (unpublished); YBFP 39: 67–68.
2 BF to PSH, May 13, 1782, FP 37: 363 (unpublished).
3 BF to PSH, April 26, 1783, FP 39 (unpublished). YBFP 39: 503–4.
4 Van Doren, *Benjamin Franklin*, 700.
5 Van Doren, *Benjamin Franklin*, 702.
6 PSH to BF, September 28, 1783, FP (unpublished); YBFP 41: 51–52.
7 Lopez and Herbert, *The Private Franklin*, 273.
8 BF to PSH, December 26, 1783, FP (unpublished); YBFP 38: 218.
9 Lopez, *Mon Cher Papa*, 98.
10 Lopez, *Mon Cher Papa*, 99.
11 Lopez, *Mon Cher Papa*, 100.

12 WF to BF, July 22, 1784, FP (unpublished); YBFP 42: 432–35.

13 BF to WF, August 16, 1784, FP (unpublished); YBFP 43: 10–12.

14 Henri-Maximilien Grand to WTF, August 19, 1784, FP 43 (unpublished).

15 PSH to WTF, November 18, 1784, FP (unpublished).

16 PSH to WTF, November 22, 1784, FP 43 (unpublished).

17 PSH to WTF, November 24, 1784, FP 43 (unpublished).

18 PSH to BF, October 25, 1784, FP (unpublished); YBFP 43: 211–13.

19 Lopez and Herbert, *The Private Franklin*, 269.

20 Lopez and Herbert, *The Private Franklin*, 269.

21 Lopez and Herbert, *The Private Franklin*, 269.

22 PSH to BF, April 26, 1785, FP (unpublished).

23 BF to PSH, May 5, 1785, FP (unpublished).

24 BF to PSH, July 4, 1785, FP (unpublished).

25 PSH to BF, July 23, 1785, FP (unpublished).

26 PSH to BF, July 23, 1785, FP (unpublished).

27 MB to BF, Saturday morning, 1785, FP (unpublished).

28 MB to BF, July 10, 1785, FP (unpublished).

29 Lopez, *Mon Cher Papa*, 298.

30 Benjamin Franklin Bache Diary, Dr. Franklin's Return from France, in 1785, July, FP.

31 MH to BF, July 1785, FP (unpublished).

32 BF to MH, July 19, 1785, FP (unpublished).

33 Benjamin Franklin diary, 1785, FP (unpublished).

34 Benjamin Franklin diary, 1785, FP (unpublished).

35 Benjamin Franklin diary, 1785, FP (unpublished).

36 Benjamin Franklin diary, 1785, FP (unpublished).

37 Van Doren, *Benjamin Franklin*, 731.

38 Van Doren, *Benjamin Franklin*, 732.

39 BF to John and Sarah Van Brugh Livingston Jay, September 21, 1785, FP (unpublished).

40 BF to PSH, October 30, 1785, FP (unpublished).

41 JM to BF, October 1, 1785, FP (unpublished).

42 BF to PSH, May 30, 1786, FP (unpublished).

43 BF to JM, September 21, 1786, FP (unpublished).

44 Van Doren, *Benjamin Franklin*, 751.

45 PSH to BF, October 17, 1786, FP (unpublished).

46 Van Doren, *Benjamin Franklin*, 751.

47 Van Doren, *Benjamin Franklin*, 744.

48 Benjamin Franklin's Speech in the Convention of the Constitution, September 17, 1787, FP (unpublished).

49 Gillespie, *A Book of Remembrance*, 23.

50 BF to Alexander Small, December 17, 1789, FP (unpublished).

51 BF to George Whitfield, June 19, 1764, FP (unpublished).

52 PSH to Thomas Viny, May 5, 1790, FP (unpublished).

53 Franklin, *Almanacks*, 206.

Adams, Charles Francis, ed. *Letters of Mrs. Adams*. 2 vols. 2nd ed. Boston: Little, Brown, 1840.
————. *The Works of John Adams: The Second President of the United States*. 2 vols. Boston: Little, Brown, 1856.
Agricultural Resources of Pennsylvania. Southeastern Pennsylvania Historic Agricultural Region, c. 1750–1960. http://www.phmc.state.pa.us/portal/communities/agriculture /files/context/southeastern_pennsylvania.pdf.
Alsop, Susan Mary. *Yankees at the Court: The First Americans in Paris*. Garden City, NY: Doubleday, 1982.
Amacher, Richard, ed. *Franklin's Wit and Folly: The Bagatelles*. New Brunswick, NJ: Rutgers University Press, 1953.
Bailar, Benjamin F., ed. *The Benjamin Franklin Bailar Collection: A Postal Historical Study of America's First Postmaster General*. New York: Robert A. Siegel Auction Galleries, 2015.
Bailyn, Bernard, ed., with the assistance of Jane N. Garrett. *Pamphlets of the American Revolution: 1750–1776*. Cambridge, MA: Belknap Press / Harvard University Press, 1965.
Benjamin Franklin Papers, Library of Congress. https://franklinpapers.org/framedVolumes .jsp.
Benjamin Franklin's Letters to Madame Helvétius and Madame La Frete: With an explanatory note by Luther S. Livingston. Cambridge, MA: Harvard University Press, 1924.
Berkin, Carol. *Revolutionary Mothers: Women in the Struggle for America's Independence*. New York: Alfred A. Knopf, 2005.
Bridenbaugh, Carl. *Cities in the Wilderness: The First Century of Urban Life in America*. New York: Capricorn Press, 1964.
Bronner, Edward B. "Village into Town 1701–1746." In Russell Frank Weigley, *Philadelphia: A 300-Year History*. New York: W. W. Norton, 1982.
Bunker, Nick. *Young Benjamin Franklin: The Birth of Ingenuity*. New York: Alfred A. Knopf, 2018.
Butterfield, L. H., ed. *Adams Family Correspondence*. Vol. 4. Cambridge, MA: Harvard University Press, 1963–73.
Butterfield, L. H., Leonard C. Faber, and Wendell D. Garrett, eds. *The Adams Papers, Diary and Autobiography of John Adams*. Vol. 4. Cambridge, MA: Harvard University Press, 1961.
Calhoun, Arthur V. *The American Family in the Colonial Period*. Mineola, NY: Dover Publications, 2004.
Caulfield, Ernest. "The Pursuit of a Pestilence." *Proceedings of the American Antiquarian Society*, 40. https://www.americanantiquarian.org/proceedings/44807204.pdf.
Cleary, Patricia. "She Will Be in the Shop: Women's Sphere of Trade in Eighteenth Century Philadelphia and New York." *Pennsylvania Magazine of History and Biography* 119, no. 3 (July 1995).
Conner, Paul W. *Poor Richard's Politicks: Benjamin Franklin and His New American Order*. Westport, CT: Greenwood Press, 1980.

Coss, Stephen. "What Led Benjamin Franklin to Live Estranged from His Wife for Nearly Two Decades?" *Smithsonian Magazine*, September 2017.

Cummings, Hubertis. *Richard Peters: Provincial Secretary and Cleric, 1704–1776*. Philadelphia: University of Pennsylvania Press, 1944.

Declaratory Act. March 16, 1766. http://www.stamp-act-history.com/documents/1766-declaratory-act-original-text/.

Ellis, Joseph J. *American Dialogue: The Founders and Us*. New York: Alfred A. Knopf, 2018.

Federalist Papers Project. www.thefederalistpapersproject.org.

———. "Rules and Maxims for Promoting Matrimonial Happiness." https://thefederalist papers.org/founders/franklin/benjamin-franklin-rules-and-maxims-for-promoting-matrimonial-happiness-the-pennsylvania-gazette-november-19-1730.

Fisher, Daniel, and Mrs. Conway Robinson Howard. "Extracts from the Diary of Daniel Fisher, 1755." *Pennsylvania Magazine of History and Biography* 17, no. 3 (1893): 263–78.

Fisher, David Hackett. *Albion's Seed: Four British Folkways in America*. New York: Oxford University Press, 1989.

Fleming, Thomas, ed. *The Founding Fathers: Benjamin Franklin; A Biography in His Own Words*. New York: Newsweek, 1972.

Franklin, Benjamin. *Poor Richard's Almanacks*. New York and London: Paddington Press, 1964.

Franklin Institute. "Benjamin Franklin's Glass Armonica." https://www.fi.edu/history-resources/franklins-glass-armonica.

Fry, Jennifer Reed. "'Extraordinary Freedom and Great Humility': A Reinterpretation of Deborah Franklin." *Pennsylvania Magazine of History and Biography* 127, no. 2 (April 2003).

Gillespie, Elizabeth Duane. *A Book of Remembrance*. Philadelphia and London: J. B. Lippincott, 1901. https://archive.org/details/abookremembranco1duagoog/page/n32/mode/2up.

Gratz, Simon. "Some Material for a Biography of Elizabeth Graeme." *Pennsylvania Magazine of History and Biography* 29, no. 3 (1915).

Guillois, Antoine. *Le Salon de Madame Helvétius: Cabanis et les idéologues*. Paris: Calmann, Levy, 1894; Adamant Media Corporation, 2002.

Hallahan, William H. *The Day the American Revolution Began, 19 April 1775*. New York: William Morrow, 2000.

Hart, Charles Henry, ed. *Letters from William Franklin to William Strahan*. Philadelphia: J. B. Lippincott, 1911.

Isaacson, Walter. *Benjamin Franklin: An American Life*. New York: Simon & Schuster, 2003.

Janney, Samuel Macpherson. *The Life of William Penn: With Selections from his Correspondence and Autobiography*. 4th ed. Philadelphia: Friends Book Association, 1876.

Kerber, Linda K. *Women of the Republic: Intellect and Ideology in Revolutionary America*. Chapel Hill: Chapel Hill Institute of Early American History and Culture, University of North Carolina Press, 1980.

Labaree, Leonard W., ed. *The Papers of Benjamin Franklin*. Vols. 1–4, 11. New Haven, CT: Yale University Press, 1959, 1961, 1967.

Labaree, Leonard W., Ralph L. Ketcham, Helen C. Boatfield, and Helene H. Fineman, eds. *The Autobiography of Benjamin Franklin*. New Haven, CT, and London: Yale University Press, 1964.

Lemay, J. A. Leo. *Benjamin Franklin: Writings*. New York: Viking (Library of America Series), 1987.

———. *The Life of Benjamin Franklin: Journalist, 1706–1730*. Vol. 1. Philadelphia: University of Pennsylvania Press, 2006.

———. *The Life of Benjamin Franklin: Printer and Publisher, 1730–1747*. Vol. 2. Philadelphia: University of Pennsylvania Press, 2006.

———. *The Life of Benjamin Franklin: Soldier, Scientist and Politician, 1748–1757*. Vol. 3. Philadelphia: University of Pennsylvania Press, 2009.

Lepore, Jill. *Book of Ages: The Life and Opinions of Jane Franklin*. New York: Vintage Books, 2014.

Lingelbach, W. E. "William Penn and City Planning." University Archives and Record Center, University of Pennsylvania, 403. https://journals.psu.edu/pmhb/article/viewFile/30007/29762.

Lippincott, Horace Mather. *Early Philadelphia: Its People, Life and Progress*. Philadelphia and London: J. B. Lippincott, 1917.

Lopez, Claude-Anne. *Mon Cher Papa: Franklin and the Ladies of Paris*. New Haven, CT, and London: Yale University Press, 1966.

———. *My Life with Benjamin Franklin*. New Haven, CT, and London: Yale University Press, 2000.

Lopez, Claude-Anne, and Eugenia W. Herbert. *The Private Franklin: The Man and His Family*. New York: W. W. Norton, 1975.

Mason, Ann Gere. *The Women of the French Salons*. December 13, 2008. General Books, 2010. eBook #2528 https://www.gutenberg.org/files/2528/2528-h/2528-h.htm.

McDowell, Edwin. "Darker Side to Franklin Is Reported." *New York Times*, August 18, 1987.

Michel, Franz, et al. "Philadelphia: Descriptions of Eighteenth-Century Philadelphia before the Revolution." In *American Notes: Traveling in America, 1750–1920*, in *American Memory*. Library of Congress, at hdl.loc.gov/loc.gdc/lhbtn.02374. http://nationalhumanitiescenter.org/pds/becomingamer/growth/text2/philadelphiadescriptions.pdf.

"Militia Act 25 November 1753." https://founders.archives.gov/documents/Franklin/01-06-02-0116.

Morgan, Daniel T. *The Devious Dr. Franklin: Colonial Agent; Benjamin Franklin's Years in London*. Macon, GA: Mercer University Press, 1999.

Morgan, Edmund S. *Benjamin Franklin*. New Haven, CT, and London: Yale University Press, 2002.

Mulford, Carla. J. *Benjamin Franklin and the Ends of Empire*. New York: Oxford University Press, 2015.

Nash, Gary B. *First City: Philadelphia and the Forging of Historical Memory*. Philadelphia: University of Pennsylvania Press, 2002.

Norton, Mary Beth. *Liberty's Daughters: The Revolutionary Experience of American Women, 1750–1800*. Boston: Little, Brown, 1980.

Oberg, Barbara B. *The Papers of Benjamin Franklin*. Vols. 29, 34. New Haven, CT, and London: Yale University Press, 1992.

Papers of Benjamin Franklin. Sponsored by the American Philosophical Society and Yale University. Digital edition by the Packard Humanities Institute. www.franklinpapers.org.

Riley, Edward M. "The Deborah Franklin Correspondence." *Proceedings of the American Philosophical Society* 95 (1951).

Roelker, William Greene, ed. *Benjamin Franklin and Catharine Ray Greene: Their Correspondence, 1755–1790*. Philadelphia: American Philosophical Society, 1949.

Schaeper, Thomas J. *France and America in the Revolutionary Era: The Life of Jacques-Donatien Leray de Chaumont, 1725–1803*. Providence, RI: Berghahn Books, 1995.

Schiff, Stacy. *A Great Improvisation: Franklin, France, and the Birth of America*. New York: Henry Holt, 2005.

Schloesser, Pauline. *The Fair Sex: White Women and Racial Patriarchy in the Early American Republic*. New York: New York University Press, 2002.

Seavey, Ormond. *Becoming Benjamin Franklin: The Autobiography and the Life*. University Park: Pennsylvania State University Press, 1988.

Skemp, Sheila L. *Benjamin and William Franklin: Father and Son, Patriot and Loyalist*. Boston: Bedford Books of St. Martin's Press, 1994.

———. *The Making of a Patriot: Benjamin Franklin at the Cockpit*. New York: Oxford University Press, 2013.

———. *William Franklin*. New York: Oxford University Press, 1990.

Smyth, Albert Henry. *The Writings of Benjamin Franklin*. Vol. 7. New York: Macmillan, 1905–1907.

Stuart, Nancy Rubin. *Defiant Brides: The Untold Story of Two Revolutionary-Era Women and the Radical Men They Married*. Boston: Beacon Press, 2013.

———. *The Muse of the Revolution: The Secret Pen of Mercy Otis Warren and the Founding of a Nation*. Boston: Beacon Press, 2008.

Tise, Larry, ed. *Benjamin Franklin and Women*. University Park: Pennsylvania State University Press, 2000.

Turgot, Anne-Robert Jacques. *The Monthly Anthology, and Boston Review: Containing Sketches and Reports of the Philosophy, Religion, History, Arts and Manners*. Boston: T. R. Watt, 1811.

Van Doren, Carl. *Benjamin Franklin*. New York: Penguin Books, 1988.

Virginia Resolves on the Stamp Act, 1765. https://www.encyclopediavirginia.org/Virginia_Resolves_on_the_Stamp_Act_1765.

Waldstreicher, David. *Runaway America: Benjamin Franklin, Slavery, and the American Revolution*. New York: Hill and Wang, 2004.

Winthrop, John. *The Journal of John Winthrop, 1630–1649*. Cambridge, MA: Harvard University Press, 1996.

Wood, Gordon S. *The Americanization of Benjamin Franklin*. New York: Penguin Press, 2004.

Zagarri, Rosemary. *Revolutionary Backlash: Women and Politics in the Early American Republic*. Philadelphia: University of Pennsylvania Press, 2007.

Ziff, Larzer, ed. *The Portable Benjamin Franklin*. London: Penguin Press, 2005.